ALWAYS A PEOPLE

D1218296

ORAL HISTORIES OF CONTEMPORARY WOODLAND INDIANS

Collected by
Rita Kohn, *Senior Editor*
and W. Lynwood Montell, *Associate Editor*

Introduction by R. David Edmunds

Michelle Mannering, *Project Consultant and Associate Editor*

Oil Portraits by Evelyn J. Ritter

Portraits photographed by
Pierson Photographics

ALWAYS
A
PEOPLE

INDIANA UNIVERSITY PRESS
BLOOMINGTON AND INDIANAPOLIS

© 1997 by Rita Kohn, W. Lynwood Montell, R. David Edmunds, and Michelle
Mannering

Oil portraits © 1996 by Dr. Michael Shinkle and Mrs. Linda Shinkle

All rights reserved

No part of this book may be reproduced or utilized in any form or by any means,
electronic or mechanical, including photocopying and recording, or by any information storage and retrieval system, without permission in writing from the publisher.
The Association of American University Presses' Resolution on Permissions consti-
tutes the only exception to this prohibition.

The paper used in this publication meets the minimum requirements of American
National Standard for Information Sciences— Permanence of Paper for Printed
Library Materials, ANSI Z39.48-1984.

Printed in Singapore

Library of Congress Cataloging-in-Publication Data

Always a people : oral histories of contemporary Woodland Indians / collected by
Rita Kohn, senior editor, and W. Lynwood Montell, associate editor ; introduction by
R. David Edmunds ; Michelle Mannering, project consultant and associate editor ; oil
portraits by Evelyn J. Ritter.
p.   cm.
Includes index.
ISBN 0-253-33298-2 (alk. paper)
1. Woodland Indians—History. 2. Woodland Indians—Biography. 3. Woodland
Indians—Portraits.   I. Kohn, Rita T.   II. Montell, William Lynwood, date.
E78.E2A58   1997
973'.04973—dc21   96-53025

1 2 3 4 5   02 01 00 99 98 97

SOCIAL SCIENCE DIVISION
CHICAGO PUBLIC LIBRARY
400 SOUTH STATE STREET
CHICAGO, IL 60605

R01703262l5

To

RAYMOND O. WHITE, JR.

Whose vision guided this project to fruition

The Press, the authors, and the subjects are grateful to the people and foundations listed below whose generosity made publication of this book possible:

MICHAEL AND LINDA SHINKLE

MR. AND MRS. DAVID A. GALLIHER

ROBERT AND JOY GOLLIVER

SHERMAN AND MARJORIE ZEIGLER FOUNDATION, INC.

Contents

PORTRAITS AND ORAL HISTORIES

Foreword

"The Woodland People Are Coming Home"

Michael Shinkle and Linda Shinkle

We are thankful to so many for making this project possible. Ed and Virginia Ball and Rosemary Ball Bracken set the stage at the Minnetrista Cultural Center in Muncie, Indiana. They introduced us to Miami Indian Tribe of Indiana Tribal Chairman Raymond O. White, Jr., and his wife, Karen, and to Nick and Verona Clark. The bond between Nick, Ray, and Mike grew as they shared their dream to try to provide a place for the Woodland People in their ancestral territory.

The enthusiasm of the three of us and our families seemed to be infectious. We were able to attract unusually fine talent to help the project move ahead, one plateau after another. Evelyn Ritter's remarkable painting talent was just one part of what she brought to the project, for she was genuinely interested in the many fine people she met and painted. Rita Kohn's uncanny ability to sense the urgent need to capture the words of the subjects, and to quickly assemble her capable colleagues, Lynwood Montell, David Edmunds, and Michelle Mannering, has made this project unique.

A simultaneous effort, the development of the Minnetrista Council for Great Lakes Native American Studies [MCGLNAS] as a consortium of Woodland tribes to find ways to study and honor their culture, has provided a base for long-range activities. This kind of enthusiasm "to bring the Woodland People home" continues with still another phase, Prophetstown State Park, near Lafayette, Indiana. Leaders from local government, industry and academia representing the Indiana communities of Lafayette, Battle Ground, Muncie, and Indianapolis, have come together with state officials to focus on making the Prophetstown of 1811 live again, after 185 years.

In our minds, this extraordinary, multifaceted effort could not be happening without some divine intervention. We can feel the same electricity that was evident in the establishment of MCGLNAS and the development of "Always a People" with the Prophetstown Foundation Board members. We are pleased and will always be thankful for the friendship and love of the Woodland tribal members who have made this small, ongoing and growing bit of cultural renewal well worth all the dedication of time and resources.

Michael Shinkle   Linda Shinkle
MIKIANI   ZITAKANA

February 16, 1996
Peoria, Illinois

Preface

"Making a Book Is a Journey"

Rita Kohn and W. Lynwood Montell

Always a People, the book and the title, came about because Linda and Mike Shinkle acted on a suggestion made in 1991 by Ray White, at that time tribal manager of the Miami Nation of Indians of the State of Indiana, Inc., who was installed as principal chief on February 14, 1993. He served until his death on March 3, 1994. Chief White had strong opinions about the need to speak of Woodland Nations through the original words of The People, sentiments echoed in the text of his interview in the following pages. Ray White was concerned about the omission of Woodland history, culture, tradition, and commerce from mainstream books and was distressed by errors in those works in which People of the Great Lakes have been mentioned. He was passionate about using the present tense and about detailing current accomplishments and future goals, and adamant about correcting the damaging "Indian as victim" image.

It was the high respect for Ray White among his peers that enabled him to bring together, after a hiatus of some 150 years, leaders of Woodland Nations to again unite as a confederacy. The original confederacy, in its traditional functions of preserving peace and harmony among Woodland Nations, predates European intervention on the North American continent. The current confederacy seeks to restore, preserve, and renew Woodland culture. Publication of this book was part of Ray White's vision for realizing that task, thus he went on to gain the personal support of Woodland leaders for the making of a book that would feature a few but that would honor all.

"If you are willing to make the journey, I will help you." Ray White made this pledge to Rita Kohn during the 1991 Winter Meeting of the Minnetrista Council for Great Lakes Native American Studies (MCGLNAS) in Tulsa, Oklahoma. That assistance came in the form of instruction on protocol, explanations of traditional ways, interpretations of "historical" events from alternative perspectives, and lessons in how to listen "the Indian way" and how to know when silence is a significant statement.

Prior to Rita Kohn becoming a part of the project as senior editor for the book, individuals had been designated by their Nations or tribes to have their portraits painted, and thus to be subjects for the oral histories. Ray White, with Nick Clark, the founding executive director of MCGLNAS, helped to develop a list of appropriate topics to cover in the oral history interviews. That list and an outline for the book were shared with Elders and leaders who offered their counsel and made changes. The revised documents were then sent in advance to those to be interviewed. Each person was also free to add or delete topics according to his or her experiences.

In keeping with protocol, Elders among the Woodland People of Indiana chose Frank Bush, Spiritual Leader of the Potawatomi Indian Nation Inc. AKA Pokagon Band of Potawatomi Indians, to be the first to be asked to contribute to this collection. It took four years for the circle of interviews to be completed. Thus, following the initial meeting with Mr. Bush in Bradley, Michigan on July 8, 1992, Rita Kohn went on to record the words of Elder Lora Siders, Miami Nation of Indians of the State of Indiana, Inc. at the Miami tribal offices in Peru, Indiana; Miami Spiritual Leader Wap Shing, at his home in Lebanon, Indiana; Assistant Chief Michael Pace, Delaware Tribe of Indians of Bartlesville, Oklahoma, during a visit of return to ancestral lands, now known as Conner Prairie, in Fishers, Indiana; and Chief Richard Snake, Delaware Nation Council, Moravian of the Thames Band, near the Moravian Reserve in Ontario, Canada.

This handful of oral histories comprises work done with the assistance of an Indiana Heritage Research Grant. These narratives represent three major facets of Woodland history and a major theme of this book: removal from the Woodland People's traditional homeland, retention of some of their homeland, and their return. The remainder of the work for the project was done without any grant or funding assistance.

The next set of narratives was collected between December 10 and December 18, 1994. The late Ruth Montell accompanied Lynwood Montell and Rita Kohn to Oklahoma for the interviews conducted with

Chief Floyd Leonard and Elder Sharon Burkybile of the Miami Tribe of Oklahoma; Chief Don Giles of the Peoria Indian Tribe of Oklahoma; Chief George "Buck" Captain of the Eastern Shawnee Tribe of Oklahoma; Chief Charles Dawes of the Ottawa Indian Tribe of Oklahoma; Chiefress Victoria Daugherty, Elder Emma Greenfeather Donaldson, Elder Billie Smith, and Chairman Don Greenfeather of the Loyal Shawnee Tribe; Elder Lucy Blalock, Elder Joanna J. Nichol, Spiritual Leader Edward Leonard Thompson, and Chief Curtis Zunigha of the Delaware Tribe of Indians; President Lawrence Frank Snake of the Delaware Tribe of Western Oklahoma; Elder Helen Rameriz and Henryetta Ellis of the Absentee Shawnee Tribe; and Elder and Tribal Judge Grace Thorpe of the Sauk and Fox Nation.

In May 1995 Rita Kohn, accompanied by her husband, Walter, traveled to Canada to interview Elder Beulah Timothy of the Delaware Nation Council, Moravian of the Thames Band at her home in Bothwell, Ontario; and Chief Leroy Dolson of the Munsee-Delaware Nation at the tribal building in Muncey, Ontario. Linda and Mike Shinkle interviewed their cousin, Chris Schenkel, who had been adopted into the Miami Nation of Indians of the State of Indiana. In mid-June, Lynwood Montell, with the aid of a small grant from the Faculty Research Committee of Western Kentucky University, traveled to the Minnetrista Cultural Center, Muncie, Indiana, to interview Nick Smith of the Loyal Shawnee Tribe; Historic Preservation Officer and Tribal Judge Patricia Hrabik of the Lac du Flambeau Band of Lake Superior Chippewa Indians; and Elder Keller George of the Oneida Indian Nation. Storyteller and Historian David Lee Smith of the Winnebago of Nebraska sent Lynwood Montell a self-recorded interview.

On October 27 and 28, 1995, Rita Kohn traveled to Michigan with Michelle Mannering to interview Rae Daugherty, Tom Topash, Dan Rapp, and Philip Alexis, four Elders of the Potawatomi Indian Nation Inc. AKA Pokagon Band of Potawatomi Indians. On March 11, 1996 Rita Kohn traveled to Peru, Indiana, with Michelle Mannering to interview Francis Shoemaker, former chief of the Miami Indian Nation of the State of Indiana.

While the original intention was to have an interview with each person whose portrait was painted, ultimately this was not possible either because of death or because of scheduling difficulties. As a result, in some cases we have been fortunate to have the use of other people's work. Noel Bauwens of Mishawaka, Indiana, has allowed us to include our transcription of the video interview he conducted with Chief Ray White on March 6, 1993. The Peoria Indian Tribe of Oklahoma has granted us permission to reprint the biographical sketches of Chief Guy Willis Froman and Chief Louis E. Myers from the book *The Peorias: A History of the Peoria Indian Tribe of Oklahoma* [Miami, OK: The Peoria Indian Tribe of Oklahoma, 1991]. The Delaware Tribe of Indians has granted us permission to reprint the memorial to Chief Lewis B. Ketchum from their newspaper, *Delaware Indian News* [Volume XVI, Issue IV, October 1995]. Dee Ketchum has allowed us to add his words about Lewis Ketchum.

The interviews were recorded on audiotapes and, where desired by those being interviewed, on videotapes. The videotapes were recorded for the sole use of the contributors and were given to each participant with the gratitude of the editors. Each session averaged approximately ninety minutes in length. The narrators put no restrictions on the editors' use of any or all information provided by them. Following publication of this book, the editors will return the audiotapes to each narrator.

The contents of each session were transcribed verbatim. A copy of the full transcription was sent to the narrator with a request for corrections, additions, and deletions. A transcription, corrected and verified by both narrator and editors, was then returned to each contributor. A version culled from that document became each narrator's entry for this book.

Since language, both written and spoken, is fraught with political connotations, we decided to capitalize Elder, Nation, and The People because to do so shows respect. We also recognize that spoken language cannot always be adapted verbatim into print. Thus, in transferring from tape to type we "unsplit" infinitives, deleted false starts, and corrected verb-noun disagreements wherever it seemed appropriate to do so. In making these changes, however, we did not alter the voice of any speaker. The original texts were also condensed to allow the book to be a manageable length. But, while all original words are not included, the words printed are the words spoken with the rare exception of corrections in syntax. In no way does publication of these oral histories represent any editorial interpretations of what was actually said.

In instances where multiple spellings exist, we made choices based on the preference of the person being interviewed. Thus, while the "official" name is Sac and Fox, we used the preferred Sauk and Fox in the texts of narratives. Other multiple spellings have been resolved for Piankashaw, Ho-Chunk, and Ojibwa. Munsee is the name of The People; Muncey is the name of the city in Ontario; Muncie is the name of the city in Indiana. Some people use powwow as one word, some use pow wow as two words, some use pow-wow. We decided to go with powwow.

Tipi is the preferred spelling among The People in the United States; in Canada the spelling is tipee. Councilor is the preferred spelling in the U.S.; councillor is the preferred spelling in Canada. Some people refer to a nation in the collective singular, others in the plural. Since most Woodland People add an "s" to the name when they speak, we followed this preference when it was used. Spelling Woodland Nations' words in English is fraught with difficulty. Variances in language for each Nation are mirrored in transliteration to English. We standardized the word for Original People to read Anishnabe throughout this book.

Two other editorial matters deal with format. Presentation is in alphabetical order by name of the narrator. This does indeed show the breadth of The People from A to Z. For the identification with each portrait we used a standard entry to include: Name/Nation/Position within that Nation/Date and Place of Birth [and date of death].

The point of view of *Always a People* is first person oral history. The editors began this project with an agenda: first, to highlight the Great Lakes-Riverine group of the Woodland Nations of the Northeast; and, second, to allow The People to show us through their own words that their culture is alive and well despite four centuries of contact and 150 years of forced assimilation.

A word regarding the portraits will suffice. Unlike transcribed interviews, oil portraits, once painted, cannot easily be changed to reflect desires of the subject. Thus, we offer the portrait of Emma Greenfeather Donaldson with apologies. Mrs. Donaldson would have preferred to be shown in her Shawnee dress because, as she states, "That is who I am. A full-blood Shawnee." In four instances there are no portraits to accompany the oral histories.

We wanted these oral histories to be accessible to general readers who might be unfamiliar with Woodland history, culture, tradition, and geography. David Edmunds's Introduction provides that essential background. In addition, we felt that in putting forward stories of Peoples whose major ties are to the Great Lakes-Riverine region, we had to be careful not to diminish the relevance of other Indigenous groups. Michelle Mannering's understanding of diverse cultures and her expertise in editing have served this book well in her capacity as consultant, associate editor, and author of the Afterword. With the help of these two valued colleagues we hope we have attained our desire to bring honor to all Indigenous People.

We take a moment now to mourn the passing of Chief Raymond O. White, Jr., Chief Guy Willis Froman, Chief Louis E. Myers, and Chief Lewis B. Ketchum. We are richer for their journey among us.

A final comment regarding the making of this book. Despite support from the leaders of the seventeen Nations and tribes represented in this work, we did not obtain outside funding for collecting the oral histories. We made the decision to go ahead anyway. We did not wish to add another broken promise to the long list in white and indigenous history. We also made the decision to return profits from this book to The People through a Woodland Nations Scholarship to be administered through the Indiana University Foundation. It was at a Woodland powwow at Minnetrista Cultural Center, Muncie, Indiana, in June 1992 that Don Greenfeather said to Rita Kohn, "Many things, many people will try to stop you from accomplishing this task, but you must not allow anything or anyone to deter you. You must push forward." So we pushed forward with the gentle kindness of Linda and Mike Shinkle, who wrote letters of introduction, hunted up addresses and telephone numbers we needed, and then underwrote the cost of photographing the portraits for inclusion in this book.

The five years from 1991 to 1996 can be described as short or long in linear terms. But, in the reality of Woodland cycling, time takes on a fuller dimension within, through, around, and beyond space to become much more than something you have or don't have, or spend, or lose, or gain. Time-space becomes a joy, much like sunrise and sunset. This is just one of the insights to be encountered through the words of the Anishnabe, The Original People, whose ancestors were here centuries before pioneer settlers came down the rivers or along the paths.

The central issue of *Always a People* deals with uncovering and making public the vibrancy of the Woodland People as a distinctive, related, cohesive, Native American Culture with not only an ancient and important heritage but also an equally significant tenacity to endure. They have evolved in part through a rebirth of cultural activities, although most were removed from their ancestral lands and were subjected to government policies designed to destroy their culture. We set out on a journey to make a book that would honor twentieth-century Woodland People. It turns out that it is they who honor us with their words, their friendship, their example. For this we say "Megwitch," thank you.

Rita Kohn,
Indianapolis, Indiana

William Lynwood Montell,
Bowling Green, Kentucky

Acknowledgments

The People whose portraits and words make this book have our sincerest appreciation. They opened their homes, their hearts to us. They entrusted us with their sacred words. There is no greater gift.

To members of tribal headquarters staffs we say thank you for helping us set up interviews. We are especially grateful to Renda and Gregory D. Ballew.

At the outset of this project Lou Anne Bush gave Rita Kohn a pouch in which to place the stories that would be collected. This pouch now is filled with the songs of The People and in this Lou Anne is honored. Sara Buchwald, award-winning producer of the videotape "The Onliest One Alive," provided professional assistance during the initial stages of this project. Sara and Rita together attended powwows and Woodland workshops and traveled to Michigan for the first interview.

Dr. Nancy Conner encouraged Rita to seek funding for the initial stages of the project. This led to receipt of an Indiana Heritage Research Grant funded jointly by the Indiana Historical Society and the Indiana Humanities Council. The grant was awarded to the Minnetrista Cultural Center in Muncie, Indiana, and covered costs for travel, tapes, and transcribing the first five interviews. Owen Glendening served as the project director.

When there was a need for letters of support for the project the following people not only sent us encouraging endorsement at that time but have continued to care about what we are doing. Once again we say thank you to Frederick E. Hoxie, Director of the D'Arcy McNickle Center of the Newberry Library; Robert M. Taylor, Jr., Director of the Research Projects and Grants Division of the Indiana Historical Society; Douglas E. Evelyn, Deputy Director of the National Museum of the American Indian; Pamela J. Bennett, Director of the Indiana Historical Bureau; Virginia G. Smith, Executive Director of the Kentucky Humanities Council; Charles H. Daugherty, Executive Director of the West Virginia Humanities Council; Dennis G. Kelly, Superintendent, Lyons Township High School District 204, LaGrange, Illinois; James W. Brown, Associate Dean, Indiana University School of Journalism at Indianapolis; Martin Zanger, Associate Director, Wisconsin Humanities Council; Doug Foard, Executive Secretary, Phi Beta Kappa; Charles E. Parrish, Historian, Louisville; Gwen Yeaman/Meda Kikalakaniqua, Woodland Basketmaker/Historian; Charles Turek Robinson, author of *Asleep beneath the Meadows: The Indian Archaeology of Rehoboth, Massachusetts*; DeMaris Gaines, Director of Native American Studies at Northeastern Oklahoma A&M College.

When we wanted to know if the oral histories had meaning to general audiences we received help from eighth-grade students, their teachers and the library staff of the Park Tudor School of Indianapolis during a 1993 program on Woodland People. Mary Mills of Indianapolis read and commented on the first oral history we collected.

Programs and papers on the project and the oral histories were presented by Rita Kohn before the Genealogy Committee of the Delaware County Historical Alliance; at the Minnetrista Council for Great Lakes Native American Studies 1992 Conference at the University of Tulsa; at the opening of the exhibition of the Shinkle Woodland Portraits Series at Miami University of Oxford, Ohio; and, with Lynwood Montell, at the 1995 Conference of the Hoosier Folklore Society at Indiana State University. We are grateful for the comments from those who attended.

Research centers whose collections have been especially useful include the Walter Havighurst Special Collections of the Miami University Libraries, Oxford, Ohio; Woodland Cultural Centre, Brantford, Ontario; Mitchell Indian Museum, Kendall College, Evanston, Illinois; Stratford Public Library, Stratford, Ontario; the resource library of the Minnetrista Cultural Center, Muncie, Indiana; Philbrook Museum, Tulsa, Oklahoma; Gilcrease Museum, Tulsa, Oklahoma; and the Newberry Library, Chicago. Individuals whose special knowledge has been an asset include Helen Tanner, Rosemary Daugherty, Robin McBride Scott, Gwen Yeaman, Darryl Stonefish, Robert and Leona Moses, Jimmy Sky, and, foremost, James E. Rementer.

Staff members and students at Western Kentucky University who assisted include Larry Danielson, Head of Modern Languages and Intercultural Studies; David Lee, Dean of Potter College of Arts, Humanities and Social Sciences; and Rachel Wessel, Clay Jackson, and Cathy Currey, all of whom helped to transcribe taped interviews. Special mention must be made of graduate student Kimberly Comstock, who compiled a bibliography of essential titles. The Faculty Research Committee of Western Kentucky University provided a small stipend to Lynwood Montell to defray some of his out-of-pocket expenses.

Generous donations from Michael and Linda Shinkle, Mr. and Mrs. David A. Galliher, Robert and Joy Golliver, and the Sherman and Marjorie Zeigler Foundation, Inc., made possible the full-color printing of the portraits in this volume. Their support provides a wonderful visual gift for which we are all grateful.

John Gallman, Director of the Indiana University Press, who believed in this project from the very beginning, Kenneth Gladish, Director of the Indianapolis Foundation, who said we'd get it done no matter what, and Paul Richard, Vice President of the Indianapolis Children's Museum, who helped in a dozen ways, are the kind of people who are nice to have around when a project is as tough as this one has been.

We especially highlight the dedication of James W. Brown, Associate Dean of the Indiana University School of Journalism at Indianapolis, for his steadfast support and computer expertise and for his assistance in setting up the Woodland Nations Scholarship Fund, which will be administered through the Indiana University Foundation. A significant portion of the royalties from this book, as well as monies from other projects undertaken by the editors, will help support this effort to give something back.

Our families, who have put up with tightened budgets, trips they never expected to make, long sessions of silence while we sat hunched over computers transcribing endless hours of tapes and then proofread and proofread again and again, and retyped those documents, deserve some kind of award.

And, finally, for each other as colleague we have been grateful. Never once during the years of working together have we had a cross word. It has been a wonderful experience.

Rita Kohn
William Lynwood Montell
David Edmunds
Linda Shinkle
Michael Shinkle
Michelle Mannering

About the Portraits

Each portrait, oil on canvas, measures 20" X 24", is framed, and has been exhibited with the Minnetrista Cultural Center traveling exhibition, "People of the Turtle," and independently as "A Portrait Collection: Twentieth Century Woodland Native American Leaders." The portraits have been shown in prominent locations in the states of Illinois, Indiana, Michigan, Ohio, Oklahoma, and Kentucky.

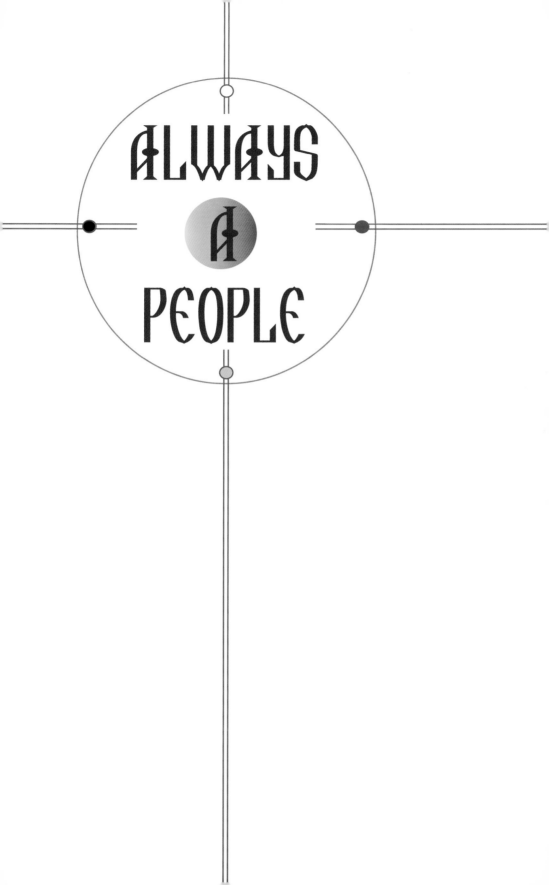

Introduction

"PAINT ME AS WHO I AM"
Woodland People at the Beginning of the Twenty-First Century

R. David Edmunds

When one looks at a map of Ohio, Indiana, Illinois, Michigan, and Wisconsin—states that comprise what was once the Northwest Territory—Native American place names emerge in profusion: Chillicothe, Muncie, Mississinewa, Kankakee, Peoria, Chicago, Decorah, Wausau, Pokagon, and Pontiac: all Native American names (among many others) reflecting the region's significant Indian heritage. Today, on the northern periphery of these states, reservation communities of Native American people who once claimed the region continue as reservoirs of tribal tradition. Yet scattered throughout these states, or resident in Oklahoma, Canada, or Nebraska, are other communities of Indian people who still occupy or once occupied this homeland. Although many of these communities are not large, they remain as important focal points for their members, many of whom have combined their Native American heritage with the changing demands of the twentieth century.

Indian people markedly shaped the region's history. In the pre-Columbian period they erected impressive urban and ceremonial centers along the Ohio, Mississippi, and Crawfish rivers, including Cahokia, an urban and ceremonial complex opposite modern St. Louis that encompassed eighty earthen mounds and during the twelfth century supported a population of over 10,000 inhabitants. Cahokia's trade networks stretched from the Rocky Mountains to the Appalachians, and from the Great Lakes to the Gulf of Mexico, but the city was virtually deserted when the first Europeans penetrated the upper Mississippi Valley. Yet vestiges of its influence and the Mississippian culture that it epitomized could be found among Indian people in the southeastern United States well into the sixteenth century.

Most of these Woodland People welcomed the French when traders, missionaries, and French officials entered the region in the latter half of the seventeenth century. Eager to acquire European trade goods, the village dwellers also sought allies against the Iroquois, who were well armed by Dutch and British traders, and who were expanding into the western Great Lakes. The Woodland People also listened to the Black Robes, Jesuit priests who offered a powerful, new medicine, which after a few decades often was combined with traditional tribal beliefs to create a syncretic Catholicism that met the needs of the tribal communities.

The growing relationship between many of the Woodland People and the French encompassed several dimensions. Throughout the seventeenth and eighteenth centuries the tribespeople became more dependent upon European trade goods, and although women still planted their gardens of corn, squash, and beans, many of their husbands extended their trap lines to secure sufficient pelts to trade to French merchants for items that once had been luxuries, but now had become necessities. Meanwhile, the tribes' political ties to New France were strengthened as growing numbers of warriors journeyed eastward to assist Onontio (the tribespeople's name for the governor-general of New France) in his wars against the British.

The French connection was enhanced by biological ties. Throughout the seventeenth and eighteenth centuries, many Frenchmen took Native American wives, and these marriages, some tenuous, some permanent, produced a growing number of mixed-blood or métis children. Integrated into tribal kinship networks, the métis functioned in both French and Indian societies, often serving as cultural brokers between European and Native American communities. Many exercised considerable economic and political influence within the tribes since their close relationship with French officials enabled them to both control and distribute French largesse, and in turn they often rallied their kinsmen to serve in the French interest. By the late eighteenth century the differences between the tribal communities and the creole French (French colonists born and living in the Great Lakes region or Mississippi Valley) had so diminished that both sides had formed a "middle ground," a Great Lakes culture that incorporated values and traits from both sides. Indeed, as historian Richard White argues, the Indian and white worlds "melted at the edges and merged," producing a culture in which it became unclear "whether a particular practice or way of doing things was French or Indian."[1]

The tribes, and members within the tribes, differed among themselves in their subscription to this "middle ground" of politics and culture. Not all tribes (particularly the Foxes or Iroquois) welcomed the French embrace, but among the tribes represented in this volume, the Peorias, Miamis, and Potawatomis, and to a lesser degree the Ottawas, Chippewas, Sauks, and Winnebagos, all walked the middle ground during the latter decades of the eighteenth century. In contrast, the Delawares and Shawnees, who often befriended and traded with the French, also maintained significant contact with the British. The Oneidas, an integral part of the Iroquois Confederacy, generally were allied with the British during the colonial period.

Of all the tribes represented in this volume, the Peorias developed the closest ties with the French. Members of a very loosely allied group of tribes some scholars have called the "Illinois Confederacy," the Peorias lived in eastern Iowa when they first met the French, but in the early seventeenth century they moved to Pimitéoui, a village on Lake Peoria. During the colonial period the Peorias and their kinsmen became closely allied with the French, but they suffered from attacks by the Iroquois and by tribes from Wisconsin. By mid-century, their numbers were much depleted, and they retreated to the American Bottom, located along the Mississippi River opposite modern St. Louis. In southern Illinois the association with the French accelerated, and many Peoria women married French farmers or traders. Jesuit missionaries converted additional members of the tribe, and the Peorias joined with the Cahokias, Kaskaskias, and other members of the much-diminished "Illinois Confederacy," further attaching themselves to the creole community. After the French and Indian War, the Peorias followed the French across the river into Spanish Louisiana where, like many of the creoles, they supported the Americans during the revolution. During the first third of the nineteenth century, the Peorias ceded their lands in Illinois and were removed to a small reservation in eastern Kansas where, in 1854, they merged with the remaining Weas and Piankashaws, former members of the Miami Confederacy, a loose alliance of tribes in the Wabash Valley. Still threatened by advancing American settlement, in 1867 the Confederated Peorias exchanged their lands in Kansas for a small reservation in modern Ottawa County, Oklahoma. In 1873 the Confederated Peorias again merged with other Miamis living in northeastern Oklahoma to form the "United Peoria and Miami." Attached to the Quapaw Agency, a unit of the Bureau of Indian Affairs which administered federal services to the neighboring Quapaw tribe, in 1940 they were incorporated under the Oklahoma Indian Welfare Act as the "Peoria Indian Tribe of Oklahoma." Today they number 2,200 individuals, and their tribal offices are located at Miami, Oklahoma.

The early history of the Miami people closely parallels that of the Peorias. The Miami language is so similar to the language of the Peorias and other members of the Illinois Confederacy that many linguists believe they are dialects of the same tongue. The Miamis first encountered the French in Wisconsin, where they had fled to avoid the Iroquois, but early in the eighteenth century they returned to Indiana and formed a confederacy of loosely allied tribes. The confederacy was comprised of the Miamis proper, who were scattered in several communities on the headwaters of the Wabash and Maumee rivers; the Ouiatanons or "Weas," who occupied villages near modern Lafayette and Logansport; and the Piankashaws, who resided further downstream, in the lower Wabash Valley. Like the Peorias, the Miamis became closely associated with the French, although part of the Piankashaws, led by their chief La Demoiselle, or "Old Briton," moved to the Miami River in Ohio and formed a temporary alliance with British traders between 1747 and 1752. During the American Revolution most of the Miamis and Weas, even those with French ancestry, supported the British while many of the Piankashaws were friendly to the colonists. In the post-revolutionary period the Miamis, led by Little Turtle, an influential chief from Kekionga, a village near modern Fort Wayne, spearheaded the Native American resistance to American control of Ohio and Indiana. In 1790 and 1791 Little Turtle and his allies twice defeated major American expeditions, including a stunning victory over Arthur St. Clair in November 1791 which inflicted the greatest losses ever suffered by the United States (630 men killed) in its military campaigns against Native Americans. By 1794, however, Little Turtle and most of the Miamis had come to terms with the Long Knives, and few Miamis fought at Fallen Timbers, a battle in which the tribes suffered a major defeat. Following the subsequent Treaty of Greenville (1795), the Miamis gave up their claims to lands in Ohio, and the Weas and Piankashaws withdrew from the confederacy.

In the early nineteenth century the Miamis strenghthened their ties to the United States. Most rejected invitations to join the political and religious movement championed by Tecumseh and the Shawnee Prophet, and after the War of 1812 mixed-blood Miami leaders such as Jean Baptiste Richardville and Francis Godfroy attempted to cooperate with the Americans. Active in the fur trade, some of these acculturated mixed-bloods were shrewd businessmen who amassed personal fortunes (Richardville reputedly was the richest man in Indiana when the state joined the union in 1816), but they could not protect the lush Miami homeland from settlers. Eventually the Miamis were forced to cede most of their remaining land in Indiana. In response, Richardville, Godfroy, and others offered their fellow tribespeople refuge on tracts of privately held lands, but federal troops forced most of the Miamis to remove to a new reservation on the Marais des Cygnes River in Kansas in the 1840s.

The federal government recognized the Miami community on the Marais des Cygnes as the "official" Miami tribe, and all tribal annuities (payments for previous land cessions) were paid in Kansas. But the western Miamis were hard pressed to retain their new lands. Like the Peorias, they were overrun by white settlers in the post–Civil War period. In 1867 the tribe signed a treaty providing for the allotment of their reservation, and some western Miamis received small individual tracts of land in Kansas, where they attempted to settle as small farmers. Others were removed to Oklahoma, where in 1868 they were attached to the "Confederated Peorias." In 1873 seventy-two Miamis who previously had received small farms in Kansas moved to Oklahoma where they joined the Peorias, Weas, and Piankashaws. In 1939 the Miami Tribe of Oklahoma incorporated under the Oklahoma Indian Welfare Act, and today the tribal government occupies offices in Miami, Oklahoma. The tribe operates a profitable trucking company and maintains a ceremonial center north of Miami. In 1990 their tribal enrollment numbered 1,450.

Yet many Miamis either remained in, or returned to, Indiana. Federal officials reported that the removal parties of 1846 contained over 323 Indians, but that an additional 148 Miamis remained on private land held by the Richardvilles, Godfroys, Slocums, or the descendants of Metocina, a chief from the Mississinewa River region. By 1855, as refugees returned from Kansas, the population increased to 300, and the

Indiana Miamis, whose tribal government no longer was recognized as valid or "official" by the federal government, outnumbered their kinsmen in Kansas. Since they shared in none of the tribal annuities (payments), the Indiana Miamis relied on hunting, fishing, gardening, and "day work" obtained in the farms and villages near their communities. Some worked in Peru, a railroad center on the central Wabash where the Wallace Circus wintered and provided both seasonal and regular employment to tribe members. The federal government did allow the Indiana Miamis to patronize the Indian Health Service, and also enrolled their children in Indian boarding schools, but in 1897, in the infamous Devanter decision, the federal government reversed its position and declared that the Miamis no longer were Indians.

Until that time, the small Miami reserves in Indiana, like all tribally held Native American land, were subject only to federal jurisdiction, and exempt from state and local taxation. The Devanter decision removed all Miami lands from tax exemption and did much to break up the Miami communities. Now forced to seek employment across the state, the Miamis scattered up and down the Wabash. Some relocated to Indianapolis, others to Fort Wayne, yet they still periodically assembled for family meetings, traditional ceremonies, and other gatherings. Like other Hoosiers, many suffered in the Great Depression.

Since the 1950s the Indiana Miamis have repeatedly sought federal recognition from the government. They have yet to achieve success. Although they adhere to their Native American identity, the federal government refuses to recognize them as Indians. Undeterred, they maintain tribal offices in Peru, Indiana, and count a tribal membership of about 2,700. They remain optimistic, but at present their future is uncertain.

The Pokagon Potawatomis have been more fortunate. Closely related to the Ottawas and Chippewas, the Potawatomis also first encountered the French in Wisconsin, but traditionally they occupied a broad swath of country bordering the southern shores of Lake Michigan and stretching eastward across southern Michigan to Detroit. During the eighteenth century, as the Peorias and their allies withdrew toward St. Louis, Potawatomi tribespeople established villages down the Illinois River to Lake Peoria, and across northern Indiana from the Kankakee River to Fort Wayne. Like the Miamis and Peorias, the Potawatomis also maintained a close relationship with the French, and were, with the exception of the Peorias, the most loyal of all the western

tribes in supporting Onontio. Potawatomi warriors repeatedly journeyed as far east as Montreal, New England, and New York where they
fought with the French against the British. Potawatomi women also
intermarried with French traders, but the tribe was more populous than
either the Peorias or the Miamis, and the traders' mixed-blood children,
although important as community leaders, initially exercised less influence than the métis among the Peorias or Miamis.

During the American Revolution, Potawatomis from the Detroit and
South Bend regions generally assisted the British, while their kinsmen
near Lake Peoria and in southern Wisconsin remained neutral or half-
heartedly supported the Americans. Potawatomis from Michigan and
northern Indiana joined with Little Turtle and other militants to oppose
the American occupation of Ohio, but tribal support for Tecumseh and
the Prophet came primarily from Potawatomi villages along the upper
Tippecanoe, Kankakee, and Fox rivers. After 1815 the Potawatomis
were clustered into several loosely knit communities. One community
was centered in southeastern Wisconsin, stretching from Milwaukee
down the Fox River into northern Illinois. Often intermingled with the
"United Potawatomis, Ottawas, and Chippewas" who were located in
the modern Chicago region, they were led by mixed-blood or métis
traders such as Alexander Robinson and Billy Caldwell. Another community, although smaller in number, still resided near the north shore of
Lake Peoria, while other Potawatomis remained scattered along the
headwaters of the Tippecanoe River in northern Indiana. A small community, sometimes called the Huron Potawatomi, remained in several
villages along the Huron River in southeastern Michigan, while a much
larger community was centered along the St. Joseph River, near modern
Niles, Michigan, and South Bend, Indiana. Similar to the community
near Chicago, the Potawatomis near South Bend also contained a significant mixed-blood population.

Between 1815 and 1840 the Potawatomis signed twenty-nine separate treaties with the United States through which they relinquished
most of their homeland in exchange for government annuities and
reservations in the trans-Mississippi West. During the 1830s federal
officials removed the Potawatomis from northern Indiana and southern
Michigan to a reservation on the Osage River in eastern Kansas, while
their kinsmen from Illinois and Wisconsin were relocated to a tract of
land near Council Bluffs, Iowa, but in 1846 both groups were consolidated at a new reservation west of modern Topeka, on the Kansas River.
There they remained until 1861, when part of the reservation was di-

vided or "allotted" and many of the more acculturated Potawatomis received individual private allotments (acreages) and were bestowed with American citizenship by the federal government. Other Potawatomis, more conservative tribespeople, were transferred to a small reservation near Mayetta, Kansas. Known as the Prairie Band Potawatomi Tribe of Kansas, today they number over 4,000 individuals.

Following the Civil War, many of the "Citizen Potawatomi" (those who had accepted small allotments in Kansas) were swindled out of their allotments, and in 1867 they moved to a new reservation near Shawnee, Oklahoma. Today, incorporated as the Citizen Band Potawatomi Tribe of Oklahoma, they number over 22,000. Most are acculturated mixed-bloods, and many have been active in a resurgence of Native American economic activity which emerged in the 1980s.

Not all the Potawatomis went west. Some tribespeople from Michigan and northeastern Indiana fled the removals and sought sanctuary in Canada where they still remain in permanent communities on Walpole Island in Ontario. Others retreated into the forests of northern Wisconsin and Michigan's Upper Peninsula, where they subsisted through hunting, fishing, and lumbering. In 1913 the federal government established two reservations for these refugees, one at Hannahville in Menominee County, Michigan, and the other in Forest County, Wisconsin. The Hannahville community numbers about 200, while the Forest County band has an enrollment of approximately 800 individuals.

Two other communities of Potawatomis remained in Michigan's lower peninsula. One, in Calhoun County, was comprised of members from the Huron Band. Their descendants still reside on a small state reservation near Battle Creek, and currently number about 820. The other community, the Pokagon Potawatomis, live in southwestern Michigan, near modern Dowagiac and Rush River.

The Pokagon Potawatomis originally were part of the greater St. Joseph Potawatomi community, but many trace their lineage back to Potawatomi villagers who early converted to Roman Catholicism. Prominent among these Potawatomis was Leopold Pokagon, probably of Ottawa or Chippewa origin, but married to a niece or daughter of Topinbee, the most prominent leader among the St. Joseph Potawatomis. When Topinbee died in 1826, Pokagon emerged as one of the more influential St. Joseph chiefs, and, supported by métis trader Joseph Bertrand, he allied himself with Catholic priests and purchased land for his followers near Silver Lake. Through an appeal to the Michigan

Supreme Court, he was able to exempt his "Catholic followers" from removal, and after he died in 1841, his son Peter succeeded him as the leader of the Pokagon community. Throughout the nineteenth century, the Pokagon band repeatedly petitioned the federal government for their fair share of Potawatomi annuities (usually paid only to Potawatomis in Kansas or Oklahoma), but they met with limited success. Meanwhile, many subsisted as hunters, fishermen, gatherers, and agricultural laborers, while Pokagon women crafted baskets that they traded for necessities.

In the twentieth century the population slowly dispersed from the Silver Lake region, seeking employment in the growing industrial base of northern Indiana and southwestern Michigan. After 1900 the federal government generally ignored the Pokagon people, but in 1934, the Pokagon Potawatomi Business Committee attempted to organize under the provisions of the Indian Reorganization Act and renew their formal recognition from the government. Hard-pressed by financial obligations, the federal government was reluctant to extend "new" recognition to Native American communities who no longer possessed a communal tribal land base and, after several cursory investigations, denied the Pokagon petition.

Although denied federal recognition, the Pokagons retained their Potawatomi identity. Most were Catholic; they continued to elect their business committee; and many members met to celebrate the more traditional parts of Potawatomi life. They organized powwows, established programs to teach and perpetuate their cultural heritage, and, led by their Business Committee, again sought federal recognition. Finally, sixty years after their first petition, they were successful. In September 1994 the federal government recognized the Pokagon people as the Potawatomi Indian Nation, Incorporated. Today the tribe maintains an office in Dowagiac, Michigan.

The Delawares first encountered Europeans in coastal regions of New York and New Jersey, and by the middle of the seventeenth century they were trading with Dutch, Swedish, and British colonists. In the early eighteenth century they migrated to Pennsylvania, where they were heavily influenced by the Iroquois. By the 1750s they were living in western Pennsylvania and eastern Ohio where Moravian missionaries converted several hundred tribespeople who then separated into Christian villages. During the American Revolution some Delawares fought with the British, others assisted the Americans, while the

Moravians attempted to remain neutral. Yet the warfare of the revolutionary period sparked a Delaware diaspora. After American militiamen massacred over ninety Moravian Delawares at Gnaddenhutten, Ohio, in 1782, many of the Moravian Delawares fled north into Canada. Other Moravian converts, accompanied by their kinsmen, moved to eastern Indiana. In 1789 another group of Delawares migrated to southeastern Missouri; others sought sanctuary among the Senecas. By 1800 the Delaware people were scattered in a wide arc from Missouri to New York.

Many of the Delawares attempted to walk the white man's road. The Moravian converts in particular settled down on small farms, erected log cabins, and attired themselves in a manner similar to their non-Indian neighbors. Other Delawares on the White River in Indiana and in Missouri also combined farming and hunting like their white neighbors, and most members of the tribe endeavored to cooperate with the Americans. Delaware leaders such as Anderson, White Eyes, and Killbuck opposed Tecumseh and the Prophet, and while some younger warriors fought with the Shawnees and British during the War of 1812, many Delawares assisted the Americans.

In 1818 the Indiana Delawares ceded their lands east of the Mississippi and joined other western Delawares in new villages on the James Fork of the White River in Missouri. Some of the Delaware tribespeople who earlier had fled to Missouri moved to the Sabine River in east Texas, where they lived near the Texas Cherokees. Pressured by the white frontier, and preferring better access to the bison herds, in 1830 the Missouri Delawares accepted a new reservation on the Kansas River just east of modern Lawrence. By mid-century, Texas had forced the Cherokees and Delawares formerly living along the Sabine River back into Oklahoma where many of these Delaware refugees formed new communities near the Wichita Mountains. Led by Black Beaver, these new communities adopted economic patterns similar to neighboring Caddos and Wichitas, and relied extensively upon hunting buffalo on the plains.

In 1866 the Delawares in Kansas ceded their lands and one year later relocated in northeastern Oklahoma, inside the Cherokee Nation. Known as the "Registered Delaware," they established their own Business Committee and continued to receive Delaware annuities, but were administered as part of the Cherokee Nation and participated in Cherokee politics. In contrast, the western Delawares, who had settled near the Wichita Mountains, were assigned a reservation in modern Caddo

County, Oklahoma, which they shared with the Caddos and Wichitas. In 1891 this reservation was allotted, but federal officials enumerated the western or "Absentee Delawares" as Caddos or Wichitas, not Delawares. Although the western Delaware community remained intact, they were not recognized as "Delawares" by the federal government from 1895 until 1936 when they organized under the Oklahoma Indian Welfare Act. Today the Delaware Tribe of Western Oklahoma maintains tribal offices in Anadarko and enrolls a population of over 1,100. Other Delaware communities also continue at three reserves in Ontario. Moraviantown and Muncey are located on the Thames River, while the third is on the Six Nations Reserve on the Grand River.

Like the Delawares, the Shawnees also were a people scattered by the European invasion. The Shawnees believe that the Master of Life placed them in the Ohio Valley, and early French accounts, although vague, indicate they occupied villages in southern Ohio and northern Kentucky. In the late seventeenth century, as the Iroquois expanded, the Shawnees split into several groups. One group fled westward into Illinois. Another sought refuge among the Creeks in Alabama. Others moved eastward, finding sanctuary along the Susquehanna River in Pennsylvania. Yet after 1700, as the Iroquois withdrew from the west, the Shawnees returned to their homeland, and by the 1750s they had reestablished villages in central and southeastern Ohio.

Prior to 1700 some Shawnees had traded with the French, but by the middle of the eighteenth century most had developed ties to the British. Some Shawnee warriors assisted the French during the French and Indian War, and many Shawnees joined in Pontiac's Rebellion, but the Shawnees generally were allied with the British throughout much of the eighteenth century. They opposed colonial expansion into Kentucky and Ohio and staunchly supported the British against the Kentuckians during the American Revolution. In the postwar period the Shawnees were leading proponents in the multi-tribal coalition that opposed the United States until the Battle of Fallen Timbers.

Following the Treaty of Greenville (1795), the Shawnees attempted to live in peace with the Americans. During the American Revolution part of the tribe withdrew from the fighting and moved to southeastern Missouri where they were granted land by the Spaniards. In Ohio, the majority of Shawnees, led by Black Hoof, welcomed missionaries and attempted to embrace the government's acculturation program. Yet socioeconomic conditions among the tribe deteriorated, and in 1805

Tenskwatawa, the Shawnee Prophet, emerged as the leader of a new religious revitalization movement. By 1809 Tecumseh, the Prophet's older brother, had transformed the religious fervor into a militant, pan-Indian political movement designed to centralize power and prevent the further cessation of Native American lands. Black Hoof and many other Shawnees opposed Tecumseh, and during the War of 1812 the tribe split over support of the British or the Americans.

Following the War of 1812, the Shawnee Prophet and a few followers temporarily remained in Canada, but in the mid-1820s they returned to Ohio where they were removed with other Shawnees, first to Missouri, then to Kansas. In the west the Shawnees split again into three bands. During the first two decades of the nineteenth century, many of the Shawnees who earlier had moved to Missouri became associated with the western Cherokees and Delawares, even following the latter two tribes to Texas. When these tribes fled north into Oklahoma, the Shawnees who accompanied them established new villages along the Canadian River, east of modern Oklahoma City. Since they took no part in the allotment of lands in Kansas, they were known as the Absentee Shawnees.

In 1825, following the federal government's purchase of Shawnee lands in Missouri, those Shawnees who had not joined the Cherokees and Delawares, and new Shawnee migrants from Ohio were consolidated on a reservation in eastern Kansas. Disputes over religion, acculturation, and their relationship to the federal government divided them into two groups, and many of the former Missouri Shawnees, led by Black Bob, eventually joined with the Absentee band in Oklahoma. The Kansas reservation was allotted in 1854, and some of the Kansas Shawnees then moved to Oklahoma, forming a new community within the Cherokee Nation. Other Kansas Shawnees joined with a small party of Senecas on a small reservation in modern Ottawa County, Oklahoma. Since many of these former Kansas Shawnees supported the Union cause during the Civil War, they were known as the "Loyal Shawnees."

Today all the Shawnees are a relatively acculturated people who retain a pride in their heritage, but also have adjusted to the challenges of modern life. The Absentee Shawnees, incorporated under the Oklahoma Indian Welfare Act, operate tribal offices at Shawnee, Oklahoma. The Loyal Shawnees are under the jurisdiction of the Cherokee Nation but have a tribal building in White Oak, Oklahoma. Also incorporated under the Oklahoma Indian Welfare Act is the Eastern Shawnee Tribe of Oklahoma, which maintains tribal offices at Seneca, Missouri. Their enrollment numbers 1,700. Other small communities of Shawnee people, while not "officially" recognized by the federal government, still reside in Kansas, Missouri, and Ohio.

The Sauk and Fox people were two separate tribes until the 1730s when they joined together after a conflict with New France. Both tribes first encountered the French in Wisconsin, and both the Sauks and the Foxes occupied northern Illinois, southern Wisconsin, and eastern Iowa during the eighteenth century. During the American Revolution they generally favored the British, but by the War of 1812 they were divided in their loyalties. Some Sauks and Foxes, led by Black Hawk, fought with Tecumseh and the British, while others remained neutral or gave at least limited support to the Americans.

During the first third of the nineteenth century, they concentrated their villages along the Mississippi River from Dubuque to Rock Island, where their largest village, Saukenuk dominated the mouth of the Rock River. In 1804 a party of Sauk and Fox warriors inadvertently signed a treaty at St. Louis in which they ceded all Sauk and Fox lands in northern Illinois, Wisconsin, and Missouri for a small payment, but since white settlement had not reached the region, the tribe ignored the cession. By the early 1830s, however, American settlement had crossed the Illinois River and threatened the Sauk and Fox homeland. In 1830 American officials demanded that the Sauks and Foxes withdraw to Iowa, and part of the tribe, led by Keokuk, complied. Others, led by Black Hawk, an aging but militant war chief, refused to abandon Saukenuk and only removed to Iowa after being threatened by the Illinois state militia. On April 6, 1832, Black Hawk and about 2,000 Sauks and Foxes, including almost 1,500 women and children, returned to Illinois in a futile attempt to peacefully reoccupy Saukenuk. Their return panicked frontiersmen and precipitated the "Black Hawk War," a desperate attempt by the Sauks and Foxes to retreat back to Iowa while being pursued by state and federal forces. A series of battles and skirmishes occurred before July 20, 1832, when most of the fleeing Sauks and Foxes were either killed or captured at the Battle of the Bad Axe, in southwestern Wisconsin.

As punishment for their involvement in the Black Hawk War, the Sauks and Foxes were forced to cede part of their lands in Iowa, and between 1836 and 1842 they exchanged the remainder of their Iowa land base for reservations in Kansas. Political and cultural divisions that had been exacerbated by the Black Hawk War continued to plague the tribe. Keokuk, followed by his son Moses Keokuk, led the "progressives," while the conservatives were led by Mokohoko. In 1867 the Sauks and Foxes agreed to the sale and allotment of their reservation in Kansas, and many then moved to a new reservation between the Cimarron and Canadian rivers in Oklahoma. In 1886 Mokohoko's followers, who initially had refused to leave Kansas, were escorted to the new reservation by federal troops.

In Oklahoma, organized as the "Sauk and Fox Nation," the tribe established a formal statutory government with a tribal court system. Many tribal members pursued small scale agriculture or stock-raising. In 1890 the reservation was allotted, but the Sauk and Fox tribal government continued to function, and the tribe was able to retain many of its traditions and ceremonies. Today, the Sauk and Fox Nation, more recently organized under the Oklahoma Indian Welfare Act, maintains tribal offices in Stroud, Oklahoma. The Sauk and Fox tribe enrolls about 1,600 members. In addition, a small reservation occupied by about 160 Sauk and Fox people is located astride the Kansas-Nebraska border at Reserve, in northeastern Kansas. The Mesquakies (Foxes) own and occupy a 4,300-acre settlement near Tama, Iowa.

The Lac du Flambeau Chippewas are part of the populous Chippewa people who occupy a broad swath of territory from the upper Ottawa River Valley, across southern Ontario and northern regions of the Great Lakes states, to the plains of North Dakota and Manitoba. In the colonial period the Chippewas were much involved in the fur trade and, like the Potawatomis, Miamis, and some other tribes, they developed close economic and political ties to the French. Since the Chippewas were such a numerous people residing over an extended territory, it is difficult to characterize their early relationship with the United States, but certain bands of Chippewas, primarily from northern Michigan and Wisconsin, supported the British during the American Revolution and the War of 1812. During the late eighteenth and early nineteenth centuries, however, they expanded their range to the south and west, gradually pushing the eastern Sioux from Wisconsin and eastern Minnesota.

Residents in the northern forested areas of the Great Lakes region, the Chippewas initially were not as threatened by American settlement, which spilled over onto agricultural lands in the southern parts of these states. In 1854 Chippewa leaders in northern Wisconsin signed a treaty establishing several reservations, including an 85,000-acre tract surrounding Lac du Flambeau. Led by Awmose (the Wasp), Kenishteno,

Megeesee (the Eagle), Oscawbaywis (He who Waits), Quewezance (White Fish), Negig (the Otter), and other chiefs, the Lac du Flambeau Chippewas continued to hunt, fish, and harvest wild rice. Although part of the reservation was allotted during the 1890s, the tribe, through individual or tribal ownership, still retains control of approximately 45,000 acres. In the twentieth century some Chippewa men have found seasonal work in the lumber industry, while others have left the reservation seeking employment in Green Bay, Milwaukee, or neighboring communities.

Since the 1980s the Lac du Flambeau Chippewas have developed a tourism industry, focusing particularly on sport fishing and the Lake of the Torches Casino. They also own and operate their own sawmill and electric company, and tribal members own and manage many small businesses on the reservation. Interest in traditional Chippewa culture remains an important part of Lac du Flambeau life, and tribal members participate in the Drum Society and other ceremonial or social activities. The tribe also operates a tribal museum.

The Lac du Flambeau Band of Lake Superior Chippewa Indians is organized under the Indian Reorganization Act and is governed by a twelve-member, elected tribal council. Tribal enrollment numbers slightly over 2,700 individuals.

Closely associated with the Chippewas and Potawatomis, the Ottawas also are a people of the northern forests; but in the colonial period their homeland was the region north of the Grand River in lower Michigan. Early in the seventeenth century, they served as traders at Michilimackinac, but like other Great Lakes tribes during the middle 1600s they fled to Wisconsin to escape the Iroquois. After 1700 they returned to Michigan, establishing villages at Detroit and as far south as northern Ohio. During the colonial period they also were associated with the French, and following the British occupation of Detroit, Pontiac, an Ottawa war chief, sparked a revolt against the British which spread from Pennsylvania through Indiana. Ottawa warriors supported the British in the American Revolution and during the War of 1812. By the early decades of the nineteenth century, Ottawa villagers had settled with Potawatomi and Chippewa villagers at Chicago, while small communities continued to occupy locations along the Maumee and Auglaize rivers in Ohio. Following the War of 1812, other Ottawas fled north to Ontario, where they joined with kinsmen at villages on Walpole and Manitoulin islands.

In 1821 the Ottawas ceded all their lands south of the Grand River in Michigan, and fifteen years later they relinquished their claims to the remainder of the lower peninsula in exchange for annuities and several small reservations between the mouth of the Muskegon River and the Straits of Mackinac. Most of these reservations were allotted in the nineteenth century, but Ottawa communities still remain on or adjacent to reservations at Grand Traverse and Little Traverse Bay. Other Ottawa communities remain active in Canada.

The Ottawas residing in Ohio ceded their lands to the federal government in two treaties (1831 and 1833) and were removed to a reservation on the Marais des Cygnes River in Kansas in 1836. In 1862 these Kansas Ottawas agreed to the allotment of their reservation and sale of their surplus reservation lands. In the turmoil of the Civil War many of the Ottawas lost their allotments, and in 1867 most of the tribe emigrated to Oklahoma where they received a reservation in modern Ottawa County. The Oklahoma reservation was allotted in 1892, and most of the Ottawas became small farmers or ranchers. An informal tribal government functioned until 1938, when they were incorporated as the Ottawa Tribe under the Oklahoma Indian Welfare Act. In 1955 the tribe was terminated, and the federal government withdrew its recognition until 1978 when the Ottawas in Oklahoma were reinstated as a federally recognized tribe.

Today the Ottawas continue to function as farmers and businessmen, and they are eager to reestablish a tribal land base in Oklahoma. The tribe is governed by a business committee established according to their constitution, which was formulated in the 1930s. The Ottawa Tribe maintains a tribal headquarters in Miami, Oklahoma. Their current enrollment is approximately 1,600.

The Ho-Chunk or Winnebago people are a Wisconsin tribe who traditionally spoke a Siouan language more closely related to the languages of the tribes of the prairies and eastern plains than to those of their woodland neighbors of the Great Lakes region. They first encountered the French in the Green Bay–Fox River region of Wisconsin where the Winnebagos were at war with the Foxes, Ottawas, and many other tribes. By 1700 they had entered into the French trade network and had withdrawn to Lake Winnebago. From there they expanded along the Wisconsin, Black, and Rock rivers, occupying much of southern Wisconsin and part of northern Illinois. They assisted the French against the Foxes and fought with the British during the American Revolution.

Winnebago warriors were among the most devoted followers of Tecumseh and the Shawnee Prophet, and the Winnebagos suffered more casualties than any other tribe in the Indian defeat at the Battle of the Tippecanoe, in 1811.

Following the War of 1812 the Winnebago homeland in Wisconsin was threatened by white settlement. During the 1820s American lead miners continually trespassed upon tribal land south of Prairie du Chien, and in 1827 Red Bird, a local chief, led a small party that killed several settlers. Red Bird surrendered to American authorities and died in prison, but in 1829 the federal government used the "Red Bird Uprising" as a pretext to demand that the tribe relinquish claims to much of its land in south-central Wisconsin. Subsequent treaties in 1832 and 1837 surrendered almost all the remaining Winnebago territory in the state, and in exchange the Winnebagos initially received a large tract of territory in northeastern Iowa and southeastern Minnesota. Part of the tribe moved to this region, then exchanged it for two reservations in Minnesota, finally moving to the Blue Earth River, near modern Mankato, where they attempted to walk the white man's road as small farmers. When the Minnesota Sioux rose up against the government in 1862, the Winnebagos at Blue Earth took no part in the hostilities, but anti-Indian sentiment was so intense that the Winnebagos were forcibly removed to Crow Creek in South Dakota, where many of them starved during the winter of 1862-63. They abandoned the lands on Crow Creek and in 1865 negotiated for a new reservation, just north of the Omahas, in northeastern Nebraska. In the 1890s much of this reservation was allotted and passed from Winnebago possession. About half of the Winnebagos in Nebraska eventually returned to Wisconsin, but others settled on small homesteads adjacent to Winnebago, a town near the eastern edge of the remaining Nebraska reservation. Some tribespeople continued to farm their allotments, while others worked at seasonal jobs in the region. Both the Dutch Reformed and the Roman Catholic churches maintained missions in the community, but early in the twentieth century many Winnebagos also became followers of the Peyote faith.

In 1936 the Winnebago Tribe of Nebraska organized under the Indian Reorganization Act, and the tribe currently is governed by a nine-member tribal council and operates the Winne Vegas Casino. The reservation population numbers about 1,200.

In 1837 part of the Winnebagos refused to remove from Wisconsin and took refuge among the heavy forests in the west-central sections of the state. Led by Dandy and Yellow Thunder, these tribespeople "lived off the land" until 1881 when they were permitted to establish homesteads in regions generally unwanted by whites. Two Winnebago enclaves developed: one near Black River Falls in western Wisconsin, and another near Wittenberg. The Wisconsin Winnebagos remained a conservative people, and although some enrolled their children in public or mission schools, they continued to follow many of the ways of their fathers. Most still hunted, fished, gathered products from the forest, and planted their small gardens, although some sought seasonal work in agriculture or lumbering. By the mid-1920s a community of Winnebagos had settled near the Wisconsin Dells, where they sold their crafts and performed for tourists. Meanwhile, others moved, in growing numbers, to urban areas such as Milwaukee or Minneapolis. Many Winnebagos fought in World War II, and following the conflict they formed the Winnebago Veterans organization, a group which also pursued the land claims of both the Wisconsin and Nebraska Winnebagos before the Indians Claims Commission, a federal agency established in 1946 and designed to provide legal access to the tribes so that they might contest the fraudulent sale of their lands, primarily transactions conducted in the nineteenth century.

In 1963 the Wisconsin Winnebagos organized under the Indian Reorganization Act, and at that time were recognized by the federal government as the Wisconsin Winnebago Tribe. In 1994 they adopted a new constitution and officially changed their name from the "Wisconsin Winnebago Tribe" to the Ho-Chunk Nation. The Ho-Chunk Nation functions under a government composed of four branches: a general council, legislature, executive, and judiciary. They maintain tribal offices in Black River Falls, and have initiated a broad spectrum of community services for tribal members. They currently operate their own construction company and three casinos or bingo halls. Their tribal enrollment numbers approximately 5,000.

Unlike the other tribes represented in the interviews, the Oneidas were part of the Iroquois Confederacy, and their traditional homeland was in upstate New York. A loose political confederacy originally comprised of five (Mohawk, Oneida, Onondaga, Cayuga, and Seneca), and later six (Tuscarora) tribes, the Iroquois league early developed close ties to the Dutch and British, bringing it into conflict with many of the French allied Algonquian tribes discussed above. Throughout the colonial period the Oneidas were closely allied with the British, and like other members of the Iroquois league they became heavily dependent upon British trade goods. Unlike the Algonquian tribes to their west, the Oneidas were more sedentary, living in large, permanent villages near Lake Oneida and planting extensive fields of corn and other vegetables.

In the American Revolution most of the Oneidas and Tuscaroras broke with other members of the Iroquois league and supported the Americans. When the war ended American officials promised the Oneidas that they would retain possession of their territories, but in the postwar period the tribe sold several tracts of land to the state of New York. Meanwhile the tribe split into two parties, one Christian, the other primarily followers of the Seneca Prophet, Handsome Lake. Encouraged by missionary Eleazar Williams, in 1823 one party of Christian Oneidas purchased a tract of 500,000 acres from the Menominees, and during the 1830s they moved to Wisconsin. In 1838 Oneida leaders in New York signed the Treaty of Buffalo Creek, which provided for their removal to Indian Territory, but most Oneidas refused to go and during the 1840s most emigrated to Ontario, while a few joined relatives in Wisconsin. About 200 Oneidas remained in New York.

In Wisconsin the Oneidas settled near the head of Green Bay, where they engaged in fishing and farming, and leased some of their lands to white-owned lumber companies. In 1892 their reservation was allotted and many eventually were forced to sell their individual tracts, or lost them to taxes. Many Oneidas moved to Green Bay where they worked at various occupations, but the tribal community retained medicine societies, kinship groups, religious organizations, and other social units. In 1934 the Oneida Nation of Wisconsin incorporated under the Indian Reorganization Act, and since the 1960s has aggressively sought to become economically self-sufficient. Today the Oneida Nation of Wisconsin owns and operates the Oneida Radisson, which is located near the Green Bay municipal airport; several retail establishments; and other enterprises. They maintain tribal offices at Oneida, Wisconsin, and enroll approximately 12,000 tribal members.

The Ontario Oneidas settled on the Thames River, near Westminster. Most Canadian Oneidas also remained Christian, although the Longhouse Religion of Handsome Lake attracted other members of the community. Originally most Canadian Oneidas either farmed on their reserve or worked as agricultural laborers for Canadian farmers, but in the twentieth century they have sought employment in London or Westminster. They are governed through an elected tribal council authorized by the Canadian government and accepted as legitimate by all Oneidas who are not members of the Longhouse religion, which maintains its own hereditary council.

The Oneida community in New York lives on a small reservation near Vernon, and in adjacent communities. They pursue a broad range of economic opportunities, and although many live on the Onondaga reservation, they have retained their Oneida identity. The Oneida Indian Nation of New York was incorporated under the Indian Reorganization Act, and all enrolled adult members of the tribe are members of the Oneida General Council. A business committee of nine members administers tribal business. The tribe owns and operates a casino, bingo hall, recreational vehicle park, and convenience store.

* * * * * * *

The individuals featured in this volume are members of the tribes discussed above, and as the tribal sketches indicate, the separate tribes all have their own particular histories. Individual tribal members are part of that history, and "being Winnebago" is different from "being Miami," which is different from "being Oneida," etc. Yet there are certain shared patterns of experience that emerge from the interviews, and that form part of the continued Woodland Peoples' consciousness.

First, almost all of the individuals featured in this volume are the products of a rural upbringing. Today almost half of the Native American population of the United States lives in major urban areas, but most of the adults, like the individuals in this book, were raised in rural Native American communities. They currently may reside in Tulsa, Milwaukee, or Chicago, but they trace their roots back to a specific place, a rural location that embodies much of their identity and that still serves as "home." For those tribal people who still retain their reservations, the tribally held land remains a "wellspring of Indianness," a place where many plan to retire, no matter how long they have been absent. Yet even those people whose reservations were allotted retain strong attachments to their families' rural homes. Frank Bush fondly remembers growing up on the "Bush homestead" in rural Michigan where his family contracted to raise cucumbers, and where they supplemented their income through picking berries or raising vegetables in the garden. Lora Siders, Floyd Leonard, and others recall childhoods spent on farms where money sometimes was in short supply, but where families joined together to produce much of their food. Other subjects mention hunting or fishing to supplement their gardens, and almost all describe their rural childhood as a formative period in their lives: a time of limited economic opportunity, but a span of years in which they learned to be self-reliant, and a time when their parents taught them the values that have shaped their lives.

Almost all of the individuals featured in this volume are of mixed ancestry. Some are entirely of Native American descent, but very few of these people claim descent from only one tribe. Of course, there is considerable historical precedent for intertribal marriages, and European accounts from the colonial period often mention that prominent tribal leaders frequently were of mixed tribal ancestry. Sauks, Foxes, and Kickapoos often intermarried, as did Potawatomis, Ottawas, and Chippewas. Tecumseh, the great Shawnee war chief, was the son of a Shawnee father and a Creek mother, and Pokagon, the leader from which the Pokagon Potawatomis take their name, was born among the Ottawa or Chippewa tribes.

Within the past century this process has accelerated. The concentration of many tribes in Oklahoma and the establishment of numerous federal and private boarding schools brought people together whose tribal communities originally were separated by considerable distance. As all tribal people know, "Haskell marriages" (Native Americans who met and subsequently married after attending Haskell Institute or other boarding schools) are rather commonplace. Moreover, the development of large intertribal powwows and the urbanization of the Native American population in the half-century since World War II also have contributed to this phenomenon. As Indian people have relocated to cities, they have associated with other urban Indians, regardless of tribal affiliation. Urban Indian centers, often housed in a storefront or religious institution, have become important meeting points for people from many tribes, and programs sponsored by such centers provide a medium through which urban Native Americans from different tribal communities can meet and interact.

Urbanization also has facilitated intermarriage with non-Indians. As indicated above, many of the Woodland People have a long history of intermarriage with Europeans, and almost all of the subjects featured in this volume come from mixed-blood families. Yet in the twentieth century, particularly since World War II, these relationships have increased. Recent statistics illustrate that more than fifty-five percent of unmarried urban-dwelling Native American women will marry non-Indians, and all available evidence seems to indicate that this percentage will increase. Indeed, with the exception of several rural, reservation-based communities in the West, most Native American families now acknowledge that part of their ancestry is European. Obviously, such a heritage does not make them "less Indian," but it does illustrate that Native American people, like other Americans (and people throughout the world), are part of a constantly shifting genetic pattern.

Regardless of their ancestry, all of the individuals whose interviews are included in this volume share a very deep and abiding commitment to their families. Today (as in the past), at powwows, intertribal meetings, or on college campuses, when Native Americans initially meet and attempt to become acquainted, most discuss family ties, looking for some mutual, if distant, kinship relationship that will place their friendship in its proper perspective. Like Native American people everywhere, they know that family always has been the very warp of tribal society, and they are acutely aware of extended kinship ties often deemed distant or unimportant by non-Indians.

Most of the subjects remember a childhood surrounded by members of their extended family: aunts, uncles, and particularly grandparents. Within tribal societies kinship terms such as "grandmother" or "grandfather" transcend the usual family or generational definitions ascribed to such titles in English, and envelop a much broader and more honored or reverential meaning. Since many Native American children traditionally were reared or cared for by their grandparents, it is not surprising that many of the interviews illustrate such affection. Sharon Burkybile describes how she "worshiped" her grandfather, and Philip Alexis remembers his grandmother as a "special friend." Other subjects talk fondly of their close relationships with grandparents, aunts, and uncles, and most relate that the time and experiences they have shared with their families are the happiest moments of their lives. Some, like Michael Pace or Helen Rameriz, are concerned that their children continue to adhere to their family obligations, but all share a love for their children and grandchildren that seems to ensure that the tribal community will continue.

All of the subjects come from tribal communities that have overcome almost insurmountable difficulties, but that have persisted. Uprooted repeatedly, forced to seek temporary residence at a series of locations across the eastern and southern United States, communities of Shawnees and Delawares have maintained a sense of cohesion that has triumphed over a series of geographic dispersions. Peorias, Potawatomis, and Miamis, long subjected to an extended acculturation, still maintain tribal communities that adhere to their sense of identity and that are mutually supportive to their members. Throughout most of its existence, the federal government incorrectly assumed that Native American people would acculturate and be completely assimilated into the mainstream of American society. Indeed, until the 1930s (and even later in some instances) the primary focus of most federal policy makers was to destroy the tribal communities and disperse Native American people among the non-Indian majority. Ironically, although whites have systematically (through statute or custom) attempted to deny African-Americans, Asian-Americans, and other ethnic minorities access to full participation in American society, most have assumed that Native Americans, separated from their former tribal communities, would eventually become full members.

In contrast, the individuals featured in this volume, like other Indian people, have tenaciously clung to their sense of community. They obviously are individual human beings, but more importantly, they see themselves as part of a larger tribal community with whom they share economic resources and cultural values. According to Emma Greenfeather Donaldson, "We were always taught to be good and kind to each other and not to be angry or have bad feelings in our hearts. . . . help each other, and be kind to each other, . . . and if you do, you're going to find out that you are going to be blessed." And as David Lee Smith adds, "When I get old I want to be here among The People, not someplace else with other people. I want to be with the people I know; the people I grew up with. And when I die here, I want to be buried here among The People so my spirit can roam."

If the fabric of tribal community is woven from many strands, perhaps the most frayed and fragile thread is language. Relatively few of the Woodland People featured in this volume are fluent speakers of their native tongues, although almost all hold some proficiency in their language. Yet all would agree that the retention or resurrection of tribal languages is a key factor in maintaining tribal communities. Surely no facet of tribal culture has come under greater attack. From the colonial period through the twentieth century, government officials, missionaries, and most educators have consistently endeavored to force Native American people to relinquish traditional languages and adopt English. In both boarding schools and the public school system, Indian students were forbidden to converse in their native tongues, or even punished for doing so, and because very few Indian agents were fluent in the tribal languages all official negotiations or other "business" between the tribes and the federal government also was conducted in English. Since the 1960s many tribal communities have made a concerted effort to develop and utilize bilingual materials, but during this period the tribal communities, like other communities across the United States, have been subjected to the most sophisticated electronic media "blitz" in all of recorded history. As linguists readily admit, it is very difficult to speak and think in a language when one is surrounded by a plethora of voices, both live and recorded, that converse in another tongue. All the subjects realize that they and their children must interact with the non-Indian world, and all understand that fluency in English is necessary for such interaction, but they are eager for their communities to retain a fundamental knowledge of their tribal language as a keystone of their community's identity. Only time will tell if the new tribal language programs will be successful, but so far the prognosis is, at best, guarded.

Other facets of community life most certainly have been strengthened and retained. Almost all of the subjects specifically mention the pride they have taken in their community's adherence to traditional values or ceremonies, and those tribes who have lost some of their traditional ways have made a concerted effort either to resurrect part of their heritage or to establish new cultural patterns that will buttress the community's sense of identity. In a pattern as old as tribal society itself, many of the traditions continue to be passed down from grandparents to grandchildren, quietly taught and reinforced through both instruction and personal example. Leonard Thompson remembers when he and other Delaware children "would sit over in the corner on the floor, but didn't say anything . . . and listened to the old people tell stories" of witchcraft and the Delawares' great trek from the Ohio Valley. Billie Smith, a Loyal Shawnee, remembers the lessons taught to her by her aunts and other tribal Elders, especially Susan Flint, who instructed her about medicinal plants and which ceremonies to perform before hunting animals or using natural products from the forest. Smith, who has passed these stories on to her children, has retained much of her traditional beliefs, but she fears that some may be forgotten within the next generation.

Many of the communities are taking steps to ensure that Smith's fears will be unfounded. Since the late 1960s the tribal communities have been strengthened by growing numbers of young adults who are determined to revitalize their societies. Almost all of the tribes represented in these interviews now sponsor formal classes in tribal languages, traditions, or crafts. Educators like Tom Topash have developed new curricula and instructional materials designed to explain and illuminate traditional tribal ways, while others, such as Curtis Zunigha, are working closely with museums and other institutions to ensure that tribal members will have greater access to their collections. Beadwork, ribbonwork, and basket making are now being taught at tribal centers, and beautifully crafted items are being produced, both for domestic consumption and for sale to the public. Unquestionably, the renewed pride in tribal identity and the interest in revitalizing tribal traditions have gone hand in hand. As Patricia Hrabik points out, "Not to practice cultural traditions is losing your identity somehow. I am just now beginning to learn and appreciate the beauty of some of the old ceremonies and the way of speaking to our Creator in the old traditional way."

The ceremonies, both old and new, continue. Some communities, such as the Oneidas, the Lac du Flambeau Chippewas, and the Absentee Shawnees, have been able to retain many of their ceremonies, passing down ritual and tradition through the generations. Unquestionably the vagaries of time and relocation have changed some parts of these celebrations, but the central, essential meaning of the ceremonies remain the same. As Victoria Daugherty points out, her grandmother, mother, and older sister all have served as head dancer among the Loyal Shawnees, and the position has been "handed down from generation to generation." Within other communities, old ceremonies also continue, although they have been altered by outside influences over which The People have little control. Unquestionably, as many tribes were concentrated together in Oklahoma, new rituals and beliefs were adopted from neighboring tribal communities, or even from the dominant American society. In this context, Native American people have participated in a worldwide pattern of religious and cultural syncretism shared by all people throughout recorded history. Ritual and ceremony, like all facets of culture, continue to integrate new traditions, and to evolve through time. Tribal communities, like all communities, are dynamic organs of change.

Within the past decades many of these communities have labored diligently to regain ceremonies that once seemed almost lost. Until the 1930s federal officials discouraged many traditional ceremonies as part of the Bureau of Indian Affairs' program to force acculturation upon the tribal communities. Consequently, although these traditions were still remembered or celebrated by tribal Elders, during the middle decades of the twentieth century they were not practiced by other members of the community. More recently, however, many of these ceremonies have been embraced by growing numbers of tribespeople eager to reaffirm their ties with the past and to strengthen their tribal identity. As Don Giles mentions, the Peorias did not resume their Stomp Dance until 1992, and their first powwow was held in 1994, but tribal members now look forward to these occasions as opportunities for Peorias to assemble and assert their sense of community. Meanwhile, Elders whose wisdom once was associated with the past are treasured as storehouses of ceremonial knowledge that help communities reaffirm their own identities. Unquestionably Frank Bush serves as such a resource for the Pokagon Potawatomis, but all of the Elders featured in the volume have contributed to the retention and revitalization of tradition and ceremony in their communities.

In conclusion, who are these people and the communities they represent? What do their experiences, their lives, and their values tell us about modern Native American people? Not surprisingly, one reader who examined preliminary drafts of the interviews commented that the individuals featured in this volume undoubtedly were Indians, but they were not what he expected. They seemed remarkably "like everybody else." When asked to elaborate upon his description, he commented that most worked at "regular jobs"; their children attended public schools; they seemed to reside in modern housing; and most lived interspersed within the non-Indian community that surrounded them. Most did not live on isolated reservations in the Far West, nor did they make their living through "traditional" economic practices, such as hunting or fishing, herding sheep, or the manufacture and sale of jewelry, pottery, or craft items.

Indeed, the subjects of this volume are real people who do not fit the stereotypes often associated with Native Americans. Yet ironically, most modern Indian people throughout the United States also do not fit such stereotypical images. Unfortunately for most non-Indians, "authentic" Native Americans—that is, "real Indians"—are associated with a way of life that ended late in the nineteenth century, but that continues to be portrayed and romanticized in the popular media. Consequently, "real Indians" should wear feathered headdresses and moccasins, not baseball caps and running shoes; they should ride on horses, not in pickup trucks; and they should hunt deer and buffalo, not work in factories or as small businessmen. In addition, within the past decade, as modern Native American leaders have successfully utilized tribally owned land to establish tax-sheltered enterprise zones or gaming centers, they have been condemned by many non-Indians (who often envision such economic activity as a threat) for misrepresenting their people and debasing their culture.

But Native American cultures have never been "fixed in stone." Like other cultures throughout the world they have continued to evolve. The tribal people featured in this volume, like Native Americans everywhere, are the products of that evolution. They are modern Indian people living in a modern society. They have combined their Native American heritage with the demands of life in the late twentieth century. They are members of tribal communities that are adaptable yet tempered by a strong sense of their tribal past. Although many do not fit the general public's stereotypical image of "Indians," all of the subjects in this volume have retained a strong sense of their tribal and Native American identity. As Grace Thorpe points out, "There was no particular time in my life when I was proudest to be an Indian. That's just something you take for granted. You don't go around saying something. You're just who you are, I guess." Thorpe's sentiments are echoed by Philip Alexis, Potawatomi tribal leader and businessman, who informed artist Evelyn Ritter that "you can paint me under one condition, that you don't paint me as a 1700 or 1800 Indian. You have to *paint me as who I am*. This is who I am. I am Phil Alexis. . . ."

NOTE

1. Richard White, *The Middle Ground: Indians, Empires, and Republics in the Great Lakes Region, 1650-1815* (Cambridge: Cambridge University Press, 1991), p. 50.

PHILIP V. ALEXIS

Potawatomi (Pokagon Band)

Executive Director, Confederated Historic Tribes, Inc.

Born February 25, 1938, in Watervliet, Michigan

I was born in my grandmother's home on Pleasant Street in Watervliet. My mother is part Ottawa, Grand River Band. She lived in the Bradley area when she was young. My father was a Potawatomi. He grew up around Watervliet and Hartford. Actually, they lived in Rush Lake, which was one of the old Indian settlements.

My Dad came back with skills from Mount Pleasant Indian School. He worked a lot on farms. We moved around a little. We lived in Watervliet, and we lived in the old Indian settlement at Bowesville-Hartford. Some of the people still don't believe that I lived there, but I did. It was the old shacks—tarpaper shacks, stuff like that. My Dad worked for various farmers. Our lives kind of changed when he went into the service when I was small. He went into the Air Force. We lived in the Army housing unit in Benton Harbor. When he came back he ran a sawmill, with a few of the other guys. Then we moved over around Dowagiac.

We lived right across the county line, about a half-mile from the county line. I went to Eau Claire High School and graduated from there as the salutatorian of the class of 1957.

I got a football scholarship and went to Albion College in Michigan. I was a three-time all-state football player. Then I got hurt and ended up with a bad knee and I quit, so I didn't finish school. I should have, but I never did. I went two years to college.

During those years when I was real young, my grandmother was kind of my favorite friend. She was my dad's mother. She did a lot of things with me, and I think that's where a lot of the Indian awareness things came back. My grandmother was known as one of the medicine

28

Philip V. Alexis

Potawatomi (Pokagon Band)

Executive Director, Confederated Historic Tribes, Inc.

women of the tribe. So she taught me about medicine and how to make baskets, to do all that stuff even though I was really young. That went on until I was about a freshman in high school.

I could identify the tree that she used to make baskets. I pounded the bark and made the strips. The guys all did that—the men. They made the handles and the ribbings on top of the baskets. And the women did all the weaving. The women split and smoothed the strips for weaving the baskets.

When you strip the bark off the tree, it comes off anywhere from one-quarter inch to one-eighth of an inch. You can split that, sometimes four times. And that's why it gets real thin and smooth. Then you smooth it with a knife.

That got started again around 1975 when I asked the members [of the tribe] if they could remember how to make baskets. Julia Wesaw said, "Well, we can still make the baskets but we can't find the wood."

And I said, "Well, if I find the wood, will you make me a basket?"

And that's how we started. I left the hall and was gone twenty minutes and came back with a black ash tree, and they've been making baskets ever since. That was about twenty years ago. This became known as the Potawatomi Basketmakers Exchange. We started out doing it among ourselves, because [most of the members] lost the skills. So we formed a project and started a little co-op made up of Elders. My dad [Mark Alexis], Mike Daugherty, Dan Rapp, and myself were the ones who got the wood. At first, they didn't know how to recognize it. Then we got a grant from the Michigan Council for the Arts to put together the co-op. I was going to videotape the cutting down of a tree, but I didn't. I got out of the jeep with a camera but changed my mind, said, "I'm not going to do it." So the only ones who knew how to identify the tree were my dad, Mike, Dan, and myself. My dad has passed away. The only ones who know how to identify the tree now are Dan, myself, my sons, and maybe Dan has taught somebody else, too.

The basketmakers in the Pokagon Band became real famous. They were written about in numerous articles in the basket journals in the country. Julia Wesaw and Agnes Rapp and Barbara Paxson, a non-Indian, went to the Smithsonian and participated in Michigan on the Mall part of the Smithsonian Folklife Festival [held each July 4]. It was a real honor for them to do that. We were sending fliers and brochures there by the case. Out of that they got all kinds of citations from numerous arts projects. But it was the whole basket co-op, and they were the two older ones. A lot of the art work was done by Barbara Paxson, and

I'm the one who paid her to do it. She built up a trust with the basketmakers; they trusted her. So I could send Barbara with Agnes and some of the other people anywhere in the country, and I knew that Barbara would get it done, and get there on time.

My background is business. I worked for the Whirlpool Corporation. Then for ten years I worked for Modern Plastics. So I know what meetings are like and what deadlines are like. I show up on time. I make hard decisions; I'm just used to doing that.

The Confederated Historic Tribes of Michigan [CHTM] are a group of unrecognized tribes in the State of Michigan that are seeking federal recognition. I'm the executive director. I know all kinds of anthropologists and historians, legal people, and all of the system. At one time, there were six tribes that were members of CHTM, but now we're down to two. Four of them are now federally recognized tribes. I am on the White House Task Force on federal recognition.

The Pokagons have an office on the campus at Notre Dame. It's old; it was there when I was working there. Michigan State has a Native American Institute. I'm the former chairman of Michigan's Commission on Indian Affairs. I'm the one who created the institute at Michigan State—free tuition for Indian kids in universities in Michigan [and] Indian outreach [personnel] who work for the Department of Social Services.

The Michigan Commission on Indian Affairs is unique. Minnesota has a commission, and South Dakota does. Michigan's was created by Governor Milliken in 1974. Before that, they had task force commissions. But, in 1974, the governor had legislation introduced, and the commission was created by [Michigan's] House and Senate and placed in the governor's office. So the governor appointed Indian people to the commission. There were nine the first year. I was on the first Indian Commission. I accepted in honor of Mike Daugherty, who had asked me to serve.

When I was on it, we were empowered to do anything. They could hold hearings with different departments on Indian issues; ask people to come in—subpoena them if they had to—to make testimonies. They could apply for and receive funds on behalf of Indian people in the state. We created the Department of Social Services. We created twenty-nine Indian centers in the state of Michigan. We brought federal money in to fund them, gave them corps management staff, worked with the Department of Labor to set up the Indian centers. The commission has kind of gotten away from that now. It has been taken out of the governor's office. It is now in the Department of Civil Rights.

The Confederated Historic Tribes got started when the chairmen of each of the unrecognized tribes sat down with each other and talked about strategies to address the need for working on acknowledgment [federal recognition], and in having a voice in the things we were trying to do. Instead of just the Pokagon saying stuff and then the people up in Sault Ste. Marie or Pshebestown [an Indian settlement] saying something else, or the ones over in Brutus saying something different, we decided we'd all come together and we'd try to do it all together. We cooperate on a lot of issues.

I was the chairman of the Pokagon Potawatomi, then I resigned the chairmanship and became the tribal operations manager. Then I took on the job of putting together the staff for the Potawatomi Indian Nation, Inc. I resigned the position as operations manager of the tribe and took the position as director of a small business center in Lansing under the American Indian Business Development Consortium. So I did a lot of economic development in the state for the Indian tribes and created all of the Indian businessmen's councils.

In the meantime, the meetings that I started with the other groups about putting together a confederated historic tribes came to the point that the Michigan Commission on Indian Affairs said that we would give the Confederated Historic Tribes $40,000 to start their staff. They came and asked me to do it. So I said, "Okay, I'll go do that. That'll be fun." So that's what I've been doing.

It depends on what the tribes want. I'm the director; I'm controlled by a board. They tell me what they want. Whatever they want, I try to find the ways or resources to address their desire to do that.

I talked about my grandmother being the link with my remembering the ways of the Potawatomis. When I was growing up, nothing really was happening to link me with the Potawatomi ways. We were all being encouraged not to speak our language, not to do certain things. So a lot of that went undercover; we didn't share that with other people. Certain families did things among themselves. I can't tell you who they are because they wouldn't want me to do that. But my mom and dad could and I can still speak our language because we spoke it at home. But we didn't speak it outside on the street. We spoke it with other people who came and visited and they knew that, too. Even the medicines. We kept all those values, and they were hidden. I don't think [many people] can talk to you about the huckleberry marshes—what happened at the huckleberry marshes. But Frank Bush could. Frank could tell you. Each one of the family groups had different areas where they went and picked huckleberries. A lot of people don't realize where the powwow came from, like the Kay-Boom-A-Kay Powwow. That means "we quit picking huckleberries." It was a celebration. At the end of picking huckleberries, when I was growing up, all of the camps came together, and we had a huge pot of food and we danced—a big celebration because we were all going back to school. All the families got together. But we stopped doing that from maybe the 1950s or late '40s, until we started doing it again at the Kay-Boom-A-Kay Powwow at South Bend, Indiana.

A lot of The People forgot all those things. They forgot how to get black ash trees; they forgot some of the medicines. So today they don't even know what it is. Some people come to my house. They ask, "What's that? Where did you get that?" See, they don't know [the traditions].

So what was happening when I was growing up is that a lot of people lost some of those things, and some of the families have kept them. So now in Pokagon, there's a huge awakening. People now are talking to Frank Bush and talking to Clarence White and other people. Clarence is kind of Frank's protege.

A camp [like at huckleberry picking time] was made up of an extended family. One family would be aunts and uncles and cousins—first cousins. They'd all be close relatives, but they'd be staying there in tents and houses, shacks, and everything else. Margaret Rapp [Dan's wife] could talk about the huckleberry marshes. She wasn't in our camp. She was in the next camp with her family. Same way with Frank. Frank Bush was in a camp farther down in a different area with his family.

What was amazing to me, what I couldn't understand until maybe ten years ago when my dad and I used to talk about a lot of things, I said, "Dad, how come you don't know all these things? You know, your mother told you this. She had to, because she told me." He said, "Philip, it's very simple. She told me but I didn't listen. She told you and you listened." And that's what he said. "She knew that you were listening, so she kept telling you. And that was the reason, because I didn't listen." I'm already telling it to my grandchildren. And they listen.

When I first got on the Pokagon council I was twenty-five. The council was made up of Elders. There was no one else younger than fifty or fifty-five, so I was like a real young kid. I was appointed to a seat. I had all these different ideas that came from a business background, a non-Indian background to some extent, and I knew how to do things in the community. That's why I was asked to serve on the council. [When

I was first asked to serve] I said, "No, I know nothing about Indian business. I go to your meetings once in a while and sit in the back and listen, and you're always talking about treaty areas and other stuff that doesn't make any sense to me." They said, "We're asking you because of things you can do."

At the time, I was on the school board, coached a football team, and did other things. So I came to the council with these other ideas because I was ready to look at education at a time when they were still involved with land claims payment. Then, too, there were separate groups arguing over the name. I said, "The main thing we want is acknowledgment, status as a tribe. We don't care what the name is." Once we agreed to that we started working for acknowledgment.

Each of the groups within the tribe had donated land to Notre Dame, had a relationship with the Catholic Church. There's documentation on that. Many Potawatomi Indian people, just because of the French being Catholic, became Catholic. The Indians related to the French because they were traders and hunters similar to Indian people. The early Potawatomi had a trust in the French because they weren't coming here to take our land. They were here to trade with us and work with us. They were similar, so we adopted some of their ways, and one of them was Catholicism. When the British came, they came after land, which we didn't relate to. The French people came with a different mission. Many Indian people saw that and appreciated it, and part of the Indian acceptance of the French was their religion. Catholic churches now are doing a lot of Indian stuff in them. There are some similarities, like at the Catholic Church in Silver Creek and in Dowagiac. The tribe has forty acres at Rush Lake, where there's an old Catholic Church and cemetery with a lot of Indians buried there. It was an old settlement.

For my portrait I said, "You can paint me under one condition, that you don't paint me as a 1700 or 1800 Indian. You have to paint me as who I am. This is who I am. I am Phil Alexis, the businessman."

From an oral history interview conducted October 28, 1995,
at Battle Creek Inn, Battle Creek, Michigan.

LUCY SADIE PARKS BLALOCK

DELAWARE

ELDER, DELAWARE TRIBE OF INDIANS (BARTLESVILLE, OKLAHOMA)

BORN JUNE 14, 1906, IN ALLUWE, NOWATA COUNTY, OKLAHOMA

My father was a Delaware but was enrolled as a Cherokee. On the roll it says, "George Parks, Cherokee/Delaware." His roll number was 31306. The tribal roll was prepared two years before I was born. I was a "too late." I didn't get on the roll. I didn't get an allotment. My mother was of the Eastern Delaware but was also on the Cherokee roll; roll number 32099. She was of the Wolf Clan. My father's parents were Eastern Delaware of the Wild Turkey Clan. My father was a farmer. He had land that was allotted from the government. So they had their own land. We didn't live on a reservation.

When I was a little girl growing up, the house we lived in was just like the houses you see now. It was a three-room house with two rooms downstairs and one upstairs. We first lived in the little village of Alluwe, Oklahoma, but we eventually were on a farm when we moved to Copan, Oklahoma, when I was five years old.

When we were living at home, I remember that my father and I were buddies. We were like everyday buddies. I talked to him, and everything he did I was right there. If he was greasing the wagon, I was there. I sure missed him when he died in 1920.

I didn't start school 'til I was seven years old. We went to a public school, a white school. And the white kids made fun of the Indian kids, so we had a hard time. The white kids would say, "Hi chief." Whether you were a girl or boy didn't matter. We Indian kids thought, "That's wrong; that's not right. They don't know any better." Yet, we didn't say nothing. They'd say, "Hi, chief; hi chief."

I went to school for ten years. [Nine were at a white public school.] I went to Chilocco Indian Agricultural School for one year.

35

Lucy Sadie Parks Blalock

Delaware

Elder, Delaware Tribe of Indians

When I was in the Indian school, I had a close friend. She was of the Sauk and Fox Tribe. We were pals, friends, bosom pals. When there were parties, we went together. And once a month the school had what they called a Town Day. Students could go to town for their shopping. Had fun. The girls had a girls' town day, and the boys had a boys' town day. It was a different day. Arkansas City, Kansas, is where we went. Chilocco was south of there. We caught the train and rode it up there. That wouldn't be over six miles. Our matron always went along to see to it that everybody behaved properly. That was the main thing about the Indian schools—they made sure that you behaved properly. I got the money I spent when I went to town from my folks. They got little royalty checks—oil royalty checks. So I'd write home and send for a couple of dollars.

When I was at Chilocco, things were pretty much uncivilized. They would not let us talk our Indian language at school. If we did, they punished us. Maybe we'd have to work as punishment—scrub the floors. When they said, "Don't do this, and don't do that," you had to do what they said. If you disobeyed and didn't do what you were supposed to do, and they caught you, that's when you got punished.

I knew all my life that I was an Indian. All my life. Because the Delaware language was spoken in my home I grew up with the language. Right now I'm the Eastern Delaware language teacher. I'm teaching adults. This is at the Indian Center in Bartlesville, Oklahoma. We're doing this because they lost their language; they did not speak the language when they were growing up. Most of the Delaware kids, when they got teased that just killed their spirit. They got ashamed. And that's why they didn't want to learn their language; they wanted to be white. But for me, as much as they teased me, I wasn't about to quit my language. I stuck to my guns.

The old traditional ways of living I knew as a child are not being practiced today. Back then they had the Big House [ceremony], football games, and tribal dances, like what they called the Doll Dance and Stomp Dances—Indian dances. I remember them as a child.

Indian Football is a game where men play against the women. That's an old game they still play today. But now it's just the young people. Older men and women no longer play. But they used to play. Even at my age—old. It is just like a tug of war. That's what it is. Indian football, feasts, and Stomp Dances are what we still do. There were several dances back then. [I liked] the dance they call Turkey Dance. It's a woman's dance. Women danced in single file. They do that yet. My young granddaughter can lead that dance.

My mother and father and my brothers and sisters spoke our Native tongue back then. My mother did not speak English. She knew it, but she just wouldn't do it. When we took her to the store, we had to interpret just what she wanted to buy. Had to be right there to interpret. "She wants this," even if it was a spool of thread. One of us kids had to be there to talk for her. I think she could speak English, but she was just stubborn. My father got along good with the white people. They liked him. He was popular. They knew he was an Indian, but they liked him. He talked broken English. Like when he'd say "maybe," he'd say "neby."

It's a great advancement for the young people today to commune with the white people, but I do think it's a shame that our young people don't know their language. Once I'm no longer able to teach the language class that now has thirty-one students, there's nobody else to take my place.

A long, long time ago when I was a child, there were elderly women who knew how to make baskets and stuff. But that is lost, too. Nobody in the tribe has any idea how to make a basket. In my tribe there was an elderly old woman, Lucy D. Lewis, who was the official storyteller. You'd go to her, say on wintry evenings, give her some tobacco and tell her that you want her to tell some stories. And she might spend half a night telling stories like fairy tales, legends, and things like that. I especially like the stories about the Delaware Big House. The Big House is a religious ceremony. They called the building The Big House—xking we kowan—"The Big House." You know, like white people have their church. This xking we kowan was a Delaware church. They had that every fall. You camped there. It lasted twelve nights. They sang songs and talked and prayed.

We use that *xk* in my language classes now. We used *xk* for that sound, ku-g-g-gh. You have to be able to say that some if you expect to know how to count or talk Delaware, because it is used a lot in the language. I told a class, "You've got to say this." They said, "Oh, I can't say that. I can't." I'd tell them, "You have to know how to make that sound if you expect to talk Delaware or if you expect to count. And you can." They did.

If this were my last chance to speak to future tribal generations, I would tell the young people to continue to learn their language. It is so important that our children and grandchildren and great-grandchildren know about the way life used to be.

From an oral history interview conducted December 12, 1994, at the headquarters building of the Miami Tribe of Oklahoma, Miami, Oklahoma.

SHARON BURKYBILE

MIAMI

MEMBER, MIAMI TRIBAL DEVELOPMENT COMMITTEE; LIAISON
BETWEEN MIAMI UNIVERSITY, OXFORD, OHIO, AND THE
MIAMI TRIBE OF OKLAHOMA

BORN 1943 IN PICHER, OKLAHOMA

When I was born my father was serving in World War II, and I didn't actually see him until I was four years old, other than in pictures. I can remember the day that he came home from the service. I was outside playing. He walked up and said, "Are you Sharon Kay Ross?" I looked at him and said, "Yes, are you my daddy?" He said, "Yes." I remember that like it was yesterday, even though I was only four.

My dad was a miner, and I suppose he probably made as much money as anyone else did in Ottawa County, Oklahoma, at that time. But he came home from the war with a drinking problem.

We moved to Metaline Falls, Washington, in 1956, and we were out there about six months. My dad worked there in the mines. When we came back they bought the house for $75. That was really something; we had something that belonged to us.

When I was thirteen and fourteen, I would go out with my next door neighbor, who was a girl my age, and sit in the car and listen to the radio. Not that our car had a radio in it, because it didn't. But we would string extension cords outside and bring the radio in the car and sit there and talk and listen to the radio. That was kind of our little getaway out there. It was kind of a neat thing to do.

Her family somehow found out that they were Native American, or Indian, and were put on a roll. And we'd always attend the Quapaw Powwow and Stomp Dance. My aunt and uncle would take us there, and they would sit in the car or sit on the bleachers until the wee hours of the morning, watching us stomp dance. We had a really good time.

I first realized that I was an Indian when I was very young. I didn't know what an Indian was. All I remember is when Daddy was in Italy,

39

Sharon Burkybile

Miami

Member, Miami Tribal Development Committee; liaison between Miami University, Oxford, Ohio, and the Miami Tribe of Oklahoma

he sent me a white fur coat, hat, and muff. And I had real long hair, and Mom kept it in Shirley Temple curls. And I can remember being downtown, and I think I had cut a big hunk out of my bangs. I can remember someone saying, "Oh, there's George and Dorothy's pretty little Indian girl. Look what she's done to her bangs."

And I didn't know whether that was good or bad. You know, I thought, "I'm Indian." I didn't know the difference between Indians and white people or anything like that until I got older, I think as a teenager, and because my dad was having problems. That's when I really realized that I felt discriminated against, but I didn't really know why.

I understand why we were called Indians in the very beginning when we were The People. But Indian is what I grew up with, even though it's something that Columbus hung on us. Native American is just something that the government is doing—changing things around, labeling people all over again. I know who I am, and I'm proud of who I am. I don't ever really feel discriminated against now as I did as a child.

My kids are aware of their heritage, and they're all very proud of it. When we moved to Springfield, Missouri, eighteen years ago, we didn't know any Indian people there. But we always tried to bring our kids home to Oklahoma for the Fourth of July and over Labor Day and to White Oak [Oklahoma] for ceremonies there. Our children's names are Wanoka, Hiwannah, Turtle, and Newakis.

There was no particular time in my life that I haven't been proud to be an Indian. I've always been proud of who I am. I worshipped my grandfather McCoontze. He seldom talked, but I can remember when he would come to visit us. He would sit there and I would sit and look at him and think "Oh, you're really something." I'd go to town and someone would say something about Grandpa. He walked with a cane. And he drank a lot, but I'm still proud of him.

I'm seven-sixteenths Indian. My maternal grandmother McCoontze was a little Choctaw, and my grandfather McCoontze was full-blooded. He was half Miami and half Ottawa. His father, Peter McCoontze, was second chief of the Ottawa Tribe. My mother, Dorothy McCoontze Ross, was part Miami, part Ottawa, and a little Choctaw. And my dad, George Ross, also had Indian blood in him.

The racist term for Indian was "blanket." My husband said whenever anybody called him that, that's when he would really get after them. To me, because of the problems of alcoholism with male members of my family, I naturally didn't like the term "drunken Indian." They'd say, "That drunken Indian."

When I was a child at the Whitebird School in Picher, my cousins moved over from Quapaw. They were Quapaw and Miami—full-blooded. Some of the other kids called them "niggers." I was ready to take on the whole elementary school. I can remember saying, "If they are, I am, too! Don't you say that!"

I can remember as a small child my grandfather and my mom always attended our tribal meetings, which were annual events held during the second weekend in September. I remember them being held at the courthouse. And, of course, back then the courthouse didn't have air conditioning, and it was hot in September. They would go on and on and on, forever and ever. And you always heard about this money. My grandfather didn't talk very much, but he'd say, "Someday, Grand-daughter, you're going to get money." And, God love him, he lived to get one payment. And that was always what I heard about. As I got older it seemed there wasn't anything about money in the meeting notices. Then we noticed there was hardly anyone there. And then the next year there was something about per capita payment; then the whole place was packed.

I used to beg my grandfather McCoontze, "Grandpa, teach me how to talk Indian." And he'd just kind of look at me. I do not speak our Native language. He taught me a few things when I was a kid. He'd teach me [Indian for] rabbit and water and things like that. But whenever I asked him, if he'd been drinking he'd just laugh. I really feel like, back then, that was their way of protecting the younger generation, because they were shielding us from the unpleasant things about our past.

My grandpa always told Mom and me never to use peyote. I don't know why, but that's what he said. I don't know if that was because Miami women or Ottawa women years ago weren't supposed to take the medicine. But that's what he told us. Our youngest daughter has attended a meeting and taken peyote and was not bothered by it. But it's something that I couldn't do because that's what Grandpa told me.

We don't do things as a Miami tribe here in Oklahoma. We do not have our Green Corn or ceremonies and things like some of the other tribes have. We do have an annual catfish dinner around the Fourth of July and our annual meeting. But there are no ceremonial things that we do. So the things that I know and the things that I have picked up through the years have been the things from the other tribes here. We're in a county of thirty-something thousand people, and eight tribes were relocated to this area. We have so many intermarriages. My mother-in-law was full-blooded Loyal Shawnee and Delaware, and when we had her feast when she passed away, we tried to get the most traditional people to carry everything through just like we thought it should be done.

Going to the cemetery has always been a very big thing with my mom and me and even with my children and my youngest brother. I can remember that, when I was a small child, both my grandmas made flowers. We always made our flowers out of crepe paper and paraffin wax, and then later on my grandma Ross learned how to make flowers out of tissues. You know, when they came out with colored tissue paper, or Kleenex. And we made flowers out of that. And today I still make all of my floral arrangements for the cemetery. I don't actually make the flowers like I used to. But I buy flowers and make all my arrangements. My husband always teases me about my flowers. He says, "You'd have made a good professional mourner back in the olden days."

If my mother were to die, I would bring her to my home. And she does want to be buried here. We have a burial plot. My first baby passed away when she was six weeks old, so I've had a cemetery plot since then. My grandmother and grandfather McCoontze are buried on my lot, and there's a place for my mom and dad there, too. So she would definitely be brought to our home, not just to a funeral home. If that should ever have to happen, we would be there with her, and we would never leave her.

On November 11, 1994, our first granddaughter, Jaquetta Jenkins, was born. Within an hour after birth we were told she had many birth defects with little hope of living more than a few short days. Our Grandfather [one Native word for God] was good to us, and we took her home after one week. She improved, gained weight, and we all had hope. At five weeks old she became very ill and was admitted to the hospital. Once again we were faced with the same words from the doctors that we all had planted in the back of our minds but refused to believe. On December 24, 1994, at 6:10 A.M., our precious baby was called to join our loved ones in heaven.

She touched so many lives in her short six weeks. A small town and community in Fordland, Missouri, got together to raise funds to help with expenses. It made me cry tears of joy to know our daughter and son-in-law and grandchildren had so much love and respect in the community. It was also comforting to know that there is still compassion for others in this world.

When it was time to make the final arrangements, my husband and I had great concerns. There were things we wanted to do, as Indian people do, when a loved one is called away. We were not sure that the funeral director would understand that we needed to sit up with our child, so as not to leave her until we knew it was time for her spirit to travel. But once again Grandfather was with us; we were permitted to do what we were taught to do.

We smoked cedar and stayed all night with her. Her seven-year-old brother Justin sat on my lap beside her casket. I explained to him why we were staying with his sissy. He wouldn't leave; he stayed, too. He kissed her, touched her hand, told her he would miss her. And as we sat together, I could sense the pride that our ancestors would have in knowing that we were still trying to teach our young our Indian way of life.

After the services at the funeral chapel, my husband and I wrapped her in a blanket. He made sure her bundle was intact, along with her eagle feather in her hands. When the minister from the church said his last words at the grave our friend John Hernandez took over, and he prayed in his Native tongue and relayed messages of how one so small with such a short life had touched so many hearts. And then we stayed with her and covered her grave with dirt. And once again our grandson took the responsibility for his sissy. He worked and did his very best until the deed was finished.

I know in my own heart that our little Jacquetta carries the love and strength of her seven-year-old brother on her journey to our Grand-father's home in heaven. I told my grandson that night by the casket that she is part of us. We brought her into this world, and as long as she's here we will stay with her, take care of her, see to all her needs. I know he'll always remember and pass that on to his own grandchildren.

I want everyone to know how proud I am to be an Indian and how much it has meant to me. I've always tried to live up to what I feel are the ways of our people. And that is to be good to others, to share what we have, to always welcome everyone into your home and into your heart, and always make them feel like they're extra special.

I am the ceremonial leather dressmaker in my tribe. I'm presently cutting out my forty-fifth dress. But we still have the lady who taught me. I learned from a little Cherokee lady, Pauline Whitebird. She's married to the last living full-blooded Quapaw, Robert "Bob" Whitebird. They live in Quapaw. I would feel safe to say that she's made probably over three hundred ceremonial dresses. We basically make our dresses exactly alike. I just tell people how I love to make the buckskin dresses. It's a lot of work, cutting the fringe. I do bead work only for my family. I don't do beadwork for other people.

My husband was a truck driver until about eleven years ago. We raise buffalo now. We're trying to breed to get white buffalo. We have one that has a white face, and someday, when she has a calf and that calf has a calf, we'll have a pure white buffalo. The market for white buffalo is great.

If this were my last chance to speak to future tribal generations, I'd like for our young to take more interest in our people and their direction. This is not an easy task, and it is one without glory. Our tribal members should be employed in our tribal office and be trained to take charge of our own programs. And they should strive to see to it that our tribal government keeps members well informed and involved in meaningful activities.

As for non-Indian people, now and in the years ahead, I'd like for them to remember that minority people are very special and have many special talents. I believe in cultural sensitivity. Not all members of any one race are alike, be they Indian, Hispanic, Blacks, or Islanders. This is something we all need to understand, and with this mutual understanding our world will be a better place to live.

> *From an oral history interview conducted December 12, 1994, at the headquarters building of the Miami Tribe of Oklahoma, Miami, Oklahoma.*

FRANK BUSH

Potawatomi [Pokagon Band]

Spiritual Leader and Head Veteran Dancer, Potawatomi Indian
Nation, Inc., AKA Pokagon Band of Potawatomi Indians

Born in Shelbyville, Michigan

My father worked for the railroad so we had a house in
Shelbyville, Michigan, close to his work. That was the old Pennsylvania
Railroad. When he got near retirement age we moved over here, in this
settlement [east of Bradley, Michigan]. It's not a reservation any more.
It was a reservation at one time, but [the government] allotted fourteen
or fifteen families around this surrounding area. They allotted depending on how big the family was—ten, fifteen, twenty acres and so on. It
happened a long time ago, when there was no industry here. [There
was] nothing to keep up the taxes. That's how the government decided
to go into private ownerships, and the people then started paying taxes.
Some sold out, but most of us retained the old homestead. We have ten
acres that was the Bush homestead. Nine and a half acres. We donated
a half-acre for the [Methodist] Church. That goes back to the Bradley
Indian Mission, to a man named Selkirk. [Selkirk] Lake property is
named after him. He was a missionary, and he started a church. He
started out with an old log church in a different location not far from
here, but this church building was dedicated in 1914, I think it was.
They've remodeled it, made it bigger, and things like that. But he was
the one that brought the Methodist religion into this area for the Indian
people. We have our own cemetery, the old Indian Cemetery. That's
further down the road from the church.

The earliest memory that I can recall is that my mother, to keep our
family income coming in, made baskets and every now and then, we'd
go to the biggest city closest to us, Plainwell—that's south of Bradley
about fifteen miles—and people would order baskets from her. For us
boys, it was our job to get the timber and pound out the splints and

46

Frank Bush

Potawatomi (Pokagon Band)

*Spiritual Leader and Head Veteran Dancer,
Potawatomi Indian Nation, Inc.*

divide them. When the baskets were ready to be delivered we'd get on the train to Plainwell. It didn't cost us anything to ride the train because my father had a pass, so that was our transportation. We'd do that about every two or three months.

When I was growing up and going to school we had to walk a mile to the next road. We didn't have school buses in those days. Going to public school we first started learning English. My father and mother always taught the Native language when we were young so English was a new language for us and a new language for the family. Folks could understand it, but they always talked Indian. Even as a group around here, whatever we did, if we were playing, we'd talk Indian. It was strange to our folks that they had to learn a different language, the English language. We'd go to school and learn that language, and when we were on the playground we would talk our Native language. Teachers would hear us, and they would call us in, and they'd give us a good talking to, and maybe a slap across the hand or something like that. That's so we would talk English. We would come home, and we would kind of forget that we were talking English. There were five brothers, and we would be talking English, and then we would get a little scolding from our parents. So what were we going to do? We just had to think it out. I went to grade school in Shelbyville, went to high school in Wayland. In those days we had to make our own transportation to and from school, but we got through it all right.

When I was going to high school, for the last two years, I worked and lived with a farmer close to Wayland. He had a milk route and delivered milk to all the city of Wayland. He gave me a job so that I would be closer to school.

My family would contract from other farmers to raise cucumbers. We started out with three acres. That's what we did during the summer. It would take us about half a day to pick three acres. Then it was our free time. We could go, do anything we wanted, and usually we went swimming at Selkirk Lake. The next year came along, and my father took on ten acres so we were busy all day. There was seasonal work, too, like picking huckleberries, strawberries, and cherries. That's how we supplemented our income, my father's job. We always had plenty; we always had a garden.

Modern times means changing, but spiritually [our traditional practice] was handed down to us so we continued it on, even today. We have our gatherings for the four seasons: fall, winter, spring, and summer, as they used to be when we were growing up. Some of my uncles were pastors of the Methodist Church here. Some of them would practice some modern religion. But about the middle of the week, around Tuesday or Wednesday, they would gather in different houses, and we would go along with our Native religion. That's how we are doing that today. It was just handed down.

We didn't have automobiles in those days. We had to rely on horses that we kept, and we didn't go very far, not like today when you can go to California in a day. We always managed to keep together. People in those days watched out for each other. From this house to the next house, there was always a path. From each one of these houses that path was always worn smooth. But now it's all weeds, all grown over. We don't know who's living next door. Everybody always shared what they had. Everybody always raised a big garden; everybody hunted in a different season. We don't share that any more. When some of the elderly couldn't hunt any more, our leader saw to it that everybody had their equal share. That's how we got along.

Tribal law is a lot of traditional belief. We still believe in the tribal law, but it doesn't hold too much weight in the modern courts now. There are a lot of things that have been deleted from tribal law. A lot of things we used to do have been changed. But we still practice what we were brought up with, what was handed down to us. In the modern courts now there is a lot of litigation you have to go through, with a lot of research.

The father was the head of the household, but we relied on the elderly for anything we wanted to know. My father was a good provider. That, I think, was important to his role. And he realized he had to do that somehow, and he did. There were five of us boys and one girl. We looked to our mother for just about everything we wanted to ask. She kept us together. The boys were well over six foot. My dad was six foot six. We didn't argue too much with our parents. We had a happy upbringing; we all got along.

My grandfathers lived on the Huron Potawatomi Reservation that sits southeast of Schoolcraft, southwest of Battle Creek. They were the Pamtopees. They were the chiefs and leaders of that whole band of Indians down there. That's where my mother is from, the Pamtopees and the MeeMees. They all seemed to be pretty closely related. Pamtopee was my grandmother's father's name. On the old census rolls you still can see he was mentioned as the leader.

My grandmother on my father's side was from Iowa. She was Sauk and Fox. They called her O Sage Que, Sauk Woman. My father was a

Pokagon from around the Dowagiac area. There still are a lot of Native people there in Dowagiac, Hartford, Decatur. They seem to stay by their own homeland and their own homesteads.

The old traditional religion was practiced by my grandpa. He was a Mide, a pipe carrier. Once in a while I'd stay all summer with him. He had a little place on the Pine River. There was a little island we had to get to by canoe. That's where he had his worship place—a little longhouse, a little sweatlodge, fire altar, and everything that was the old ways. I learned a lot, a lot of things that he taught me about the old religion. The children in those days, if they were invited to a traditional meeting, had no voice; we just had to sit and be quiet and learn all we could. That was the way it was in those days.

There are more people coming back to the old ways. Some of the children who were adopted and grew up in a non-Indian family had no Indian teaching. But when they get to a certain age and they realize they're different, they start searching who their parents were. So in our gatherings today, in our longhouse meetings, there are a lot who didn't know they were Indian. Now they've joined the circle and are learning about the old ways of their ancestors. People from all over the State of Michigan, even out of the state, are doing that.

We talked the Huron Potawatomi language. We had to learn it in order to know what was going on. Even today, at some of the traditional longhouse meetings, they will talk in the Native language only. So the Pokagon Potawatomi in Dowagiac and in South Bend have classes once a week so the Elders can teach the Native language. A lot of the adults are going to that class because they don't know how to talk the language or understand it. That's a good thing. Otherwise, in just a few years the language will be almost forgotten when the Elders die. One of the things we try to keep up with is our language. I remember years ago when they had the church up here everything was in our language, even the hymn books. Native language was on the left side page; on the other page it would be in English. Now they have taken all those books out. Once in a while some evangelists would come in and do the sermon in Native language. It's modern nowadays, but some of them sing the songs in Native language, too. I don't know where they took those old books.

One good thing about the Algonkian language is that while there is the Ottawa, the Ojibwa, and the Potawatomi, and their pronunciations are not the same, the words are similar enough that you can understand what people from each Nation are saying. We can go into Ojibwa country and know what they're talking about when they talk their own language.

We hear so much that is negative, yet we have people who are positive in their way of thinking. We have classes to teach basketry, tanning, beadwork, many things that pertain to the Indian culture. We still know how to make Indian corn. Indian corn, to an Anglo, is just decoration corn, and you'll see it hanging up in a store. But we still use that, and we know it has to be prepared the old way to make it edible. And there are drum-making people. Young men are joining the circle of the drum. It seems to be a surge, a comeback. They know their identity now, and that's what they want to be.

It's a ceremonial dress that we use today. We honor when we wear them, like the buckskin. We wear that in honor of that animal that gave up his life. He didn't give up his life now, but he still lives by us wearing his hide. Each article of ceremonial dress is a representation of honor. It's an honor to the animal to wear that beaver turban or an otter turban. We're paying respects to that animal. He died, but he still lives. He's still visible, and that's what each item is for.

Just a few years ago we could go to a gathering, and we could look at people's moccasins and tell what tribe they were from. They all had that distinctive marking. The Potawatomi had a crease right in the middle, and the Ojibwa had that pucker toe with beads on it. And the western tribes would have the hard-sole moccasins, all bead-covered, but theirs would not be a Woodland floral design that we use. They use geometric designs.

A man was in Alaska. By chance, he came upon a mammoth skeleton where he found the tusk. He made me a little neck piece out of that piece of mammoth tusk. He made some designs on it, made a design of the mammoth. I wear that because that animal hasn't been around for ten thousand years. And so now he's on the road again, going to different places, where I go. That's the kinds of things we put into our ceremonial dress.

I can remember when in the summertime my grandpa John Pamtopee would go to these different fairs, and [people would] peddle their wares, and they would dress up in their costumes. I'd never see anybody wearing a feathered bonnet because it wasn't the proper dress.

I made everything but the beads for my own ceremonial clothes. I did that because it was the custom to do that, to make your own, instead of buying it. You even had to kill the deer for the buckskin. We had to tan it. We buy the cloth for the shirt, but we make the shirt. We also wear the branches, the insignia, of our armed services. I have two that I wear. One is beaded on my back bustle, maybe four inches in diameter. One neck piece I wear is a brass insignia I found in the South Pacific on one of those islands. I just wear that for that purpose, that it comes from such a distance.

The Potawatomi colors are like you see in the shirt in the portrait. It's not a purple; it's not a pink; I don't know what you would call it, but it is our Potawatomi color. We usually wear colors for the four directions that we use in our religious ceremony, like the yellow is the first morning sunrise. That's the yellow color for the people in the east. The south would be the black color. West would be the red color, and the north would be the white color. Those are the directions that we use in our religious ceremonies and we try to put them somewhere in our ceremonial dress. When we dress, we pause to think and give thanks for all the that we have, especially for the animals and things they came from.

We had a grandpa here. We called him Grandpa, but he wasn't related in any way. Everybody called him Grandpa. We'd all gather to his house. He had a big oak tree down there, and everybody would gather there. And somebody would have a drum along, and he would tell us some of the stories of his boyhood days, about how he always kept a horse, up until the later part of his life. He could remember that about three miles down the road, east of here, they built the first cement bridge in this area, and they were fascinated by that bridge across that little creek. They'd go down there and just run back and forth all day long. It was fascinating to them how they mixed that mud and used it for that purpose.

He was attached to Charleson Park, over south of Hastings, where a good friend owned the park in those days. And he would go down there and he'd camp out all summer. He went back quite a few years. He lived with his aunt; Aunt Sarah is what they called her. She lived to be 113 years old recorded, and how many more years on top of that she really was nobody knows. She was active until she left this world. Right up until that day she did her own housework, cooking, and all that.

We had a good baseball team here in Bradley, and we'd go all over. We'd go into Canada and play. We had the big league scouts. They'd come over, and they'd watch us play. But that's about all. There was nothing. I'm sure a lot of those boys were good enough for the big leagues. When I was in service [in World War II], they'd send me back to the rest camp where I met Bob Feller. He was a great baseball player. And Mickey Cochran, who played for the Detroit Tigers—and all of those people. I played with them, and they'd say, "Well, when you get out look me up, and we'll get you into the big leagues," and it just never happened.

We had basketball teams, and now they're into softball. We have two or three softball teams around this area. One of our Elders played all over the United States. He played out in Nebraska. He was that good to be chosen to spend his time doing what he liked to do. He was our team manager. There were a few Indians that were in the big leagues. I was invited up to Drummund Island where Monahan had his place. They had quite a few celebrities, like Sparky Anderson and the pitcher Jack Morris who plays for the Blue Jays.

If I had to come back in a hundred years, I'd like to see that there was no alcohol or any of these mind-altering drugs or whatever, because that tears a person down no matter who he is, no matter if he's Native American or if he's Anglo. And I'd like to see some of the old ways, like the languages that would be spoken. The way we grew up, it was simple. To keep on honoring Mother Earth whatever she provides through all the gifts that we receive, to wake up in the morning, for somebody watching over us during the night. That's what I'd like to believe in. There're so many gifts that we just take for granted. We make plans; we'd be planning tomorrow. But the Creator up there has His own plans for us, and we sometimes get angry because our plans just don't work. People don't realize that. They call it luck. But somebody greater than we are is just watching over us, and we've got to accept that. That's why we try to govern ourselves in our religious teachings and religious meetings.

Elders long ago wouldn't wait seven days just to go to church for one hour on that day. They'd go to church every day. They'd pray to that rising sun for everything that has happened to them, everything that was given to them, given another day. That's what my grandpa always told them. He used to tell us that it's a day that was given to you, and you've got to appreciate that gift. And some day, when your time comes, why it'll all be planned for you; that's planned for you, no matter what. No matter what you can do to alter it, it'll never, never be altered. It just is. That's what we live by.

I've been sharing the religious part of my life that my grandparents told me. My grandfather always told me there was somebody up there higher than we were who was taking care of us. But, he said, there was going to be a lot of different groups of different religions, and they'll call the Creator a lot of different names, like God and the Messiah. But, he said, there's going to be religions that will be different from one another. And, he said, as far as me teaching you that you have to be an old traditional religion, that's not going to work. You have to take your children, you'll have to show them the different churches, how they operate.

And that's what I did. I took them to the Methodist, the Protestant, the Catholic. I took them to all these different churches. He said, my grandfather said, you can't just drum this one religion into their heads. Sooner or later they're going to make their own decisions, and that's what happened. Some of them fall into the old religion now; some of them fall in the Methodist religion. My only son up here is an ordained minister and my daughter across the street is Catholic. So we've got all of these different religions that he said they'll choose from, choose what will satisfy them. They all respect one another, and they all know that there is only one God even though you may call Him by a different name. And that's one of the teachings I remember that my grandpa told me. He said you can lead a horse to the water, but you can't make him drink.

It all turns back to the religious upbringing that I received. My grandchildren, some of them will hang onto the old religion and get as many teachings as they can because it's very important. Someday they're going to cry out for help in some kind of way. That's what I did during the war years. I asked for help many times, and I'm here today. That's what I tell my grandchildren that is important, and they seem to listen. I have eleven grandchildren, six girls and five boys, and two great-grandchildren.

My Indian name is Naswa Qua Quet. That means Eagle Weather. My grandpa gave me that name when I was very small. Eagle Weather, I imagine, is just clear blue sky.

That is another thing we still practice. People still want their Indian names. Each person has an Indian name, but he has to have a Pipe Carrier go out and fast for that. And that name will come to that person because the Creator, at the very moment you were conceived, knows your name. But you've got to ask these holy men to go out and find what that name is. I think the reason He gives you that name at the first moment is that something may happen within that nine-month period, or any time. And He can call that name, and that name will answer. Many people are asking for their names now. No two names are alike. All the names seem to fit their character.

This grandpa we call Grandpa Birch gave children their names. I've got two special places where I go to sit. It may not come the first time. I may have to go several times, but the name will come. You get clues to that name, and pretty soon you put the clues together, and that's what the name is.

Well, thank you for taking the time to come out. The interview is over so we'll say, "Megwitch." Megwitch is giving our thanks. And "Pamape" [is] someday we will meet again, hopefully. That is what we say when we greet each other or when we part. So it's never, never a goodbye, but it's just a little time later that we will meet again somewhere.

From an oral history interview conducted July 8, 1992, at the home of Frank Bush, Shelbyville, Michigan.

GEORGE J. "BUCK" CAPTAIN

Shawnee

Chief, Eastern Shawnee Tribe of Oklahoma

Born August 14, 1922, in Ottawa County, Oklahoma

We lived in an oak house my dad built. I went to a country school, Moccasin Bend District Number 5, and I went through the eighth grade there. My whole life was fairly rugged. My childhood was during the Depression. We did have plenty to eat. We lived on a farm. We raised everything we had. But we didn't have any money. But we had a lot of company. It wasn't just us. It was everybody.

My dad went to Indian school, as did all of his family. They had to; it was mandatory. They went to Seneca Indian School, which closed about 1988. I was on the school board at the time. Seneca Indian School was located near Wyandotte in Ottawa County in northeastern Oklahoma. Usually, officials picked children up when they were three or four years old, took them to Indian school, with or without their parents' consent. They had nothing to do with their own children once they were born. They belonged to, I guess, God and the Indian Agent. They were more or less brought up to fear the Indian agents because they controlled their lives, totally, just about.

Then they went on to Chilocco Indian School, in Kay County, just at the Kansas-Oklahoma state line on US77, or they went to Haskell, in Lawrence, Kansas. My dad went to both places. My brothers went to Haskell, or they went to Carlisle, Pennsylvania. That was the other school that was active at that time. That's where Jim Thorpe went to school.

In the military, when they find out you're an Indian, they sometimes push you ahead. You have to do things other people can't do, or they can do it and probably would rather you did, so you've always got the job no one else wanted to do. They thought this was the way; they thought, if you're an Indian, you're a good scout, automatically.

56

George J. "Buck" Captain

Shawnee

*Chief, Eastern Shawnee Tribe of Oklahoma
(Retired 1996)*

Prejudice? Well, my name is Captain. When I was working in intelligence for two government agencies, why, being named Captain, most people thought I was Mexican. One time I was sent across to another building to help some people out, writing. I could write good intelligence reports. There were two Texans who kind of resented that I could do these things. I walked in. They were talking, and one of them said, "What is that damned Mexican going to do next?" Then they turned around and saw me. After that I had two slaves. They were afraid I would report to the board. But I didn't.

I've had some real good friends. I think most of the time you're judged on your ability. I didn't know it, but I guess I've had an uncanny ability to figure things out that a lot of other people couldn't see. And they turned out to be right, so I kind of established a reputation. So you're recognized by your abilities, not what your race is, in most places.

One thing that my tribe has a reputation for is that they like to war. Warrior training started when you were about eight years old in the Shawnee Tribe. So they took great pride in being warriors. I think most Indians did. You look at records of World War II, you see Indians still have that.

I truly don't think there was much change in the tribal law and leadership positions when my people moved to Oklahoma, nor since we've been here. Our group, most of them came from the Chillicothe Division in Ohio. That was the group that most always produced the chiefs for the Shawnee Nation back in Indiana and Ohio. We always had a chief. My dad, Thomas Andrew Captain, was a chief for over twenty-five years. And my grandfather before him, and so forth. In Oklahoma, we weren't recognized as a tribe until 1937. Then [the federal government] set up the tribal government. The federal government knew we were in Oklahoma because they had an agency, but they gave us nothing as far as authority. But we still always had chiefs. We're the only group of Shawnees that does. You have a chairman for the Loyal Shawnees and a governor for the Absentee Shawnees. I think we stuck with the old tradition. You're a chief, and that's it.

Our Shawnee tribes haven't been together as a Nation for close to two hundred years, so about 1990 I decided it was about time. I contacted the Absentee Shawnees and I talked to the Loyal Shawnees and then I threw a dinner here, in our new tribal building. We like to eat, so we got together, and we've been trying to work together ever since. Throughout history the Shawnees have always been friends, but the

Shawnees always roamed. The Shawnees never stayed in one place. One group would move, another group would move, they'd have to figure out where they were at. In a war they got united.

When the big move came from Ohio to Kansas, they did leave some people back in Ohio. Chief Blue Jacket was one who stayed in Ohio along with several others. So there are now people in Ohio with past Shawnee ancestry. Well, they can't ever be on the Shawnee roll, but they can certainly be my friends.

I feel comfortable with the Shawnee Remnant Band of Ohio. And, to tell you the truth, those people know more about the Shawnees than do the Shawnees that live in Oklahoma because our history is there, in Ohio, or Illinois, or Indiana, Kentucky, Pennsylvania. We know we've been there. The people who came here knew our history, but they passed on. The important thing is you have to provide for families and eat every day. So when you go to a wild country, it's difficult to make a living, but they had to do it. I might add that, when you read the treaties, they ended up with fifteen hoes and two chopping axes and a blacksmith's shop. That was about it. It was up to you to make a living.

My idea is to build a museum to let people see what we've got from our past. We're the remnant of the tribes, the downfallen, the group they've made beggars out of, and they don't know the talent the Indians really had because they confiscated everything they ever had. All the art, the pottery, the knives they ever had, all went to Europe or in museums. You will see more Indian things in England and Paris, France. What I want to do with the Inter-Tribal Council is to talk about a plan to make a super stop on the highway—a museum where we can put all these things that are being returned. To keep those things in hiding is of no use to anybody. Bring the kids in, let them look. In this area, of course, people are so used to Indians being here they don't pay any attention to them. They're kind of waking up now and saying, "That's not bad; they're not the old drunks and thieves everyone thought."

When you come right down to it, we've already been stripped of everything we ever owned so they're seeing us in a different light. It used to be, if you're a Native, you're a thief. That's the way it is; a story gets started. Once we have a quality museum, we can get control of other things. We could put up different displays regularly. So that's what my hopes are.

One of the problems is that Indians have a built-in inferiority complex that was put there by the government. When you've been down so long, and put under a fist, you develop that. You have no confidence in your own ability. So if they can see what our people used to do, I think it will help us all because even though we have a number of gifted artists now, we could develop more artists.

We've been in Oklahoma since 1832, and we were still "children" clear up until the 1930s because of the federal laws and the way we were treated. You had a boss man you had to go see. You could be a millionaire, but he controlled your purse strings because you were an Indian. If you had a degree from Harvard, you were still stupid.

When I was young, the Eastern Shawnees were traditional. Now we are the least traditional of the three branches of Shawnees. When I was a child, when a Shawnee passed away, he always had full burial rites—Shawnee rites, feast at midnight, the third night after his death. That's when we would send him to the happy hunting grounds. But now most of us have forgotten how. I think the big change came with the old ones dying and younger people having to move to make a living. When people moved to Wichita, Kansas, and California and Seattle to defense plants, that changed the lifestyle of practically the whole tribe one way or the other. Even if you stayed here on our own original reservation, you took the jobs available. So we changed then and never went back. We're slowly working back. We will have our fourth annual powwow in 1995.

If you want to research the Shawnees, you've got to go back to Ohio, Indiana, Illinois, because that's where our history is. People here had no way of recording it. People couldn't read and write. It was all handed down. So when they ended up being moved three and four times, why, it got lost. Our history was in Missouri for a long time. We lived on a Spanish land grant, and then we moved to our present reservation here in Seneca, Missouri. Just about every time the Shawnees were established, they were moved. That's why we've got so many treaties—sixteen or eighteen treaties with the federal government.

My grandfather Captain could barely speak English, but he made sure his children did not speak Shawnee. "Because," he said, "you can't eat Shawnee. You've got to speak English so you can make a living in the white man's world." That was Grandpa's theory.

We have had some language classes in conjunction with the Absentee Shawnees and the Loyal Shawnees. The Cherokees are helping. We're putting together a book of the Shawnee language. The Northeastern Oklahoma A&M College in Miami has developed an Indian program. Shawnee will be taught at that college as a tribal language. There are eight tribes in Ottawa County so they'll change off.

In my case, I don't know if I lost a lot or not by not speaking our language. When I was young I sat in on many conversations by going to funerals, visitors coming to our house. They could speak Shawnee. I spoke some then. I would love to now. But you're so assimilated into our society now, there's really no place for it, except in your little group. It's been a government policy not to allow you to speak your own Native language. But now the clock is turning. You can do anything you want. It's the thing to do. To bring back your heritage is difficult, to step back all these years, because you haven't practiced it.

I do realize we're going to have to work on the children. We've had classes for the young ones to learn how to dance. The dances survived. They used to use turtle shells for the Stomp Dance, but they're so heavy, they use cans now. Cans are about a tenth of the weight of nine turtle shells or so tied to your legs. They modernized it. They've always had to improvise. So this is another way of improvising as I see it.

We've had craft classes here. They make just about anything. They can sell everything they make. Basically, there is a gift of art. It seems to come naturally to make things.

We lived on stories. We entertained ourselves. We had to. A lot of just real life. Walt Bluejacket used to come up to the house to visit my dad. They'd go south of the house and sit on an old bench. Sit there until sunset, both chewing tobacco. Pretty soon old Walt would say, "Tom," and Dad would say, "Yes?" Walt would say, "I got to go home." Dad would say, "Well, I sure did enjoy your visit, Walt." And old Walt would say, "Well, I sure did, too." And that's all that was ever said, and here they sat for three hours together. It was a silent companionship that the Indian had the capability of understanding, perhaps a closeness that they were Indian. They could look back.

The Shawnees were happy talking about old Grandma Bluejacket. She was old, smoked a pipe; they enjoyed a pipe. Even though they did not have one nickel between them, they enjoyed themselves, happy being together, not speaking a word. That's where you get the idea the Indian is silent, out of his element, but they were happy together not talking. But they had this sense of humor, knew how to get along, entertain one another.

Other tribes looked up to the Shawnees. One reason was that Shawnees were great warriors. Another is that the Shawnees believed in a female deity. They are one of the few groups in the world that did. Maybe some still do; they could be right on that. We've probably had the most famous chief of all in Tecumseh. And the Prophet was probably the greatest Medicine Man that ever lived. These two had certain character, or whatever it takes, to be leaders, to make people follow.

The Quakers were associated culturally with the Shawnees. When we dedicated the building next door, we had a gentleman speak who was a Quaker missionary. He was very old, 97. His family came here at the same time the Indians did. The Quakers worked with the Indians well. They were sincere in their belief that the Indian was a human being, which many other people did not believe. The way of the time was to leave the Indian part out—get rid of that Indian blood.

If I come back in a hundred years, I'd like to see the tribe totally independent and forget that the Bureau of Indian Affairs ever existed and the hardships my dad went through, as did all the ancestors. They truly believed the Indian agent was the most valuable person in this world. I think some of them considered him holy. They were browbeaten to that point. That's what I want to see—have enough wealth, enough benefits, that we can let them take care of themselves.

In my lifetime, the biggest change within the tribe has been going from poverty to being capable of holding good jobs. We've had many successes. I've seen so many changes since I was a kid. Up until the fourth grade I thought I was like everybody else, until all at once I found out I wasn't. What I see now is a great acceptance of Indians that wasn't true when I grew up. I think education, people working together, going to church together, have changed a lot of thought. In my time, if you were Indian, you were no good, a drunkard. You hear it so much, you start believing it. I think, if you're treated like a drunkard all your life, you'll start being one. But I see changes.

From an oral history interview conducted December 12, 1994, at the headquarters building of the Eastern Shawnee Tribe of Oklahoma, Seneca, Missouri.

RAE DAUGHERTY

Potawatomi

Elder, Potawatomi Indian Nation, Inc.

Born March 22, 1920, in Dowagiac, Michigan

My father was Michael D. Williams; my mother was Cecilia Topash Williams. My father originally had the name of Cowtuckma, but the priest gave him the name of Williams in order to make it easier for him, for the white man to relate to him. He wasn't singled out; it was something that was done with the various names. My mother was from the Tom Topash family; she was very busy, very active, in Indian affairs. They had a farm and had six children, four boys and two girls. They were prominent. The farm was not a common farm [it was privately owned by them]. They would have people come there on Sundays, or any time. My parents moved us to South Bend so we could enter a parochial school. Because we were some of those people that were committed to stay during the Removal, they thought religious parochial schooling would be good for us. I went to the Catholic school there up until junior high; then I went into the public schools and graduated from a public school in South Bend.

I married Mike Daugherty. We had four children, three girls and a boy. My father and my husband became very good friends, and because my father was active in Indian affairs, my husband naturally continued and was active until he died. He did many things; he was given the title of historian. My son is a member of the Potawatomi council and continues our family involvement with Indian affairs. I served on the personnel committee, and served on boards throughout the state. For example, I served on the Elders Council, the Indian Advisory Board, and the Board of the Michigan Legal Service. I consider myself more or less retired at this point.

My father was educated at Haskell, but was not always able to find

Rae Daugherty

Potawatomi (Pokagon Band)

Elder, Potawatomi Indian Nation, Inc.

a job in his field. Some of my earliest memories of existing [are when] they worked for a resort along the St. Joseph River. As I grew older I was aware of my father always being asked for his opinion on Indian affairs. At that time it was beginning to be difficult to be an Indian. When we were finally given the right to sue the government for claims, he became very active in that. And he succeeded; it was almost a lifetime job. My husband helped him a lot with that. We had help from lots of people. It was a struggle for many years: the hearings, finding lawyers, trying to keep the law on the books, going out and speaking to churches and asking for their support and to senators to keep it on the books. My father succeeded in gaining this, but he didn't live to see it. His life was over before the payment was made. The same thing happened with my husband. He worked all the years to achieve federal recognition for the Pokagon Band. On February 22, 1994, there were five of us who testified in Washington before the Senate for this legislative support. My husband died on the 18th and didn't get to see it. But he knew.

When I was growing up, when you are in school where there aren't that many Native American children, you are always being singled out, because you are bound to look different from all the rest of those in the class. I was a good student; I minded my "P's and Q's." So I didn't have problems.

I met a special friend when I was about eleven who lived right next to us. The war came, so she left and married. At our fifty-fifth anniversary of our class reunion she was mistress of ceremonies, and she said that everybody had to say something. She came to me and said, "This was my best friend when I was in high school." I knew what I was going to say, but she made me forget all of it because I thought that was such a kind thing for her to say. We write letters to each other. She is very kind.

I was proud to be a Potawatomi Indian always, because I lived with it all my life, being Potawatomi, who we are. It's fine, though life is a struggle. I've had many moments when I was elated, like when we testified in the House and Senate because we had things to say, and they listened to it. It was worthwhile.

There was a time when The People didn't respond. I think everybody deep down cared, but life was difficult just to have a job, raise your children, so the leadership depended on a few. It is changing because we are growing economically, and so there is a lot of interest, a lot of new people coming out. It is said that it is all right to be an Indian today. So when we had our first powwow eleven years ago a lot of families took their children, and the children really liked this. It was, "Oh, look at the dances, and here are the drums." My impression was that it was a learning thing for them. What it did was bring out their feelings that they always had—that they wanted to do it, too. This was part of the heritage.

One of the big things for The People here, in the area around Dowagiac, Michigan, was to find a job. There were so many farmers, they had to spread out. They began to go to school, and they got a job here and got a job there so they're here, there, and everywhere. Our economic development will bring them all back because there will be paying jobs. You've got to have jobs to exist.

I worked on a survey for elder care. The Elders would like to be with the other Elders; they enjoy one another. They would like to rehash their histories; they laugh a lot and are happy and funny. They like to be with one another. I think that child care is very important. Moms need help with their children; they need a baby sitter, so I think that should be looked into.

We, the Pokagon Potawatomi Indians, are recognized as a Nation in Michigan as well as in Indiana. The census shows the majority of The People live in Michigan.

My family goes back many generations in leadership. The facts of the tribe were written down by my father. I found a paper that my father had written. He spoke to the Niles Historical Society. The newspaper printed it, and it was very well put.

Until 1978, we were not allowed to practice our own religion, so it went underground because we were told not to do it. Many of the people went to schools, the Indian schools, and they weren't to speak the language. It was just kind of erased out. It was a time of darkness, but it was all a matter of families knowing it and passing it on to their offspring. When we speak of pipe carriers and medicine men, that comes about in that manner. Just being passed on. They earn it. It was not something given to them because they are the son of another pipe carrier; they have to earn that honor. I think that Tom Topash, the young Tom Topash, is the one who really made an effort to learn all of this, because he is a generation under me and he wanted to know it all. With his inquisitive mind, he really went into it. Young Tom had a longhouse; he asked different speakers to come in. It is a gathering of The People to express their feelings, what they have to say, if they choose to speak. They don't have to say anything if they don't want to. They pass the feather around, and if you don't want to say anything the feather is passed to the next person. You could just say, "Thank you for being here." You go in with a positive feeling, not a negative feeling, so it is helpful to everybody in the group. The eagle feather is the one that is passed around. Eagle feathers are earned; they are not given out freely. Someone who has been active, someone who has shown interest and who has practiced these various things, will be granted an eagle feather. They treasure the eagle feather; it is never dropped.

The language was not spoken since our religion was not practiced. The language was brought back by my husband. We have been trying to go at it grammatically, properly. They say my father spoke very good Potawatomi, but that was his manner of speaking. He always spoke properly. When the ladies get together they talk. They can say one word, and it can break them up. My father would say, "He is an old man, or he is an elderly man." The ladies would just say "old man, Kwasi," the noun with no verbs.

We want to teach them how to say "he is an old man." We want the verb tenses right; that's the process we're trying to work on. Even though my father went to Haskell, he still managed to keep the language. He started in Indian affairs when he was sixteen because he could read and write. He could speak both languages, Potawatomi and English. So he could translate and write, and that is something you don't lose when you learn it that young. He started school when he was seven. He didn't know the English language, and that was one of the reasons he wanted to make sure that when we went to school we did learn. So they spoke English at home all the time because we weren't supposed to speak the Indian language. I don't speak it well, but I remember hearing them speaking it. When I was young I didn't realize that they weren't supposed to be doing that. I don't know how the government could do that to Indian people. [The federal government] doesn't tell Italian people what they can or cannot say, and how they can say it in their own homes. It was just a bad thing.

When I testified in the Senate meeting I wrote what I had to say because I lived all of this, and I just wrote my life more or less. When it came to questions, I was asked, "What are you doing to further your culture?" [I told them about our language program.] Their response to my remarks was, "When a tribe wants to remember their language, they are a tribe." When I was asked what I personally think I said, "I just happen to think everyone should be bilingual. I think they should know their own language, but since the English language was there first in most of our lives, what can we do? But I think we should be bilingual.

I mean everybody. It is a big world and it's getting smaller, and we function better if we can understand one another."

I remember my grandparents just as my grandparents. I remember how they lived, how they would have the gathering at their house with the other relatives, friends, the Potawatomis. They were all the time gathering; that is where they found their companionship, their fun, their good times, their discussions of what was happening, what should happen.

My favorite story is about my grandfather, Peter Cowtuckma. He was a nice-looking gentleman. One year he lived in Hartford, which isn't too far from here along the Quapaw River. At one point in their lives they had a payment, annuities or something. He finished his house, and then with what money he had left he bought lumber to help build the church. They said he was such an honest man, and that is always how they spoke of him. He lived to be one hundred years old. As far as my grandmother goes, she was a good cook, a great cook. She cooked the Indian way, and she had all these sons that were hunters and fisherman. It wasn't unusual for her to fix squirrel, rabbit, muskrat, turtle. That is what they liked to eat. She would dry the corn on the roof of the barn. She cooked outside in the summertime because it was cooler, and she would have my grandfather put up a tent so she could make her baskets. These are things that I remember about my grandmother, doing basic things to exist.

The corn that we fixed was dried in order to preserve it, so that they could save for all year long. When it was dried and they wanted to eat it, the husk had to be removed. So they would use ashes to remove that husk. It had to be washed and washed and washed and then cooked, and it was good. We are going to have a Thanksgiving feast, which is traditionally done at the Catholic church. Somebody will take in a big kettle of corn soup. The recipes are not written down. My children have called me and asked me how to make this or that, and I'll try to give them some sort of recipe. My mother would do that for me, too, but for the most part it was just picking up a handful of this and a spoon of that and putting it together. You knew what the ingredients were that went in it.

I have heard that there are five hundred recipes for fry bread. I do believe that there are; I believe everyone has their own version. My mother made all kinds. She baked bread all the time. It is just that everyone made their bread their own way with whatever they had. They didn't always have everything; they made do with what they had.

My grandfather and grandmother moved to the reservation at Mayetta, Kansas, the Potawatomi reservation. She had asthma so she had to leave this region for her health. With her went one son, and he married and had a family. We went out to visit them one time. What I remember about visiting my grandmother [was that] I thought she was a very tall lady because she wore her dresses to the floor, full skirts. She might have had a bandanna around her head. She dressed as a Native American back then. My grandfather, I think, dressed more or less like the average man, but there would be times when he would be wearing his regalia, but my grandmother always dressed that way. To me, she was truly Native American, a Potawatomi lady.

I'm used to the term Native American right now simply because I am out with different groups, and I find it easier to categorize Native Americans. In our survey we did with the Elders, these were People of the Potawatomis, that was one of the questions we asked, what they preferred to be called—"Anishnabek, Native American, or American Indian." Native American seemed to be the most popular, though there would be some that would say Anishnabek. You hear us call one another Anishnabek. But when I am out in the full communities, I say Native American. Around here it's Pokagon Potawatomi now.

If I could come back in one hundred years I would like to see what we call a sovereign Nation. I would like to see the tribe's land base here maintained as much as possible as it was in the olden days because they speak of Mother Earth, they speak of the Creator, and they always speak of living with the land. I would like to see that a reality. And getting down to practicalities, I would like to see us have a community. I don't want us to be living on top of one another but just be within close contact of everybody like we used to be.

I would like my children and grandchildren to benefit from my pride of being who I am. Be proud, be proud. I would like to see the white community learn the truth, the history. I would like this to be taught truthfully. Honesty can be the best answer to all of this. We are all here together. Let's make it good.

From an oral history interview conducted October 27, 1995, at Dowagiac, Michigan.

VICTORIA DAUGHERTY

Shawnee/Delaware

Elder, Head Lady, Loyal Shawnee Tribe

Born 1918, in White Oak, Oklahoma

Out where I live near White Oak, Oklahoma, that's where there used to be several Indians residing. But anymore they've all moved off for jobs. They left here, I'd say, within the last twelve to fifteen years. Whenever it started getting to where they couldn't find jobs around here, they started looking elsewhere. Most of them went to Tulsa, Claremore, Miami, and Bartlesville.

Lincoln didn't have nothing on me. I was born in a log house. We had a log house, and it was a pretty large one. We had a little porch with a breeze-way there and one room out the side. Our kitchen was built out of logs, but then part of it was board. And we had altogether seven rooms. We had three little rooms upstairs. And then we had four downstairs. My mother and father had a room to themselves, and the girls all slept in one room. I never did feel a need for some private space that belonged just to me.

I went to a little country school—Kelly School. And when I got into the eighth grade, I had to transfer to White Oak, because Kelly School didn't go any farther. I went to White Oak all my four years in high school. The reason I stayed in school was the fact that I played basketball, and I loved it. You had to make certain grades to play.

Back in my elementary school—the one-room Kelly School—practically all the students were Indian. The high school here at White Oak had very few Indians because most of them went to government schools and then on to boarding schools.

I never did get any whippings at home. My parents always talked to us. My dad got us at the table and talked to us. And that would hurt us

70

Victoria Daugherty

Shawnee/Delaware

Elder, Head Lady, Loyal Shawnee Tribe

more than anything. We girls would all cry when he talked to us. We never would talk back to him.

I remember we were at this ceremonial dance, and the dance is supposed to be a fun dance. My mother was the Head Lady. She always took the first lead, and then the others followed her. One particular time we sat over there and were talking to some of our friends. We didn't dance. So my dad never said anything until next morning at the breakfast table. He said, "You girls did something last night that you should never do. Any time you see the Elders get up and dance, you get up and dance with them."

When I was little, we spoke our Native language at home. Actually, that's all my mother talked. When we went to the store after I got older, I'd have to interpret for her. She could talk English, but it was broken. Different kids would make fun of her. They would ask her to say it again, or something—something she didn't pronounce right, you know. And she'd say, "No." She'd get mad, and she wouldn't say it.

If we were sitting around the table eating, for example, she would speak the Shawnee language. The rest of us would speak Shawnee part of the time, but we used English most of the time. But not my mother. Maybe she would say something now and then in English to us, but otherwise it was all Shawnee. My father could speak English. He had gone to school, I think, to the fourth grade. He could really figure. I had him help me with my high school math. But if us Indian kids were playing together at school we would speak our Native language if we didn't want some of the white kids to hear what we said. We didn't have to whisper. We could just talk, and they wouldn't understand us.

My people came here from Kansas after 1907. My dad remembered part of that land run from Kansas, but he was just little, I guess, when his family moved here. When I was a little girl, a teenager even, my mother and dad would sit around and tell family stories. They talked about the older generations. And they often talked about some of the hard times that they had. Tried to impress us that we thought we were having a hard time. They said, "You should be thinking about us when we were small and had some of the hard times."

My dad mentioned the move here from Kansas several times. And he evidently got it from somebody else. But he was telling about what hardships they had encountered. When I think about those times, the main thing that goes through my mind was the way they were treated.

And how they had to hide to keep away from the white attackers. The white people literally did attack them, physically, to do physical harm. Mother said the Shawnee would never have got into [fighting] but, she said, "they attacked us so we had to protect our families and had to fight back, you know." I'll tell you what, the Indians were treated awful.

When my dad came here as a little boy with his parents, tribal leadership was the same as it is now. The only thing, their rules were a little stricter [in Kansas and before]. For example, [before the move to Oklahoma] whenever they picked out their dancers they had to have their regular clan. They're supposed to have [a dancer from each clan]. But now we've got so few clans that we kind of switch them around [ask someone to represent a missing clan]. We can't be very strict like they were back then. If they didn't have a Turtle Clan to take that lead, they would never substitute. Nowadays, we always have to say that we are borrowing that clan to take their place, but back then they didn't do that.

My role as Head Lady is mostly in the ceremonials. In one sense of the word, I would be considered as spiritual leader of the women of my tribe. The council has a time to set for our camping. We have the different things we go by. For example, when the dogwood starts blooming, we've got to have that council meeting to set the date for the dancers to camp. After we get camped, we pick out our dancers. It works like this. The women decide. Then we go to the men and tell them what our decisions were. They do likewise and pick out their dancers. Everybody's supposed to know what they're doing at the ceremonials, but they don't. And that's where I come in. As Head Lady, I have to let them know the correct things that we do. My grandmother was tribal Head Lady. And then it was handed down from generation to generation. Then it went down to my mother. Then when she passed away, it went down to my oldest sister. Then when she was sick and had to go to the rest home, my other two sisters wouldn't accept it. They said it was too much of a responsibility. So then she asked me. I didn't want it either because I knew that I'd get a lot of resentment from different people. So she said, "Well, I'll tell you what. If you'll take that [responsibility] while I'm in the rest home, I'll always coach you on what to do."

The ceremonial chief makes the speech—the talk, the prayer—at the ceremonials. He sits in a certain place. After the dances, he makes his prayer—his talk. [My family has] had several of them in the tribe.

My uncle was. But before him there was several others [from my family].

Some things are lost when our Native language is no longer spoken. Some of the talks and prayers have to be made in our language. There is a tribe of Shawnees down in Shawnee, Oklahoma. You'd go there, and you'd see kids playing out in the yard and they'd be talking Shawnee. My sister said she was really impressed when she went down there. She said, "They were playing ball out there, throwing a ball." She said, "Them girls were holding up their hands and would holler, 'Taw-tha.'" That means, "Throw it here." And that was really impressive to her. It would be so nice if there were some way to get the Shawnee people to learn the language and pass it on.

Back a long time ago, our people even made their own caskets, you know. They used lumber, and they made the little wooden spikes to go into the casket. They never had a piece of metal in them. It was all boards. You know, 2x8's or 2x4's or whatever. But I was little, and I remember seeing the men up there fixing this one casket. About the last one, too. Some of them were hewing those little spikes out and some of them were measuring the casket for the sides and everything. And when they got through, my dad talked about that. He said, "There ain't no metal in there, whatsoever. It's all wood, you know." They always objected to having metal in any part of the casket because they said that they wouldn't get to heaven because that metal would scare the spirits away.

I am a religious person. I go to church at Holy Ghost Catholic Church. I like it there because the priest does things in such a way that it's so much like our Native people did it. They burn that incense; we burn cedar. And then they don't condemn our dances—our ceremonial dances. In fact, they'll come out and take part or even watch. And they even have their dances in their parish hall at Miami, and they've invited me to come up there and say a prayer for the [woman who's] going to be a saint—Tehkawika. She's an Indian and she's going to be the first Indian that's been canonized.

And we went up there and had a big dinner, and there was another man from, well, I guess he lives in Quapaw now. He was from Fort Smith. He talked his own language, and he made a prayer, and I made a prayer. Then we had this dinner, and after dinner, why, they moved all the tables back and they had a little powwow there. They had a great big powwow drum. And the priest even got in there and danced.

We all have a major responsibility to share our heritage with our children and grandchildren. I'd like for my descendants to know that I graduated from high school. And I'd like for them to know that I've gone to the ceremonials and had faith in that.

From an interview conducted December 13, 1994, at the headquarters building of the Loyal Shawnee Tribe of Oklahoma, White Oak, Oklahoma.

CHARLES DAWES

Ottawa

Principal Chief, Ottawa Tribe of Oklahoma; listed in *Who's Who in America* and as a biographee in *Who's Who in the South and Southwest* and *Who's Who in the World.*

Born 1923 in Peoria, Ottawa County, Oklahoma

Our horse ranch was about one-eighth of a mile from the Missouri line. And it was only about three miles from where Missouri, Oklahoma, and Kansas come together. My father was a landowner. The amount of land he owned varied anywhere from six hundred to twelve hundred acres, and then he rented pasture land and hay land in addition to that. We raised horses for sale.

I was born in 1923. I'm one of those who wasn't quite a citizen until I was a year old. I was a citizen of the Ottawa Nation. I was a citizen of the State of Oklahoma. But I wasn't a United States citizen until 1924, the year in which I was made a citizen by the Indian Citizenship Act, passed by Congress [June 2, 1924].

My mother's maiden name was Nonkeesis. That name is a corruption from the Ottawa Indian words nano keesis, which means five moons; nano being five and keesis meaning moon. It also means moon, sun, day, depending on how it's used—as a measure of time, or simply as a lunar cycle. You'll find it on the rolls and in the written material as Non Geesis, Non Keesis and Nano Keesis. And that's my Indian name [Nano Keesis].

My childhood home was of native stone. The house that I was born in had seven rooms. The house was quite modern for its time. It had a carbide gas lighting system, and that was really unique. We always had a lot of company. So the kids slept on the floor or on the couch. I spent a lot of time with my dad working the horses and riding the fences and so forth. He taught me so much about nature.

One memory that comes to mind immediately is that we had a blacksmith shop on the ranch. My dad did a lot of his own work, made

76

Charles Dawes

Ottawa

Principal Chief, Ottawa Tribe of Oklahoma

a lot of his own tools. My job was to turn the handle on the forge and to keep the fire hot. One time he asked me to take some tongs and take this piece of iron out and put it on the anvil and hold it flat. Something distracted me, and I didn't quite have it flat on the anvil, and he went ahead and hit it. It just froze me. He said, "Now, I just want to tell you, when someone tells you to do a job, you do it the way they tell you to do it." And I carried that admonition and still do. I've carried it all my life. It really is a great lesson. If someone gives you instructions, then follow those instructions. My father was seventy-one years old when he passed away. I left a promising career in the Army Air Corps because I wanted to spend as much time with him as I could.

I know exactly where I was on Pearl Harbor Day. I went the next day to Joplin [Missouri] to enlist, and the line was around the block and halfway around the third side. So I came back and didn't go in the service immediately because so many people were going in. It was a patriotic urge, and I wanted to fly. As a kid I remember that an airplane would go over very rarely, and I'd run just as far as I could to keep it in sight as long as possible.

I have never suffered from prejudice for being an Indian, never ever. As a matter of fact, it's always worked as a positive influence. It did when I was in school; it did when I was in industry; and it did when I was in the military service. But I know that the fact that I was an American Indian influenced the Air Force Board when I went up for my orals to become an officer. A couple of times they said, "You sound just like an Indian."

Where we lived next to the Missouri line was all a part of the Quapaw land. I lived and grew up in the same spot. I grew up among the Quapaw. I have a Quapaw name. I spoke Quapaw before I spoke Ottawa because more people did in this area. But what tribe you were didn't matter. You were either Indian or you weren't. There was no particular tribe to me—Ottawa, Quapaw, or Osage—not until later on when some of these entitlement programs came along. We were really assimilated in that area.

When my people first moved to Oklahoma, tribal leadership was basically the same thing we have now. We had a principal chief. Prior to moving from Kansas, we had band chiefs. And then the tribe was almost decimated. The tribe was down to 274 people. And we had five clans, or bands. Each one of them had a chief. At that time, the Ottawa Elders got together and decided, "Hey, this doesn't make any sense. We need a principal chief." And that's when that structure started, a principal chief and a council. That took place between 1860 and 1870 in that ten-year period. The first principal chief of the Ottawa was named Shawbanda. Then, when we moved down here, we moved under a principal chief, and we've had the same basic form of government since then.

We had written laws when we were in Kansas. We were one of the few tribes [that did], because we had a Baptist missionary who was also a printer. And we had twenty-eight, I believe, written laws related primarily to stealing and felonies, depending on the value. If you stole someone's horse, there would be certain penalties. There was no mention of murder or rape, acts that we consider as serious crimes against people, because I think we just didn't have those. There was the system whereby the tribe would banish someone for a real serious crime— make them leave. And when the word got around, they were just loners for the rest of their lives.

In our family it was the father who was the head of the family. My mother I'm sure had some input, but when it got right down to the final decision, it was his. That was the same with my grandparents, basically a patriarchal society. I understand that our tribe was matriarchal at one time. Certainly, women had their position in the tribe. They were very important in consultation and so forth, and few major decisions were made without their counsel.

My people's history started very early on the Atlantic Coast; then we moved west. We went as far as Mackinaw City in northern Michigan. That's where our real history begins, because it was almost a nomadic life to that point. Then we split off, with one group going to Manitoulin Island in Canada; another went to Walpole Island, Canada, just north of Detroit. Our group went down to what's now Toledo, Ohio, where the Maumee River runs into Lake Erie. Others feel sorry for us because we got in the way of colonization before they did. And we got moved out to Kansas, then later on to Indian Territory.

We were basically in the same area in the Great Lakes as the Miami of Indiana, although we didn't have a lot of intercourse with Miamis. We were very closely related to the Objibwas and the Potawatomi. These three tribes—Objibwas, Potawatomi, and Ottawa—were and still are identified as the Three Fires Council of the Great Lakes. They consider us still a member of that group.

Only twenty-five years ago, a boy went from the Wikwemikong Village to the university in Sudbury, Ontario, and later took his law degree at Toronto. He found a Queen's proclamation that very simply stated in a couple of sentences that all aborigines in Canada would be treated equally. There was nothing about ceding lands, nothing about qualifications whatever. He took it to the provincial government in Toronto and then took it on to Ottawa, and they recognized immediately what they were up against, so they started giving them all the same entitlement programs, grants, and so forth, that the others got. And they actually tried to make up for all those years when they weren't getting them. As a result, Wikwemikong Village has new schools; they have K–12; they have a new health clinic; they have a new center for aged people, a drug abuse center, and everything.

There were band chiefs prior to Shawbanda becoming the principal chief. My grandfather, William Hurr, was a chief and a councilman, one of the ones that assigned the 20,000 acres to Ottawa University so they could have a school. That's a story in itself. I just can't imagine these people who could not even sign their names. Yet some of them had the vision to foresee the need for higher education. They gave 20,000 acres for the university. And the fundraising didn't more than get off the ground till they gave 7,000 acres more right down on the Marais des Cygnes River—very prime property—and let them sell that so they could actually start the construction. Today, it's a thriving little four-year fine arts school.

Language is the greatest single loss you can have. And that, in turn, will precipitate your loss of all your other culture. You can't carry on without it. I speak my Native language. I learned it from an uncle. He really came down hard and said, "You've got to learn your own language." As I grew older, I got scared, because my son and my daughter and my wife and I were the only ones using these words. When my uncle Clarence died—he was the chief—I realized that here was something we were going to lose. I was the last one, really, that could save it, so I started gathering notes. I spent nine years collecting notes. I'd pick these words up and write them down, and then I put them together in a dictionary. We have a little over a thousand words, and I'm told that in a primitive language that's not bad. That's pretty good.

There are shades of language meaning. For example, when we ask a question, if we say, "Hi, how are you?"—aniee ahnish na—there's no inflections for questions. You can almost tell in English if it's a question; also in the Romance languages. But in our language it's the words themselves. So we can't continue. We can't carry on. I can't name babies. I can't bury our dead. There's just no way that I could do it without the language itself.

DeMaris Gaines started a Native American Heritage Program at Northeastern Oklahoma A&M College. And when I taught Ottawa history, there was only one date I made them learn. That was 1830. In the first session, I made them learn that. I told them, "That's one date that you might as well write down right now, because you're going to have to know it." I didn't tell them why at that time. Later on, I added the Snyder Act of 1921. That's the one that provides health services. But 1830 was the Indian Removal Act during [Andrew] Jackson's administration. All the Indians east of the Mississippi had to be removed westward.

We have a twenty-acre park, and the most interesting part of it is, we have our original cemetery. The principal chief, Shawbanda, died on the way down here from Kansas, and they brought his body on with them. He's the first one buried in the cemetery. Ottawa University maintains it for us.

We have twelve principal chiefs buried in the five-acre original plot. We have one Miami chief and one Peoria chief, but we have twelve Ottawa chiefs. Every chief we've had since we came here to Indian Territory is buried there. I keep telling them that I think there's more heads of sovereign nations—heads of state—buried there than at any other spot in the world. They're all identified; they're all marked. And when I die, I'll be buried there. When former Chief Louis Barlow dies, he plans on being buried there. So that's going to make two more. My son and everybody have [burial] lots there so that others with any potential to become a chief will also be buried there.

The missionaries that we had were Baptists and Friends, and they didn't make any attempt to take our rites away from us. These rites were not, in their opinion, paganistic. They had legitimate interests in the families and respect for the dead. So we still have these practices.

In some instances, the Ottawas have converted the Catholics. The Catholics were quick to realize that there's a certain mysticism in our ceremonies—in our religious rites—that is similar to theirs. And they latched onto that, whereas the Anglican church had no room for it at all. So today when you go to mass on Sunday morning in Wikwemikong, the priest has vestments that have Woodland beadwork—all of his vestments, the altar cloth, the altar boys, everybody. Then, when he takes the incense in the little long-necked burner that they use, they put this out over the congregation through the Aladdin Lamp, I call it. They don't do that [with the Ottawas]. They have a little iron pot. And they put sweet grass and cedar on some hot coals and do it exactly the same way that we do it. Then they take an eagle feather and blow it out all the way down [the aisle] and all the way back. And when they use the Holy Water, instead of using it out of this bulb-shaped thing with a handle on it in sprinkling the congregation, they take a little bowl of water and they take a cedar sprig, and they throw it out exactly the same way that we do.

I don't go to church. I professed faith and was baptized in the Christian church—the Disciples of Christ. But I don't go. I'm having a terrific struggle right now with myself as to whether I should write some of this down, because I have positive beliefs. I have a personal relationship with God that anybody can have if they go out and seek it. God talks to me. I don't hear his voice, but if I go out in a peaceful spot alone and just open up my heart and cleanse my mind of everything else, I can get a message direct from God. I do it frequently.

I am the spiritual leader of most all the tribes in this area. This means that those who have lost their burial rites, or their naming ceremonies, or how to petition God our way, they will come to me and ask me if I'll do it or ask me for advice. I don't have an official position with any of them. They just rely on me, and, of course, any time they ask, it's obligatory as far as I am concerned. Very often somebody will come up and want me to conduct the funeral rites or graveside rites; that's all they're interested in. Then they want to pay me, but I just can't do that. I'm not allowed to do that.

Clarence King was chief and spiritual leader before I was, not the immediate chief before I was, but the one before him. I am not looked upon by my people as being an intermediary between them and God. I don't know how to explain it. And not all of them subscribe to this, by the way; not all of our tribal members do. They belong to their own church, and they believe and act and go to church on Sunday—some of them everytime the door is open. But for those that do subscribe to this, and most do, they don't look at me as much as a holy man [but rather] as a knowledgeable person. There is a distinction, but they don't pay homage in any sense of the word to me, except they have respect for me for my knowledge in this realm of their lives.

Our people had shamans and people that would doctor—medicine men and women. I don't doctor. I told the medicine men up in Wikwemikong that I don't do it. We have the same medicines in many cases. And they asked, "Well, why don't you do it?"

I said, "Because I'm afraid. I'm afraid I'll make a mistake."

And they said, "You shouldn't worry about that. You're not doing anything anyway. God is the one that does it."

But I still haven't brought myself to the point. Oh, I would [in] my own family. We use a lot of Native medicines, sort of like we would use non-prescription drugs.

I've been told that there is a medicine to cure every disease that we have. I went to a retreat where we had medicine men from all over the country—people long and highly recognized as medicine men, such as Leonard Crowdog from the Sioux Nation and Frank Thomas from the Six Nations Reserve [Iroquois]. We would each one do our own little thing in the evening, and then after that we would sit around the fire and just talk. It was a week-long thing. I asked Leonard Crowdog if our people had a cure for cancer, and he said, "No, Charlie, we didn't have cancer."

I said, "Why?"

He said, "Because we didn't eat cattle. We ate wild game."

In the role as tribal chief, I am the tribal administrator—administrative officer for the tribe. I handle the business of the tribe as an elected official. The tribal chief is probably listened to more now than the earlier chiefs were, because we don't take decisions from the Bureau of Indian Affairs lying down. If they are counter to what we believe, or what we want, or the way it should be, we fight.

I'd like for my descendants and everybody [in the Ottawa Tribe] to remember me as having a vital role in preserving our language and our culture. The thing I think that I have accomplished is that I did remarkably well in industry. I was retired from a Fortune 500 Company. I've been president of my own corporation. Everything just worked out for me.

From an interview conducted December 12, 1995, at the headquarters building of the Ottawa Tribe of Oklahoma, Miami, Oklahoma.

LEROY DOLSON

DELAWARE

CHIEF, MUNSEE-DELAWARE NATION

BORN DECEMBER 18, 1941, ON THE MUNSEE-DELAWARE RESERVE

I guess they had about six feet of snow, so they couldn't get to the hospital. So I was born right here on the reservation. My parents lived on a back road. They couldn't get out.

I have three children. One boy twenty-nine years old. I had two other children I lost by accidents.

My mother worked out. My father was a hunter, farmer, and fisherman so it was an interesting life. I've always done a lot of hunting and fishing. I was taught by my father. We had a small farm with chickens and cows. I had to milk the cows after school. I rode a bicycle about four miles each day to school and from school. That's how we got to school. There was no bus service at that time, so we just rode bicycles. I guess that kept us in good shape. We had to cut our own firewood. We had to make our own butter and grind our own flour. It was quite a change from modern times. But I was lucky with two good parents who said we needed education. Both were very supportive of education. My dad wanted me to be a farmer, but farmers were having a rough time in those days, so I went for an education, which helped me get a job here. I went to grade school in the area. I graduated from technical school with a diploma. I went to work in the United States; then I worked in London, Ontario. I came back to Munsee-Delaware Reserve in 1970, and I started working as an administrator here.

An early memory of childhood is about a snake that was on the farm. In the summer we would always pick strawberries in the strawberry patch, and we would go barefoot. The snake would wind itself around my ankle. It was just a garden snake. The river that runs through the Reserve is a fishing river. This reserve is together with Chippewa land.

84

Leroy Dolson

Delaware

Chief, Munsee-Delaware Nation

We all went to school together, and we would play together. I thought they were my friends, but sometimes when we were playing they would turn on me. But we were children, and we stayed friends. We intermarried.

Because of jobs, there is a lot of moving between Canada and the U.S. In the 1960s I went to General Motors for four years. But then jobs in the States started slowing down, and people were coming back to Canada after the 1970s. We've got the freedom of the border so it's pretty easy to get the job and come back and forth between the States and Canada.

We were more traditional in my childhood because when we had health problems my grandmother would tell us which medicines to use to cure us. She knew about certain flowers, and sent us to find them. This medicine was practiced a lot in my childhood—for a cold, a cough. We would go out in the woods and fields and get what we needed, and leave a little tobacco.

We have traced our history back prior to 1565. The year 1624, when the Dutch first started moving us back, was the first migration. The Munsees were always living on Manhattan Island and what's now the states of New York and New Jersey. In the 1700s the migrations out [from our traditional lands] really began. We have tried to get the history written down to the present.

There are different speech patterns between the Munsee and Unami branches of the Delaware people. In the late 1960s and early 1970s the busing of school children started, and the assimilation started. This meant our kids began to learn our language later in life. But people before that lost interest in teaching the language to their children so we almost lost the language. There are still some people who do speak Delaware. We're trying to revive the language. We have a recording for people to listen to. We have classes. People are showing interest now. The new dictionary being developed will have the Munsee and Unami dialects. There really isn't much opportunity to speak your own Native language any more. Hopefully, at our gatherings, we'll get to teach and use our language. We tried to revive the language teaching a couple of years ago, but the language teacher died, so it took us a while to get back to it. When you lose your language, you lose your culture.

The first time I experienced prejudice was when I went to high school. There were very few Native people there. It was in the late 1950s. It was the time when everyone was going to high school off the Reserve, and to universities and colleges. There was a bias, going back to the past. It's surprising that there were people who were not aware of our culture. They still thought we lived in tipees. The worst thing is television. ·

In August of 1994 we had our first gathering of all the Delaware tribes for a three-day meeting. People came from all over—Oklahoma, Ohio, Canada. We have early records of the chief, vice chief, and warriors who ran the business of the tribe. Now we just have a chief and four councillors. Elders are still conferred with. If an Elder objects to something, a councillor listens. That's respect. The Elders are passing on the stories. It's continuous. The modern way is with the computer. We have one Wampum Belt. There is supposed to be a treaty behind each belt so we have to do the research. We have sort of lost the old traditions around being chief. When we have a gathering we have the ceremonies.

Matrilineal ways are still followed, but some things are handed down the mother line, and some down the father line. It was my grandmother on my father's side who handed a lot of this stuff down. Sometimes she used to baby-sit us, and really she was a good teacher. We think back on all the things she taught us, like the health things, to take care of ourselves.

We have a joint Anishnabek project to teach culture in the schools. It's a curriculum for all the schools, and to put on video. The language is different for each tribe. There are six hundred different Nations in Canada. They are related in some ways, but they are in different locations and have a different heritage. So there have to be differences for each in the general curriculum.

Common sense is the most important thing that was passed on to me. You think, when you have to do something, it should be done this way or it should be done this way. When you are young, you think everything should be simple, but you have to think which is the right way.

Because of our modern world, our children now should be educated at least at the college level. The children who don't have an education have lost potential. If you get your education and use it, you have a good life. Our first lawyer from the Reserve graduated a year ago [1994]. That is quite an accomplishment. We are giving scholarships to help people get their education.

I can remember, when I was seventeen, we used to have a joint administration with the Chippewa Council. Since then, we've separated, and we've come a long way. That happened in 1965. It's been thirty years. There was nothing, and now we have this building, and we have land to be developed—timber lots. We have a lot to do for the future.

I've been lucky with good parents. Today sometimes the children suffer because they don't have family. I would like to see these children get an education in both cultures, so they get on with a good life. Because of assimilation it is difficult for the children to know their culture so they get lost. You can't go out by yourself. You need your culture. I think about this quite a bit—what I want to see in the future for our Nation. We have Native economic development opportunities in Ontario. I'd like to see our Nation independent of any government support with strings attached—"You've got to do this; you've got to do that." It's been different in Canada from the U.S. It's a hard system to understand with federal and state funding. I'd just like to see our Nation self-sufficient.

From an oral history interview conducted May 15, 1995, at the Munsee-Delaware Nation headquarters building, Muncey, Ontario.

EMMA GREENFEATHER DONALDSON

SHAWNEE

ELDER, LOYAL SHAWNEE TRIBE OF OKLAHOMA

BORN SEPTEMBER 7, 1921, WEST OF WHITE OAK, OKLAHOMA

I moved to South Dakota in 1946, when my husband got out of service in World War II. We moved up there looking for employment, which he found. I've been up there for many years and raised a family up there.

In June 1994, I moved down here to Tahlequah, Oklahoma, when the Cherokee Nation gave me the job to work with them for a written Loyal Band Shawnee language. I've been trying to write down the Shawnee language in English [as a pronunciation guide to speak Shawnee].

My mother and stepdad talked our language to us from day one. There were no Shawnee people where I lived in South Dakota. We would come back to Oklahoma for our vacations, and I would visit my mother, and we would talk in Shawnee, so I kept up. When my girls were small I talked Shawnee to them, but now they do not understand it. I have four daughters, and they live in South Dakota and Minnesota. They all have good jobs. They are well educated. Their father and I made sure that those girls got their education, because we didn't.

Growing up, I used to love to play the Indian football game at the Stomp Grounds. I've always been proud of my Indian heritage. I think it's too bad they lost all of our language. The cultural traditions have not been practiced. They try to practice the best way they know how. As far as our traditional Stomp Dances, they don't do it right. It's a very sad thing. By losing our language we lose the traditional ways we worship at the Stomp Grounds. The powwows took over a lot. I have nothing against powwows; they're good, too.

Anyone can do the cooking if you're around it for a while. I was raised up that way. Our parents raised us up the Shawnee way and [the

Emma Greenfeather Donaldson

Shawnee

Elder, Loyal Shawnee Tribe

way of the] white church. All the Shawnees, we just all got together. And that's the way we were brought up; to speak the language and do the ways.

Now I'm trying to help with preserving the Shawnee language. I'm working with the linguist at Tahlequah. Sometimes I speak into the tape recorder, and sometimes it is written down. This is just the Loyal Shawnee. The language is different between the three Shawnee Tribes [Eastern Shawnee at Seneca, Missouri; Absentee Shawnee at Anadarko, Oklahoma; Loyal Shawnee at White Oak, Oklahoma.] The Eastern Shawnee have lost their language altogether, and the Absentee Shawnee speak enough that we can understand each other. They have their own language project. When Victoria Daugherty and my sister, Billie Smith, and I get together, we can talk to each other in our Shawnee language.

When I was little I wore traditional clothing. When I moved I started wearing modern up-to-date clothing. But I did that even when I went to school when I was small. We didn't wear our traditional clothing to school. We wore them when we went to dances and our traditional things, but not every day.

We were always taught to be good and kind to each other and not be angry or have bad feelings in our hearts. That's the way we were taught. Nowadays there is so much anger. The outside world brings so much of this corruption and stuff in here. What we have is a lot of the youngsters wanting to learn. They are very interested. They just do like the old timers taught us, especially, when we've got something going together, to help each other and be kind to each other, not get mad and try to hurt anybody else's feelings. Just say that I'll treat you like you treat me. And if you do, you're going to find out that you are going to be blessed. You won't have hard feelings toward anybody else.

When I go home to South Dakota, I am going to teach my own children how to talk Shawnee because they want to learn—and my grandchildren. They have never been brought up with Shawnee, but they know some of it because they would ask me. And they would ask their grandmother and their step-grandfather. My stepfather was the chief of the Shawnee Stomp Dance.

From an oral history interview conducted December 13, 1994, at the headquarters building of the Loyal Shawnee Tribe of Oklahoma, White Oak, Oklahoma.

LEROY ELLIS

Shawnee

Former Lieutenant Governor and former Governor, Absentee
Shawnee Tribe

Leroy Ellis

Shawnee

Former Lieutenant Governor and former Governor, Absentee Shawnee Tribe

HENRYETTA ELLIS

Shawnee

Member, Absentee Shawnee Tribe of Oklahoma

Born October 14, 1952, in Wax, Oklahoma

I was born about eighteen miles east of Norman, Oklahoma, in a little, one-room log cabin. It was a natural log cabin with mortar between the logs. My father's mother delivered me.

After I was born, there was just me for awhile. We lived in Oklahoma City in this little house out in a pasture. I think there were one or two rooms there in that house. Then we moved to a little house about three or four miles from that little place. It had two or three rooms—a kitchen and living room and bedroom and bathroom. By then I had one brother, and that's my first memory because my second brother was born when my brother and I were sitting on the couch. I can remember my aunt telling my brother and me to sit there and be still, be quiet. And so we were just sitting there; then all of a sudden we heard a baby crying.

My very favorite friend during my early years was Connie Sue Marson. She lived two doors over; she was non-Indian. We were really good friends until we moved. I was probably about five years old then.

Back then, in that community, I kind of felt special. We had a neighbor that lived across the alley from us. He was part Indian, so he always called me his little princess. I don't ever remember any prejudice or anything. We were treated okay, and I was the only little Indian girl in the school system. And my brothers were the only little Indian boys.

When I was in the seventh grade we moved back to the country. That's when I felt prejudice, just being Indian. There weren't that many non-Indians out there, but you could feel it. And you knew about it. This was at Wax where I was born. My mom and dad were raised out in that area. But in [Oklahoma] City, I remember one day I was walking home and looking at my skin, wondering why it was brown and everybody else's was white. That's when I was about five or six. That's when I first realized that I was different. I kept rubbing and rubbing to see why it didn't come off. I couldn't figure it out, but I don't remember feeling bad about it or anything, other than wondering, "Why doesn't that brown come off?" I didn't talk to anybody about it. I guess I just didn't think it was that big of a deal.

In terms of how the white kids acted in a prejudiced way against me, I guess by just the way they called me an Indian. It didn't sound good the way that they said it. And I couldn't understand why it hurt because I had never been treated that way before. Maybe some called me a "squaw," but I didn't understand what that was either, other than seeing stuff on television.

When I felt proudest to be an Indian was probably when I was able to begin participating in our ceremonials. That would have been at age twelve. This was the Bread Dance Ceremony. And Stomp Dancing took place when I was little, but I had to go to sleep. I remember that I would lie awake in the car. They'd put us to bed, but I'd lie there and listen to the songs. We could hear them. Eventually, I'd go to sleep.

My mom shook shells. I think people called them shackles. She had shackles made out of metal cans. I remember her shaking those. Then that's what I wanted to do; that's what I did. And I still do shake shells. At these ceremonies, my dad would get picked to go hunting.

What I'm doing now in terms of old customs and practices is what I remember watching and observing when I was a little girl. Back then, I didn't get to participate, but I was there. The only thing that I can remember specifically is that, right at the end of our dance, we had this long prayer, and they made us all sit down and listen and be quiet. So what we are doing now is basically what they were doing back then. We're trying to keep it going.

I don't speak my Native language fluently, but I can speak some. I was taught when I was little. My mom says that I was able to speak it when I was a little girl, but once I got into public school, I stopped. She was a boarding-school child, and from what I gathered, she was kind of afraid that we would be punished the way she was punished. She told me at one time that she and my dad talked about it and decided that they wouldn't go any further [in teaching us the language]. But she really regrets it now. I remember, as a child, that she would get up about 5:30 or so and fix some breakfast before my dad went to work. I could hear them in the kitchen just talking away [in our Native language]. They pretty well talked like this at home.

I did not attend a tribal school. I went to public schools. To me, you kind of lose everything when the Native language is no longer spoken because a lot of the practices are all done in the language.

If one of my grandparents could come back now and listen to the language spoken at a Bread Dance today, it would be the same language. But there is a little difference over time in the sounds. I know that by looking at old books and things and seeing some words; there are some words that were lost. But we still have Absentee Shawnee people who are fluent.

To me, I feel that if you are Shawnee, you already have the old traditions, and nobody has to teach you those. You go to those dances and things like that. Even if you don't participate and you just go to observe, you learn them. That's my feeling.

As for our language, we're getting a group together of public school teachers that have gone to this language institute and are learning the international phonetics system or something like that. Some of the older people don't understand the phonetics system, but they know the old way of spelling. So they're putting the old Shawnee and new Shawnee into English.

I typically use just the word Shawnee and not Absentee Shawnee when referring to our tribe. I guess it's because in the past, we've been going back east and meeting some people that claim to be Shawnee but aren't really Shawnee. I am Shawnee, and the term Absentee Shawnee was just given to us by the government. I don't see any difference in us and the other two groups of Shawnee in Oklahoma. We are Shawnee. And it's not our fault that somebody else named us the Eastern Shawnee or the Loyal Shawnee or the Absentee Shawnee. Originally, we were all just Shawnee.

The Bread Dance is important to us. That's what we went to twice a year. We were never told why. We just went. It was our day in church. To us, that was the day that God, or the Creator, would come and listen to just us.

I think that the ceremonials associated with the Bread Dance are perhaps even more important than the language itself. To us, this is what keeps the world going.

I'd especially like for my children and their descendants to remember me as a Shawnee woman who met her obligations. I've led our Bread Dance four times, and I like to do beadwork. I've learned how to make moccasins—the Shawnee style of Woodland-style moccasins. I know how to make our tribal clothing. And I'm always trying to learn how to do other things. I make shawls. I'm learning how to make baskets.

I don't like to sell things. I feel like whenever I sell things, I am selling myself, and I don't like to do that. It means more to me when I'm able to trade or give or teach somebody else to do it. Those are the things I like to do.

From an interview conducted December 16, 1994, at Shawnee, Oklahoma.

GUY WILLIS FROMAN

Peoria/Miami

Chief, Peoria Indian Tribe of Oklahoma, 1947-1972; Honorary
Chief for life

Born February 4, 1902, Indian Territory, East of Miami, Oklahoma

Died March 3, 1994

Mother, Angeline Eddy Froman, full-blood Peoria Indian. Father, William Henry Froman, one-half Eastern Miami Indian, one-half White. William Henry Froman was a descendant of Little Turtle, Principal War-Chief of the Miamis. Both parents died when I was quite young. My dad when I was two years old, and my mother when I was seven.

I received my education in government schools. Seneca Indian School, Wyandotte; Fort Lapwai, Idaho, Indian Sanitarium. I finished my schooling at Chilocco, Oklahoma, in 1922.

Played professional baseball from 1921 till 1932, mostly in St. Louis Cardinal organization. Married Gertrude Helm of Miami, Oklahoma, on May 18, 1928. To this union were born seven children: Elizabeth Froman Hargrove, William Henry Froman, Robert Guy Froman, John Edward Froman, David Wesley Froman, Ronald Froman, Donald Froman. We have twenty-two grandchildren and nine great-grandchildren. I worked for Eagle-Picher Mining Company from 1937 to 1967.

Elected chief of the Peoria Indian tribe in 1947 following the death of George W. Skye. At that time Leo Finley was second chief; Alice Eversole, secretary-treasurer. Councilmen were Sherman Staton and Ada Palmer. Retired as chief in 1972. At that time Louis Myers was second chief; Fannie Skye Stokes was secretary-treasurer. Councilmen were George Skye and Rodney Arnett. When retired, served on Peoria Cemetery Committee and was chairman for several years. Retired from Cemetery Committee in 1986. When I retired as chief in 1972, I was made Honorary Chief for life. When retired from the Cemetery Committee, I received a plaque in appreciation from the tribe, both honors I treasure very much.

Guy Willis Froman

Peoria/Miami

*Chief, Peoria Indian Tribe of Oklahoma,
1947-1972; Honorary Chief for life*

The Peoria Indian Cemetery is located on the west side of Spring River about ten miles east of Miami, Oklahoma. It is the final resting place of many Peoria Indians who moved from Kansas to the Indian Territory in the late 1860s. The earliest marker is dated February 1871.

According to Bill Landers, councilman of the tribe, his father, Arch Landers, told him that several miners who worked at Lincolnville died during the flu epidemic of 1917-1918 and are buried in the Peoria Cemetery in unmarked graves. The northwest corner of the cemetery was open to Indians and white people. Tom Bone, a Shawnee, was interred here. Also buried in unmarked graves are Yellow Beaver [a Wea Chief who moved to Indian Territory in 1868] and Henry Turkeyfoot.

Although for many years the Peoria Cemetery was the only property owned in common by the tribe, it was neglected and overgrown with bush and weeds. Cattle roamed freely through it; tombstones had fallen and the six-foot memorial to Baptiste Peoria [Chief of the Peoria, Piankashaw, Kaskaskia, and Wea Indians during their moves to Kansas and Oklahoma] could barely be seen above the vegetation. [He died September 13, 1873.]

In the early 1960s Peoria volunteers began a clean-up and restoration of the cemetery. In early 1984, the Peoria business committee established a trust for the perpetual care of the tribe's burial grounds. In 1983 the Peoria Cemetery and the old Peoria School were placed in the National Register of Historic Sites. The listing was the second such designation in Ottawa County [Oklahoma]. Burial in the cemetery is free for Peoria tribal members and their spouses.

On 30 May 1988 the tribe held a veterans' memorial service. The American Legion dedicated a stone monument to the veterans who are interred in the cemetery. It reads:

> In honor of our U.S. Armed Forces Resting Here:
>
> Asa John Froman, Army; Charles E. Blalock, USAF; Charles W. Blalock, Army; Jack F. Blalock, Army; William H. Blalock, Army; Harvey L. Landers, Army; Baptiste Peoria, Army; George E. Skye, Army; Lester Skye, Navy; Wilson Stand, Army.
>
> Erected by Peoria Indian Tribe 1988

> *The account above is reprinted by permission from The Peorias: A History of the Peoria Indian Tribe of Oklahoma, edited by Dorris Valley and Mary M. Lembeke (Miami, OK: The Peoria Indian Tribe of Oklahoma, 1991), pp. 206-208, 158-161.*

KELLER GEORGE

Oneida

Wolf Clan Representative to the Men's Council, Oneida Nation of New York; Northeast Area Representative for the National Congress of American Indians; President of the United South and Eastern Indians

Born 1935, on the Onondaga Indian Reservation near Syracuse, New York

I was born and raised on the Onondaga Indian Reservation, which is just south of Syracuse, New York. We didn't have a homeland when I was growing up, because the lands that our people held were taken away from us. So I grew up there even though I am Oneida. My great-grandmother's husband was an Onondaga chief. And he was also known for his carvings of the false-face masks. False-face. In Indian it's called Hatowi. It is the Society of the False-face. It's a medicine society. I belong to it. As a young child, I was very sick, and the doctors at that time didn't know what was wrong. So my mother took me to the Hatowi Society that used the healing powers. And that's how I became a member of that society. I am not a healer, but I wear my false-face and go and join in the dances and the healing ceremony that is done.

I'm not an expert in the [Oneida] language. I can understand it and speak, not as fluently as I probably would like to but enough to get me through ceremonies and casual conversations. I never learned how to write or read our language, simply because it was never taught that way. It was by word of mouth. Our language comes through the oral traditions. There is a system that is used now that has been devised by linguists on how to write the language. But we don't have a dictionary in our language.

If there's somebody in the family who went on before, you usually name somebody in your family after them. I was going to name my daughter Marilyn, but my father spoke very little English and not very good English. He couldn't pronounce Marilyn. So, I decided to call her something else. For instance, my sister's name is Lucille, but he always pronounced it Rucille. So, when he was somewhere filling out some

Keller George

Oneida

*Wolf Clan Representative to the Men's Council,
Oneida Indian Nation; Northeast Area Representative,
National Congress of American Indians; President,
United South and Eastern Indians*

papers, because he couldn't write English, he had somebody fill out whatever forms he needed. And it got written that her name was Rucille—R-u, because that's how he pronounced it. Her name was later changed by affidavit.

The Oneida people didn't have a homeland. We didn't have a reservation. About 1820 the Oneidas split into three different Oneida communities. There's one portion that went to Ontario. They sold the land that they had in New York and trekked to Ontario and became the Oneida of the Thames in Ontario, Canada. This other group went to Green Bay, Wisconsin, and settled there. They took the money that they had gotten from selling their lands in New York. Moved. But my ancestors didn't go. They weren't going to leave their lands. Even though it was taken away from them, they stayed.

I characterize my ancestors as being the survivors. They went through a hard, hard time, even though they were allies with the colonists during the Revolutionary War. They fought on the side of George Washington's army and assisted them. Through our oral traditions a story's been passed on to us that says during the year 1776-1777, when George Washington was at Valley Forge and was camped for the winter, his army was literally starving to death because the local farmers would no longer support him without payment.

There was an Oneida chief by the name of Skenandon that took his young men and trekked all the way from New York to Valley Forge, carrying corn with them. They took a young lady with them—her name was Polly Cooper—to show the soldiers how to prepare the corn and use it, because it was dry corn. If you take dry corn and eat it and then drink hot liquid or liquid on top of it, it will swell in your stomach and probably kill you. But there's a way that you use wood ashes to take the hard, outside hull off and then cook it to make your mush, corn bread, corn soup or whatever you're going to make out of it.

They took the young lady, Polly Cooper, with them, and she showed them how to prepare the corn. She stayed there for the duration of their encampment that winter. The story that is told to us is that after the war, to show their appreciation, they offered Polly money. She refused, saying that it was her duty to help George Washington's army. So, to show their appreciation, Martha Washington took her to Philadelphia, which was the new capital at that particular time, and bought her a bonnet and a shawl. Well, I don't know whatever happened to the bonnet, but the shawl—direct descendants of Polly Cooper have it today.

Even though we were allies, we were treated worse in victory than the nations of Germany and Japan in defeat. During the treaty signing, they were actually given U.S. aid to rebuild. We never had that, even though we fought on the side of the colonists who were victorious, and treaties were signed saying that this portion of land in New York State would be ours forever. The stipulation was that no lands could be sold without the concurrence of the U.S. government, which at that time was the War Department.

So we're working to settle those land claims now. But, learning a lesson from our ancestors, we still view the non-Indian, the American now living on those lands, as allies, as our neighbors. Any lands that we might recoup would be public lands and not personal property.

My people stayed because of the involvement in the Revolutionary War. The Onondagas had fought on the side of the British. That land was their land, but many of my people resided there. Actually, some of the people were given that land as payment for serving in the Revolutionary War. However, they said, "No, this land is Onondaga land, and we should give it back to them." And, George Washington, as president, left it up to the Oneida people, who gave it back to the Onondagas. But the stipulation was that Oneidas could live there.

They were probably the most prosperous land owners at that time. They had the better homes and the better this and that, but as time went on our people left that area. A group called the "Marble Hill Oneidas" were given allotments of certain lands and still have them to this day. They're basically the ones that stayed around Oneida, New York. It was the Dawes Act [1887] that introduced land allotments, and the federal government or state government declared [the rest of our land] surplus lands. The people who were given these allotments didn't have to pay taxes on them, and they still don't to this day. There's a small group of the Oneida people that live there and have managed to live there all these years.

I was born in an old, old, big house. At one time it probably had been a beautiful place. It was almost like a hotel. In fact, the name that we gave it, or that I knew it as, was Suicide Inn. Evidently, whoever had been living there had committed suicide. It had been the property of an Indian family. And, it probably was a big, glamorous place at one time, but it was run down. There was no electrical power there. There was no indoor plumbing or water. The water that we had there we had to get from a well. We used kerosene lamps for lighting. That's the way a good many of the people lived [when I was growing up]. I don't even think at that time there was electricity on that reservation at all.

My father was drafted into the Second World War. After 1945, when he came home from the war, we moved for a while to Ontario, Canada, on the Oneida of the Thames Reservation. Then we moved back to the Onondaga Reservation in New York. We lived at various places, always not being able to own any of the land or the house but renting from somebody that owned it.

My Oneida people were buried in New York on Onondaga land. They had a couple of cemeteries. Part of our teaching was that it didn't matter if you were Onondaga or Seneca or Mohawk or whatever. Our people were generous people because we were bound together under "The Great Law" as the Iroquois Confederacy. We could go onto each other's territory and live.

In ancient times, before we knew what putting fences up meant, you could go and set up your longhouse and hunt and fish, and enjoy the fruits of the land because that's what you lived from. But then we learned that this was mine and this was yours, and we adopted the European's philosophy of land ownership. The Europeans brought with them this philosophy. We didn't know what land ownership was. It was believed the Creator made that land for all of us to use. We didn't go up and put up a fence like we do now.

Now we have about four thousand acres that we have re-acquired. The Nation owns that, not individuals. But an individual is given a certain block of land, and they can live on that as long as they take care of it. They can build on it; they can live on it; and they can do as they please on it. But, it's not theirs.

In my Nation we had three clans, which were nothing more than extended families: the Wolf Clan, the Turtle Clan, and the Bear Clan. Well, that's still the way we do it. We are a matrilineal society, meaning that we follow the traditional way of ownership of the land. The women are the ones who own the title to it, not the men. It's the Clan Mothers and the women of the Nation that select who they want to be the leaders. For instance, in my position as a Wolf Clan representative to the Men's Council, the women selected me. Then they bring the candidates to all the people to be approved.

It's a process that you go through. Eventually, if we ever reach that point, then we will become "chiefs," I guess you might say. There's a long process that you go through learning the ceremonies. Because our language has been oral, there's a lot of the speeches that you have to memorize to be able to conduct the ceremonies, and just a whole lot of different things to learn.

We are attempting to do things the way they were done many years ago. In 1934 they came out with the IRA, Indian Reorganization Act. It was passed by Congress in 1934, and that's what a lot of the Indian tribes have today. We don't; ours is a traditional-type government. Other Indian nations, I think, for the most part, have all adopted the "elective system." They go out and vote every two or three or four or however many years and have written constitutions.

We have a constitution, but it's not a written constitution. Our constitution is the constitution that formed the Iroquois Confederacy. It's the "Law of the Great Peace" or, as we commonly call it, "The Great Law." Through legend, it is told to us that at that time the tribes were warring with one another, constantly battling; there was no peace. Even cannibalism was prevalent between the tribes around that area where we resided, which was from the Canadian border all the way down into Pennsylvania.

The Peace Maker came and was teaching "The Great Law," the power of a good mind to bring about peace. He was a Huron. Legend says he came across "The Great Water," meaning Lake Ontario, in a stone canoe. Along with him, he brought an Onondaga, and his name was Hiawatha. The Mohawk was the first Nation that they came upon, and they accepted their teachings. Then they came to the Senecas. Then on to the Oneida. Then on to the Cayuga. Then to the Onondagas, and the Onondagas were the last to accept it.

The story is that the first chief of the Iroquois Confederacy was an Onondaga. He was an evil, wicked man in the beginning. They said he was so evil that his hair was like snakes. His hands and body were bent and twisted. And, people were afraid of him because he was also a great sorcerer. They feared him, but by The Peace Maker and Hiawatha going to him and talking to him and preaching the power of "The Great Law," when he accepted it, it changed him. His hair, arms, and legs straightened out. He became normal.

He was made the first Tadodaho, as we call it, who is the chief (chairman) of the Iroquois' Six Nations. He carries no clan. He doesn't have a clan, because his duties are to conduct the meetings of what we call the Six Nations Grand Council. The central fire was then put at Onondaga, which was the capital of the Iroquois Confederacy. The Seneca were known as the "Keepers of the Western Door." The Mohawks were known as the "Keepers of the Eastern Door."

At that time, peace came and prevailed, and there were certain things that we were to do. They are called wampum. There are certain wampum that we have to do in time of death, in time of marriage, or when a child is born. There are certain ways the ceremonies are laid out for us, how we are supposed to do them. There are certain ways to conduct ourselves in our everyday life. Some people call it a religion, but we don't call it a religion. To us it's just the way you live your everyday life. That is what wampum means to us.

To most people wampum means money. To us, they were called wampum because you had the wampum beads, and you made these little strings of beads. And you had certain wampum—so many beads on it—that told you what you had to do, if certain prayers were to be said. So that became the way.

The third wampum is that when somebody dies you've got to have the mourning period, which is ten days. The language tells us that we can only go as far as the grave of that person; we can't go beyond. But we supply him with his clothes that he needs on his journey to the spirit world. That's why we take the sacred tobacco. We still grow the tobacco like it was done three or four hundred years ago. In fact, I'm one of the ones that grow it. I grow it for my own use. This year for the first time, because we've got the land now to do it, our Nation planted plenty of tobacco.

We use that tobacco in our ceremonies. When we pray, we take the tobacco and throw it into the fire. The smoke carries your words up to the Creator. That's what we believe. It's not a hybrid tobacco; it's the original. We call it Indian tobacco. It is a strong, green tobacco.

I learned all that I know about the old way of life from my elders, in particular from my great-grandmother, Gonahdahawia. She was born in 1850 and died in 1951. Her English name was Nancy Doxtator. Basically everybody called her by her Indian name. She lived in this little house that had an open-hearth fireplace. She wore these old, long, black skirts that came all the way to the ground and were decorated with some type of beads or shell. She could speak English, but didn't too often. When she planted, she did it in a traditional Iroquois way. First, she would plant the corn. When the corn got to a certain height, she would plant the beans and the squash all in the same line to grow around the corn.

When we used to go fishing, she had this wooden box or trough that she'd take. We'd clean the fish, and she'd throw all that stuff in that big old box. Then, when she'd go to plant, that was her fertilizer. She used to take wood ashes and throw [them] in there. I asked her why she was doing that, and she said, "That replenishes the Mother Earth." It's just like farmers do today; they take lye and put it in the soil. In those wood ashes is lye.

She taught me a lot, like in the ceremonies you go clockwise. There're reasons for that. You have the four directions, and you pray to the east because that's where the sun comes up. She was the first one who taught me that and other things.

I used to go fishing, and if I had a good catch, I'd bring her some, because I knew she'd cook it. When she'd do it, she'd wrap the fish in corn husks. She saved the corn husks and kept them green and soaked in water. She'd wrap up the fish and put it under the ashes in her fireplace. She'd cover it up with the ashes and cook it, and boy that was so good. She'd bake or make what we'd call ghost bread in English. It's simply flour and a little salt and some type of leavening or baking soda, or milk if you had it. I still love it to this day. It's called kantsyan in our language, but they call it ghost bread. I guess because it's all white flour.

Most places where you go to powwows now, they have fry bread. But when I was growing up it was called hot scums. She could take the simplest meal and make it taste so good.

She'd sit and tell me stories, things of the past. She would tell me of how they did things in their day. That's how I learned when midwinter ceremonies are held by the moon. The clan mother would say, "By the movement of the moon, it's time for this ceremony to be taking place." Now we say, "Oh, it's got to be held on January tenth," that type of thing.

Gonahdahawia's daughter was my grandmother, Mary Gonyea, who was forced to go to Carlisle Indian School. A lot of people were forced to go there. It was run by an ex-army general. He tried to regiment the Indian children by cutting their hair and having them all wear the same type clothes. He had strict discipline, but a lot of people resisted it.

There are still a few of those people alive today. One is a chief of the Oneidas; he's about ninety-four or ninety-five years old. He still tells some of the same stories. He's a little bit younger than my great-grand-mother and grandmother, but he still had to go to Haskell. He went to Carlisle first and then went to Haskell. At that time, they were shipping kids out of Carlisle—closing it down—making them go to Haskell. You stayed there at boarding school. You lost all contact with family. I guess the intention was to break that cycle, the tradition, learning who you were, then taking your identity away from you.

I remember in the 1940s when I started to school, if we spoke our language we were punished by Tabasco sauce on our tongues. All the teachers were non-Indians. The teachers called me by racist names.

There were boarding schools throughout New York State. At the Seneca Indian Reservation near Buffalo, New York, there was a place called the Thomas Indian School. That's where my mother was forced to go. Because of the way she was treated, she listened. She didn't readily teach me and my siblings the traditions and the languages. She belonged to a Methodist church. So she made me go there, but from the teachings of my great-grandmother, I was also taught the longhouse way. Whenever there was something going on at the longhouse, I went there. I sat and I listened. I learned that way, too, but on Sunday mornings I was in church. And I learned about Jesus and the Bible.

When you take the teachings of the Indian way and the teachings of the Bible, I would dare say that they parallel each other in many ways. [Here is] the creation story that the Iroquois people tell:

Before there was the earth, there was a big void between the water and the earth. This is where the sky people lived. There was this man. He was caretaker of this big tree, and his wife was very demanding. She kept after him to take the fruit of that big tree. His wife became pregnant. She wanted to see what was underneath that tree. So he pulled it up, and it left a big hole. She went to peer down there, and all she could see was darkness. The keeper of that tree was fed up with her demands by that time. So he just gave her a little nudge, and she went into that void. As she was coming down, she grasped and had certain plants in her hand as she fell.

The first ones to see her coming down were the waterfowl. Great birds flew up, got her on their backs, and brought her down. There was only water everywhere. Then they saw this giant sea turtle. So they asked the turtle if they could land on his back. So the birds landed the sky woman on the back of this giant sea turtle. They didn't know what else to do. Then they saw these things in her hand. She said she needed earth to plant these in.

Several of the sea animals dove down below the water. They came back to the top, but they were unable to get any earth until the sea otter dove down. Then, when he came to the top, in his tiny paws he had soil. They took that soil and put it on the back of the turtle, and immediately it began to grow. That's the North American continent; we call it The Great Turtle Island. The plants that she put into the earth were strawberries and tobacco.

When she gave birth, she gave birth to a daughter, and they resided there for a while. Mysteriously, the daughter became pregnant, and she gave birth to twin boys, a right-handed twin and a left-handed twin.

The right-handed twin was the good twin; he came out the right way—natural birth. The other one came through the side, unnatural birth, and it killed his mother.

The grandmother didn't know which one caused her [daughter's] death, but always thought that the right-handed twin was the one that came out the side. So she favored the left-handed twin, which was the evil twin.

As they were growing up, the right-handed twin had this corn and was roasting it over the fire. The grandmother and the left-handed twin wanted some. The good twin told them, "No, you can't have it yet because it isn't time." In anger they kicked over the roasting racks, and the corn fell into the ashes. It became hard and brittle. That's why today corn is that way and you have to use wood ashes. When you clean corn, you boil it in wood ashes and that takes the hard husk away. Then you have corn that you can use.

That's the way it's taught to us. I can go on telling the tradition of the creation for a long time. You can see where it does parallel. Being born of a virgin, et cetera, and then it goes on. The good twin went creating the animals and different things. They say that he created human beings out of the red earth. He created the ukwehu:*we,* or the real people, the Indian people. He put them there, put them out in the sun to dry. Then out of the white foam of the sea he created another being which was white, which was the white man. Then out of another soil came the yellow people and then the black people, and he had them all set out and breathed life into them. And, as all four of the races were there, the white was very dominant and started fighting with the black man. The ukwehu:*we,* or Indian person, blended into the forest and just stood there and watched them. The Creator then had to separate these people because they couldn't get along. So he put each one in a different place. He left the Indian person there, gave him instructions on how to take care of the animals, to take care of the environment, and to live off the land. He told him what plants to use.

As the good twin went about creating, behind came the bad twin, trying to destroy what he made. When the right-handed twin made man, the other one made the monkey. When he would create beautiful rivers, the left-handed twin would come and knock down the mountains which created rapids and twisty rivers. As the bad twin walked through the nice mountains, he would crumble some down, creating the uneven places to walk upon. When the good twin created the rose, the evil one came behind him and put thorns on it. The beautiful trees that he created, the other made some all gnarly and bent. The evil one made the crabapple tree with thorns [and] apples [that] are small and bitter. It goes on and on and tells these different things. Then, when the grandmother died, they took and hung her head. That's why we call it our "grandmother moon." They hung her head to brighten the dark nights. There are other legends and stories that tell how the stars got there.

I thought my grandma was just telling me stories. But she was taking that opportunity to teach me, and I didn't realize this until I was probably in my twenties. I was in the service. I came home and went to one of the ceremonies. One of the chiefs was up talking, and I thought, "I know that. I know what he's talking about. My grandmother told me that." Then I realized what she had been doing. Now we tell these stories to our children.

The longhouse is the type of house that our people used to live in. Haudenosaunee simply translated means "People of the Longhouse." It could be fifty feet wide and a hundred feet long. That's where they got the name. That was where our clans lived, entire families. One village might be all Wolf, and a little bit further down might be the Turtle Clan or the Bear Clan. Then there was the central longhouse where all the ceremonies were performed. The moon tells us when these ceremonies are to be held. There's a ceremony for each one of the time periods, or months.

I like to tell this story of how we made the decision to go into gaming. When we were discussing whether to go into gaming or not, it took us four years to decide. At one time, I was against it. Then, as I was thinking about it, I heard this story. I went to an Indian gaming meeting in Minneapolis, Minnesota. I can remember the chairman of the National Indian Gaming Association telling this story about the new buffalo. The old buffalo supplied the Indian with all his needs, as far as meat and skins used for clothing and for building the houses that they used. After the buffalo was destroyed, along came the BIA (Bureau of Indian Affairs); they were supposed to provide, according to the treaties that we signed with the federal government, housing, education, and medical needs. But they've always fallen far short of meeting the needs of Indian people. Then along comes Indian gaming, which is the new buffalo. It meets all those needs. It provides us dollars now to carry out our programs, for help to strengthen our governments, to build roads, to build schools, to build whatever it is that we need within our Nation.

Now in the modern society that we live in, when our Elders get old, what do we do to them? We ship them off to nursing homes. But the thing to do is build a center for them, where they can come. Build a center in the same place with the children, so that the ones that want to can come and see those young faces; tell them the stories of things past; teach them the traditions, the languages, the values like I was taught by my great-grandmother. These are the things that we can do now with the dollars that we receive.

I learned the Native language the way most people learn any language, just by hearing it spoken at home, just the way I learned English. Now that I've come back home and I hear it when I'm talking with Elders, I try basically to use my native language. When I'm with the youngsters, I try to use it because we're teaching the language now. You lead by example. And without your language you have no culture.

My wife's name is Shirley. Her maiden name is Miles. She's of the Turtle Clan. In our culture, we can't intermarry within the clan. I'm not supposed to marry a Wolf Clan member, or a Turtle can't marry a Turtle. That's your family; if you married into your family you would be committing incest.

My tribe's ancestry is matrilineal. You get your clan from your mother, not from your father. The leadership down through the years has been matrilineal, as far as I know, forever.

We're one of the few nations that still practice it, but there are our counterparts that branched into Ontario and Wisconsin that don't do it that way. They left the traditional way; they do it the modern way.

May of 1991 is the date that I was the proudest I've ever been of being an Indian. One of our leaders, Richard Chrisjohn, became ill. He had emphysema and passed away. I was sitting in my longhouse at the funeral. Something I could never say before was "*my* longhouse." I used to visit the Onondaga longhouse or the Seneca longhouse or the Mohawk longhouse, but it was never *my* longhouse.

I was sitting there at the funeral. There's two speakers at a funeral. One gets up and tells the family about the condolences. The other gets up and in our native language explains what's going on from what we call "the other side" of the house. This man gets up and gives his condolences to the family, and I'm sitting there. And, I'm thinking, "This is *my* longhouse."

I've had other times, as when we regained our land. I was out after we did a real estate deal, and we were walking. There was a bunch of swamps and stuff, but I thought, "That's ours. That's my land." I'm walking out through there thinking my ancestors might have gone on a hunting trip through here, and I'm walking in the same footsteps that they walked. It's mine; it's my people's. It belongs to us again. We always believed that it was ours, and now it is again. I guess those would have to be some of the proudest times.

Currently, I'm president of what is called USET. It's an acronym for United South and Eastern Tribes. It's made up of twenty-one federally recognized tribes from the tip of Maine to the tip of Florida and as far west as Houston, Texas. I was elected in November 1994. Our offices are in Nashville, Tennessee. I represent those twenty-one tribes, basically, in an advocacy role, going up on the Hill and lobbying Congress for specific needs, for specific bills that are being considered.

My official title is Wolf Clan Representative to the Men's Council of the Oneida Nation of New York. I serve as the Northeast Area Representative for the National Congress of American Indians. I also serve on the Executive Committee of the Board of Directors of the National Indian Gaming Association.

From an oral history interview conducted June 12, 1995, at the Minnetrista Cultural Center, Muncie, Indiana.

DON E. GILES

PEORIA

CHIEF, PEORIA INDIAN TRIBE OF OKLAHOMA

BORN 1948, IN MIAMI, OKLAHOMA

We had a nice home life when I was growing up. My dad worked at Goodrich, so we were well cared for, raised right here in town. We spent my high school years here in town. I went to Miami High School. There were two sisters and myself. I was thinking about childhood memories just the other day, when my son was talking about Christmas time. I guess that's probably my earliest memories. I was probably seven years old, the first Christmas I remember waking up and wondering what Santa Claus brought to me. Probably the things I best remember are when I started working with Dad. I was probably seven or eight years old. He always had a pickup truck, and we'd haul gravel and dirt into town for people and paint houses. So I started working at an early age.

Family values were, of course, different when I was growing up than they are now. There was more togetherness back then than there is now. We didn't have the TV and the things that separate the family today.

When I was elected chief, in 1991, is when I was proudest to be a Peoria. Today the leadership positions are elected. When they first came to Oklahoma, it was not an elected position but one that you just worked your way up to. You earned the trust of the other tribal members, and they confirmed you to that position.

I'd say the position of the council [elected members of the tribe who run the business of the tribe] is basically the same now as it was back then. I couldn't tell you how often general council [all the members of the tribe] met back then, but we have only two or three meetings a year. We have one annual meeting and special meetings besides that. Anything of major importance that the council seeks advice for from the general council, we call a special meeting to involve all members.

Don E. Giles

Peoria

Chief, Peoria Indian Tribe of Oklahoma

My Indian ancestry comes on my grandmother's side, my dad's side on my grandmother's side. My great-grandfather served on the council; he was a business committee member. Grandmother served on several other committees. My dad served as chaplain of the Inter-Tribal Council and other organizations.

When I was born, and during my early years, the tribe had been terminated; there was no organized Peoria Tribe. So I was not aware of traditions. I was not raised in that way, though I do remember my grandmother telling stories about the old days. But even she didn't talk much about it. My family was not raised in traditional ways. That was pretty much dissolved, although there were a few Peoria Indians that still did the old ways.

In 1992 we started having the Stomp Dance. In 1994 we had our first powwow. We have a cultural and language committee. We are trying to do a lot of groundwork now that will grow and expand in the future, which will educate more people in past traditional ways.

I did not grow up speaking the Native language. There are a few people who know some of the words. Louis Myers, who used to be the chief, who died in 1994, knew more about the language than anyone else. We have a tape of his, when he taught at Northeastern Oklahoma A&M, so we can preserve the language in that way.

There are so many occasions, not just on a daily basis but at a lot of the meetings we have, [when] it would be nice if we had people who could speak the Native language. For the crafts class, it is the older people who are teaching. But for the culture and language class, it is the younger ones who are teaching.

There have been times when I remember my grandmother talking about certain people, especially about Guy Froman, who was the chief for twenty-five years, from 1947 to 1972. He accomplished quite a few things in his lifetime. Then, my grandmother's cousin, Rodney Arnette, was chief, and she talked about him quite a bit. She would tell stories about them and the things they did. She was raised in the Peoria Territory, east of Miami, so she was always proud of her childhood and where she came from. I guess I was always listening to her stories. I guess I just always felt a part of that, and was always happy to be a part of that.

When my grandmother was growing up, you didn't want anyone to know you were Indian, even though for her it was quite visible. But you just didn't talk about it back then, so a lot of the stories, a lot of the history, was lost.

I'd like to see us off, totally free, from federal assistance. It would be nice to have the language back, to have a lot of people who are well educated and trained in the language and could instruct and teach language and cultural traditions. We're developing a pretty good land base here, trying to recapture as much of the original boundaries as possible. Right now we have 1,164 acres. When the tribe was reinstated back in 1978, the tribe had twenty-two acres. That was the only land we owned—twenty-two acres.

I can see better health care for Indians than what we now have. I think this area would be very supportive of an Indian hospital because right now the closest one is in Claremore, Oklahoma, forty miles southwest of Miami. It's understaffed, overcrowded, hard to get into. This could be an intertribal enterprise.

Intertribal cooperation has changed over the years. Currently, there are six tribes that belong to the Inter-Tribal Council—six out of the eight in the Miami area. Quapaws and Wyandottes have not come in as members. The members are Seneca/Cayuga, Eastern Shawnee, Miami, Modoc, Ottawa, Peoria. There are programs we administer that tend to hold the tribes together. It is a good place for us to discuss problems and situations.

The Peoria Tribe has a scholarship program. In 1994 we had fifty-six applicants. We provide $500 a semester, $1,000 a year. In 1994 we have $44,000 to spend on scholarships. It's our own tribal money. I think education has increased. Fifteen or twenty years ago it wasn't that important. Economic independence has increased. When the tribe was disbanded, there wasn't any federal funding at all. The people used to meet in their homes; whoever's home you met in conducted the meeting. You really didn't have anything to do or any money to do anything. Getting together was just a way for tribal members to stay in touch. Since the tribe has been reinstated, we have set aside a certain amount of funds for land purchase. The properties we have bought are used for agricultural purposes. We have plans to develop some of the property into industrial sites and businesses. We see a pretty good return on our investments in the agricultural business. In the future [the tribe] will become more involved with industrial business.

It's wonderful being in a country like the United States where you have the choices you have. You can seek opportunities. There are so many things, from each day, that a person can achieve. Strive to be a better person. Strive to do for others. Don't sell yourself short. Be proud of your heritage. Be proud of yourself and who you are. Be kind to yourself. I'd pass this word of advice on to Indian and non-Indian people.

From an oral history interview conducted December 12, 1994, at the headquarters building of the Peoria Tribe of Oklahoma, Miami, Oklahoma.

DON GREENFEATHER

Shawnee

Tribal Chairman, Loyal Shawnee Tribe of Oklahoma

Born December 24, 1946, in Wichita, Kansas

I was raised by just common people. All of us worked. We lived on a farm. My father worked out, and my mother worked out at different times. All of us had chores. We didn't have a lot of private time and space, just like a lot of other country people. All of us worked to make a living. The only really private time we had after I got older was in the evening. We would get on a horse and ride off with the guys. After we got older, one of our friends would have a car, and he'd come by. And we'd go fishing, hunting, or just different things. We hunted a lot after we got into high school. That was more or less the pastime when we had free time.

Today we live real fast, even faster than we did when I first got married twenty-eight years ago. The evenings when I was a boy at home were long. The folks would sit around and read the paper and visit. We didn't have TV. It seems things were a lot slower. We enjoyed life. The little things meant a lot more to us back then than they do now. It seems like we are working harder and even longer hours but possibly enjoying life less, because we got too interested in living and [we] forget what life and living are all about.

If there was a time when I've been proudest to be an Indian, it's probably right now. I understand it more. I'm a little bit older, and I understand what cultural identity means. When I was in college, there were several people there at the university I attended from back East, and they would discriminate against Indian people.

I had friends—non-Indian friends—who would stick up for me, whether I was there or I wasn't there, if there was some discriminatory remark made. They would contradict and ask the people if they wanted to fight about it.

118

Don Greenfeather

Shawnee

Tribal Chairman, Loyal Shawnee Tribe

Everything is lost when the Native language is not spoken and cultural traditions are not practiced. Not only our blood makes us Indian, but our language and cultural traditions do, too. When that is gone, you're no more than just sort of a business as far as a tribe is concerned.

We try to live as traditional as we can, and, thereby, whether it's the young or old we're associated with, it has to be part of our everyday life.

I've got an aunt, Lois Greenfeather, in Miami [Oklahoma], who has probably influenced me more on those lines. She tells the stories of long ago when our people left Ohio and lived in Kansas and on down to the present. The way she tells them always makes you feel proud, makes you respect the past. The feeling that she has, or leaves you with, makes you want to be proud of that; you don't want to bring reproach on the past and on who you are and on the part of people that you belong to.

One thing that always stuck in my mind is one of our elderly members who was in the removal from Kansas to Oklahoma. His name was Henry Greenfeather. When he left, the only thing that he was allowed to take was a young shoat, a young hog, and everything else was left behind. He carried that young pig almost all the way to Oklahoma. When he got to Fort Scott, Kansas, he died before they came on into Oklahoma, and he's buried there. As I heard my aunt Lois Greenfeather tell that story, she would elaborate on it and put in a lot of details. I often wondered how it was when he was told, "You're going to have to leave again." I often wondered how it was to decide if you were going to try to take anything. He wanted that young shoat.

The Shawnee ways are different. There has been a revival of traditional ways supported by our Elders and assisted by them. We have sort of pulled ourselves together. We are getting stronger. We've got goals; we're doing things to make some of those changes realities.

We don't use the word chief for my position; we use the term tribal chairman; we have an active tribal council that deals with all business matters connected with the tribe. The tribal council is made up of nine positions, in addition to the tribal chairman—vice-chairman, secretary, treasurer, five tribal council people, and a tribal historian. They conduct the business for the Loyal Shawnee Tribe. We meet here at the tribal building on the second Thursday of every month, and then in September on the third Saturday we meet here for what we call our General Council. That is when the entire tribe is invited to come, and we hold our elections. Our positions on the tribal council are bi-annual; we vote on some positions one year and the alternates the next year. The Loyal

Shawnees number 8,000. Here in northeastern Oklahoma there's probably around 6,700, but nationwide on our tribal roll, there are 8,000.

The Eastern Shawnee call the same position I hold chief. The Eastern Shawnees Buck Captain holds the position of chief. The Absentee Shawnee—their leader is governor. With us, on our tribal council, the position is chairman, and I am the present chairman.

Our positions are all the same, but they are just different titles. These three leaders come together on occasion, but it is strictly to conduct business, nothing ceremonial. There is no scheduled time, but, periodically, when there is business that interests all tribes, the bands will get together. Back in May 1992 was the first time since our removal that we have officially met as a unified group. So it is a new thing for us.

In terms of what the joint meetings do, right now the federal government is interested in cutting funds for everybody, and that includes the Native American tribes. Like the old saying, there is strength in unity, and we are all Shawnee. They're Shawnee, we're Shawnee. A lot of the issues that concern them concern us and vice-versa when we come onto new issues. It has strengthened us, has caused us to be stronger. On some things we are speaking as one voice instead of three separate voices—one loud voice.

It is causing good relationships among our people. Our people have always intermingled. I've got cousins that are Eastern, and I've got cousins that are Absentee. On the business, on the government end of it, officially we had our first meeting when the Eastern Shawnee hosted that meeting back in May 1992. Since that time we have formed a joint council. On the repatriation issue we signed an agreement; we are all together on that. In fact, in December 1994, representatives from all three groups flew out to New York to deal with some artifacts.

The Loyal Shawnee Tribe is the largest, with the Absentee and Eastern next, in that order. On the other hand, our tribe is the poorest of the three. We are Shawnee but, because of our association, we live within the Cherokee Nation's boundaries.

We were the last group to leave Ohio—the last of our folks left around 1832 and moved into Kansas. Then in 1869 we were forced to move here to Oklahoma. They settled our band, along with the Delawares to the west of us, within the Cherokee Nation boundaries. Because of that relationship, we've had to do a lot of our dealings with the federal government through the Cherokee Nation. And, in all honesty, that makes us feel secondary to the Cherokee because they have more influence with the federal government than we do. It's not all the

Cherokees' fault. We're not trying to put the blame on anybody. If we are going to blame anybody, we can blame ourselves. Back in the past we probably could have done a lot of things that should have been done but weren't, but we can't go back and change the past. We are here now, and our people have come together, and we feel like we are several years behind a lot of tribes. However, I attended the National Conference for American Indians in Denver in November 1994, and there are other tribes that are exactly where we're at, or even behind us. In Indian Country we're struggling, but our people are strong. And, like I told a gentleman a while back, we've stood up. The Loyal Shawnees have stood up, and we won't lay down again.

We're proud of who we are. We are not ashamed. I don't use the word proud in an arrogant sense. The main hurdle we have had with our people is getting them to believe in who we are and in our abilities. After the fall of Tecumseh, after we left Ohio and moved to Kansas, we got settled in Kansas, but again the government stepped in and forcibly removed the people. These older Shawnee people out here can tell you stories better than I can. I have heard Aunt Lois Greenfeather tell stories that she heard about the removal that have been passed down. That was just a bad day for our people. You can imagine, we didn't want to leave Ohio. Our people didn't want to leave Kansas, but the government came in and told our people "you're leaving."

We have the soldiers' roll when we left Ohio—the soldiers that removed our people from Ohio to Kansas and then from the removal from Kansas down here. The soldiers wrote down what the different families left with.

Our people, whether it's a person or a group of people, when their spirits are broken, then they are just fighting for survival. And when the language is gone, a lot of the heritage is gone. I don't speak our Native tongue, but our tribe is working on the language. I know words, but as far as being fluent, I'm not. The main obstacle we've had as a tribal council is getting our people to believe that we can be something, and getting our people to believe in themselves again. We don't have any money, but what we have done—this facility here we started with exactly zero money, but through the efforts of our people and with the assistance of Chief Mankiller, chief of the Cherokees, why in July 1991, the Bureau [of Indian Affairs] appraised this tribal office property for $119,000. So our people finally see that we can do things, and we can be who we are. We live within the Cherokees' jurisdictional boundaries, but under Chief Mankiller's administration—she's been our friend.

And the Cherokee Tribal Council has been our friend. They have let us be who we really are, Loyal Shawnee people.

The impact of bingo is good and bad. It has created revenue that has enabled some tribes to provide better services to the people, but then in other ways it makes a slavery to it for some people.

The elderly need to be respected. That is getting away from us. For instance, when I was young, the Elders would always eat first. The children would be the last. And it's not that way any more. We don't show respect. We sort of push the older people back, and that's not right. We need to try to get back to the right perspective.

What I want most to leave for future generations are the real traditional values of doing right. I hope I can have an influence on them to where they will really be real traditional and be honest and upright and be proud of who they are.

I found this saying of Tecumseh that I keep on my desk. If I were to leave anything behind, I would like to leave these words of Tecumseh. This is the English version of it, the interpretation:

> To so live your life that the fear of death can never enter your heart. Trouble no one about his religion. Respect others and their views, and demand that they respect yours. Love your life, perfect your life, beautify all things in your life. Seek to make your life long and full of service to your people. Prepare a noble death song for the day when you go over the Great Divide. Always give a word or sign of salute when passing or meeting a friend, even a stranger if in a lonely place. Show respect to all people, but grovel to none. When you arise in the morning, give thanks for food and for the joy of living. If you see no reason for giving thanks, the fault lies within yourself. Touch not the poisonous fire water that makes wise ones turn to fools and robs the spirit of its vision. When your time comes to die be not like those whose hearts are filled with the fear of death so that when their time comes they weep and pray for a little more time to live their lives over again in a different way. Sing your death song and die like a hero going home.

> *From an oral history interview conducted December 12, 1994, at the headquarters building of the Loyal Shawnee Tribe of Oklahoma, White Oak, Oklahoma*

PATRICIA A. HRABIK

CHIPPEWA

HISTORIC PRESERVATION OFFICER AND HERITAGE TOURISM COORDINATOR,
LAC DU FLAMBEAU BAND OF LAKE SUPERIOR CHIPPEWA INDIANS

BORN OCTOBER 30, 1932, IN ASHLAND, WISCONSIN

My mother and father lived on the Lac du Flambeau Chippewa Reservation at the time I was born. As a young girl I was given my Indian name, Wabanangkwe, by George W. Brown, Sr., the very first tribal council secretary. The name he gave me means Morning Star.

Both my parents are Lac du Flambeau Chippewa. My mother's name was Mayme Devine, and my father was Thomas William Devine. Mother was Swedish, French, and Chippewa. My father was Irish and Chippewa. Mother was about eighteen when she married my father. He was twelve years older than she. My dad's family homestead was just off the Lac du Flambeau Reservation in Manitowish Waters, but he was working on the reservation at the time. Our family never lived off the reservation. We lived in federal housing constructed of wood and painted white. It was located near the old Indian boarding school that was built about 1894.

My father was the main breadwinner in our family. He worked for the Bureau of Indian Affairs as a forester and as a fishing guide on weekends. My mother opened a little gift shop across from the pow-wow grounds in later years and enjoyed it very much. She called it the Ge Bic Shop (Ge Bic means good luck). My mother was a good house-keeper but also liked to play bridge and socialize at church.

My maternal grandmother, Amanda Peterson Gauthier, was Swedish. She came over from Sweden when she was only sixteen to work in a resort. She met my Indian-French grandfather, Charles Gauthier, who was the first policeman in Lac du Flambeau. He also was an interpreter for the French, English, and Chippewa. Amanda and Charles had seven children.

124

Patricia A. Hrabik
Chippewa
Historic Preservation Officer and Heritage
Tourism Coordinator, Lac du Flambeau
Band of Lake Superior Chippewa Indians

My father was much respected. I never knew him to do anything like lie, swear, or anything underhanded. He was a good hunter, fisherman, and dancer. My father's father came over from Ireland. His name was Dan Devine. He met my father's mother, whose name was Wai di kwe gi ji go kwe. She was a full-blood Chippewa. They met near Lake Superior in the summertime. They married and had seven children. Grandma Kate (her English name) and her children were all staunch Catholics. My father served on the first Lac du Flambeau Chippewa tribal council under the Indian Reorganization Act of 1934. However, I have found minutes of tribal council meetings written as far back as 1929.

I attended the government school, which had mostly Indian students, until the ninth grade. Then I transferred to Woodruff, Wisconsin, for the remaining three years of high school. I was a minority at Woodruff. But the kids were friendly, and I was soon invited to pajama parties, proms, and homecoming dances. I sang in the choir and played in the school band. I liked all of my teachers, but my music teacher, Jan Oxley, went out of her way to help me in music.

Most of the government buildings and boarding school here on the Lac du Flambeau Chippewa Reservation were abandoned about 1932. The boys' dormitory remains and is used for tribal offices. This is the same building that my father worked in as a forester and in which I have been working for over thirty years. The federal day school teachers were housed in a large building called the "Clubhouse." It housed about eight or ten teachers. There was a large kitchen, dining room, living room, and three bathrooms. The teachers' rooms were bedroom–sitting rooms with a wash basin. There was a doctor's house, a superintendent's house, an engineer's house, policeman's house, and the forester's house that we lived in.

Times have changed, and most housing is now at least standard or in many cases above standard. The economy is up, and most people are employed either at the tribal offices, in tribal industries, at the tribal Lake of the Torches Casino, or in logging and construction work.

I think I was the proudest to be a Lac du Flambeau tribal member when my tribe appointed me as tribal judge in 1991. About eleven years ago our tribe started its own judicial system. I will be retiring soon and two more judges are being trained. The tribe sent us to the Judicial College in Reno, Nevada, and also to the National Indian Judicial Center in California. We are called special jurisdiction judges. At this time we handle only civil cases. Most cases that I have had involve domestic abuse, custody, and conservation law offenses.

There are some organizations, mainly non-Indian people, who believe that we have no right to spear fish. One became infamous during spearfishing protests for their violent tactics, racist slogans, and misinformation campaigns.

The Lac du Flambeau Tribal Natural Resource Program began in 1936 with construction of a hatchery designed to incubate walleye, muskellunge, and white sucker eggs. Through the years, a comprehensive natural resource program developed consisting of fisheries and wildlife. A major objective is to determine stocking rates, evaluate stocking programs, estimate total harvest of fish, and determine status of existing fish populations in reservation waters.

For a complete natural resource program, there must be an integration of the fisheries program with a wildlife program. A comprehensive game management plan is being developed on the reservation with current game management activities including whitetail deer, ruffed grouse, wild rice, and eagle nesting surveys. Emergency beaver control activities and a highly professional deer registration station are also included in the program.

The Indian Self-Determination and Education Assistance Act (Public Law 93-638) was passed in 1975. It provided for maximum Indian participation in the government and education of Indian people; full participation of Indian tribes in programs and services conducted by the federal government and development of human resources of Indian people; a program of assistance to upgrade Indian education. The Lac du Flambeau band has taken full advantage of this law and now conducts its own programs with the help of highly educated tribal members. At present I work under a "638" contract to provide Land Management–Historic Preservation Office services to the tribe.

In 1953, federal law authorized a great increase in Wisconsin's authority and responsibility on Indian reservations and a decrease in the authority and responsibility of federal and tribal governments. That law is commonly known as Public Law 280. The Lac du Flambeau Band is now in the position to reassume jurisdiction over criminal and civil matters that involve Indians, if those matters arise within the reservation. Such reassumption is consistent with federal and tribal policy of Indian self-determination, and would clarify and strengthen the relationship between the tribe, Vilas County, and the State of Wisconsin. It has been the desire of Indian and non-Indian people alike that we assume more control over, and responsibility for, our own affairs. Retrocession from Public Law 280, combined with renewed awareness of our unique cultural traditions, represents a major stride for our people.

Economic conditions are better now with the advent of the tribe's new Lake of the Torches Casino. Presently the casino employs 250-260 people. It is anticipated with the $18.5 million expansion that another 200 people will be hired. Located on the shores of Pokegama Lake, the Casino Hotel Resort Facility contains the casino, hotel, and conference center. The tribe and the local community are making efforts to assure that our visitors enjoy not only their gaming experiences, but our culture and natural resources as well.

Our tribe has always had both men and women on the twelve-member tribal council. Council members must have at least one-fourth Lac du Flambeau Chippewa blood and be a minimum of twenty-five years of age. For many years we have had an even distribution of men and women. Because my family were all Catholic they were taught that they should give up the old traditional ways. I was about twelve before I began to dance and sing at powwows, and then it was to earn money. Many people are now returning to the old ways.

Ojibwa language is being taught in the Lac du Flambeau public grade school and also by the Elders Council at the George W. Brown, Jr., Museum and Cultural Center. Drumming, singing, and dancing are also taught. The museum and grade school are also instrumental in the teaching of tribal arts and crafts, such as beading, hide tanning, moccasins, birch bark baskets, yarn weaving, painting, poetry, writing, music, God's Eyes, and dream catchers.

I speak only a few words of Chippewa. I was taught those by my father. People who speak the Native tongue seem to have a better feeling about themselves. They take the best from two worlds and seem to feel good when talking with others in the old way. Not to practice cultural traditions is losing your identity somehow. In my case, many of the traditions I practice are Christian, and they mean a lot to me. I am just now beginning to learn and appreciate the beauty of some of the old ceremonies and a way of speaking to our Creator in the old ways.

On our reservation the term "Creator" is the one we hear most when people are referring to God. At the building where I work, Mildred "Tinker" Schuman often comes in with sweet grass, which she lights to make a smudge. She has an eagle feather to spread the smudge to your body. We gather this smoke to ourselves to offer prayer to start the day. If someone wishes to ask you to do something special, you will be given tobacco at the time of the request. If you take the tobacco, you must answer the request.

A spiritual attitude toward life is very important to the Lac du Flambeau Chippewa. I am privileged to work with people who are Medewiwin. They belong to the Big Drum or the Native American Church. We also have the Lac du Flambeau Bible Church, St. Anthony's Catholic Church, and the Community Presbyterian Church.

My own children know little about the old way of life. When my children went to school on the reservation, there were no language classes. I don't think they even had correct history being taught. Now, according to Wisconsin law, we have an updated Native American history curriculum.

I am teaching my grandchildren through books and stories and take them to powwows and ceremonies when they visit me. I don't believe they will ever learn the language because they live in the city, and don't have the opportunity to speak it at home.

My grandparents died when I was very young, and my mother and father were not traditional. It is only in my later years that I am getting to appreciate my Native heritage. My children and grandchildren are eager to learn also.

My favorite memory of my grandma Kate, who was a full-blood Chippewa, was when I was playing outside near her home on Clear Lake in Manitowish Waters, Wisconsin. I fell down a very steep ravine and got hurt. I remember Grandma racing down the ravine with her long full-length skirts flying. I remember her screaming "Eeaw, Eeaw." I believe the word she was yelling meant "Help, help. Something terrible has happened." That made a deep impression on me, how much she loved me, and how afraid she was that I was hurt. Usually she was very quiet and dignified. She was extremely clean and always smelled like fresh air to me. She was a sweet lady. I still treasure that memory and now tell the story to my grandchildren. Grandma could speak English, but she didn't speak it around us. She didn't like my mother very well, and spoke Indian so she could not understand.

My father used to tell me that Aunt Mary, even though she was the only girl in the family, could hunt as well or better than any of the brothers. She was a very good shot. White-tailed buck deer were, and still are, the mainstay of most Indian families living on the reservation.

My Swedish grandmother, Amanda Peterson Gauthier, provided room and board for many Franciscan missionaries at her house. She had a big house and a big family and was very warmhearted. Later on, when our first St. Anthony's Church was constructed, there was a small bedroom–living room area provided for the missionaries at the back of the church.

I never knew my grandfather, Charles Gauthier, at all. He died when Uncle Ben, the oldest of the children, was only sixteen. The rest of the children were very young, and Uncle Ben became the head of the household. He supported the family by managing the resort that Grandma's relatives had developed. We have a photo of him in his police uniform. He was very handsome.

I prefer to be called Native American or Anishnabe, which means First People or Original People. However, I take no offense at the term Indian. Most of the tribes in Wisconsin think of themselves as Anishnabe. The Wisconsin tribes are: Lac du Flambeau Band of Lake Superior Chippewa Indians, Oneida Tribe of Indians of Wisconsin, Menominee Indian Tribe of Wisconsin, Ho-Chunk Nation, Stockbridge Munsee Community, Forest County Potawatomi Community, Lac Court Oreilles Tribal Governing Board, Sokaogon Chippewa Community—Mole Lake, Red Cliff Band of Lake Superior Chippewa Indians, Bad River Band of Lake Superior Chippewa Indians, and St. Croix Band of Lake Superior Chippewa Indians. Each of these other bands or tribes has some different customs from each other. But there is a very real common link, and tribal ties are very close.

Other than Public Law 280 and the Indian Self-Determination Act the biggest changes we have experienced have had to do with Tribal Historic Preservation and the Native American Graves Protection and Repatriation Act of 1990.

In 1988, just before I retired from the Bureau of Indian Affairs, I had paraprofessional archaeological training at Deer River, Minnesota. While at this training the idea was planted in my mind to try to encourage my own tribe to train tribal members in archaeological survey and site identification. I began working for my tribe in 1988 just one week after retiring from the BIA. We submitted a grant application to the National Park Service and received a grant to train nine tribal staff members in archaeological survey techniques and site identification. The grant also required that we develop a Tribal Historic Preservation Code. Tribal people now participate in all archaeological surveys conducted on the reservation.

I have been appointed the official representative for the Lac du Flambeau tribe on the Tribal Repatriation Committee and the Wisconsin Inter-Tribal Repatriation Committee. I serve as secretary of the Inter-Tribal Committee. We hope to begin repatriating human remains and associated grave goods in the near future. The main goal of the Wisconsin Inter-Tribal Repatriation Committee is to procure lands in central

Wisconsin to be used as a burial place for those remains that cannot be identified as belonging to a specific reservation. We feel it is important for the tribes to be united as we begin this important work.

My responsibilities to my children and grandchildren are for the most part fulfilled because I have provided for their spiritual and academic education. My husband, Roy "Dean" Hrabik, who died in 1984, and I had six children, four girls and two boys. They are all tribal members and hope to some day return to the reservation. They are all in professional fields—nursing, teaching, mathematics, and biology.

A very important part of sharing tribal heritage with future generations is happening by the involvement of youth in the George W. Brown, Jr., Ojibwa Museum and Cultural Center, owned by the Lac du Flambeau band. Youth are intensely involved in many activities at the museum, including arts and crafts work, the painting of a mural depicting reservation life from prehistoric times to the present, a "Native Roots" theatre troupe, an ambassadors program, and a docent program. The ambassadors program is composed of children, adults, and Elders who visit surrounding communities doing such things as storytelling and powwow dancing. They tell the people they visit about Lac du Flambeau and, in general, create very good feelings through this cultural exchange.

In the early 1960s I worked for the tribe as tribal clerk and also served on the tribal council as treasurer for several years. I had to resign from the council when I began to work for the Bureau of Indian Affairs in 1967. I worked for the Bureau of Indian Affairs, at the Lac du Flambeau Field Office, for twenty-three years. This work involved primarily the Lac du Flambeau Band but I also dealt with the other eleven tribes in Wisconsin. My title was legal clerk, and I worked mainly with tribal land acquisition, leasing, and rights-of-way.

After retiring from the BIA in 1988, I immediately began working for the Lac du Flambeau tribe as their Realty/Natural Resource Coordinator. I served in that capacity for six years with duties of Historic Preservation Officer and Heritage Tourism Coordinator being added. In 1995, I transferred to Historic Preservation and Heritage Tourism solely.

At this time, as Historic Preservation Officer, I serve as project director of the Lac du Flambeau Chain Fur Trade Project. This involves research and archaeological surveys to locate the fur trade posts that we know were here at Lac du Flambeau. The long-term goal is to locate the posts and reconstruct them. Interpretation of the fur trade era as a complement to the George W. Brown, Jr., Ojibwa Museum and Cultural

Center is planned. Our goal is to do a complete archaeological inventory of the reservation so that we can assure protection of prehistoric and historic cultural resources.

Heritage tourism is a philosophy and effort to increase awareness of the importance of history and culture to residents and visitors to Wisconsin. The National Trust for Historic Preservation selected Wisconsin as one of four states to participate in a pilot program. The Lac du Flambeau Band was the first Native American tribe to be chosen to work with the State of Wisconsin and the National Trust on Heritage Tourism. All eleven tribes in Wisconsin are now involved. The principles of the Wisconsin Native American Heritage Tourism Initiative are to preserve and protect resources, focus on sharing and teaching, make sites come alive, and collaborate in building partnerships.

If I could come back in one hundred years, I would hope that my tribe had done a good job of preserving its cultural, sacred, and natural resources, and had regained lands lost during the General Allotment Act of 1887, called the Dawes Act.

From an oral history interview conducted June 12, 1995, at the Minnetrista Cultural Center, Muncie, Indiana.

LEWIS B. KETCHUM

DELAWARE

CHIEF, DELAWARE TRIBE OF INDIANS, BARTLESVILLE, OKLAHOMA, 1983-1994

BORN APRIL 6, 1935

DIED SEPTEMBER 20, 1995

Lewis B. Ketchum, former chief of the Delaware Tribe of Eastern Oklahoma, died Wednesday, September 20, 1995, at his home in Tulsa at age sixty.

Ketchum, a native of Bartlesville, Oklahoma, attended Bacone College in Muskogee [Oklahoma], and served on their board of directors. He attended Southwest Missouri State University with a major in marketing. He worked for Bethlehem Steel Company for nineteen years before leaving to start his own business.

In 1977, Ketchum started Red Man Pipe and Supply Company, an oil field equipment distribution firm. The company now has fifty-one branch offices [in nine states] and employs 485 people.

He was a man who loved his People and served them in many capacities throughout the years. He was elected to the Delaware Business Committee in 1978, was elected Chief of the Delaware Tribe from 1983-1994, and was elected in 1990 as Chair of the Delaware Trust Board.

He was selected posthumously for the Oklahoma Federation of Indian Women's Alice Timmons Founders Award for 1995, for his outstanding contributions. In 1987, he was named "Minority Entrepreneur of the Year" by the U.S. Department of Commerce, and was honored at the White House by former President Reagan. In May 1992, he was honored with the Mary G. Ross Award, which pays tribute to an American Indian whose life and career bring honor to the Indian people.

Through his business he donated $10,000 annually to a special scholarship fund to help finance the education of minority college students.

Lewis B. Ketchum

Delaware

Chief, Delaware Tribe of Indians, 1983-1994

He was especially interested in promoting both pride and honor in their Indian Heritage among young people.

The Reverend Wayne Hardy, in his eulogy [at the memorial services at Kirk of the Hills Presbyterian Church on Saturday, September 23, 1995], said:

> There simply is not enough time to talk about who Lew Ketchum was. He did so much that was significant, and there were so many things that were accomplished. He was so balanced in terms of his faith and his life, his work and his family, that we could go on and on.
>
> He was a mediator. From the way the family and business associates described him he was a peacemaker. But I was told he could also be a lion if it was necessary to defend the interests that were proper. And that lion heart was there for his people, the Delaware people. Other tribes sometimes called the Delawares the "Grandfather of all Tribes" because of their great position historically among the tribes. The Delawares were among the first people to meet my ancestors, the Europeans, who came ashore more than four hundred years ago. In the conflict that came with European expansion into this nation, the Delawares suffered mightily and they moved ever westward. But as they moved, they weren't just fighting, they were contributing— contributing to the history of ten states in the process of their movement. One of the great passions Lew had was to restore the federal government's recognition of their tribe as a sovereign nation. I know that process still goes on. He was a leader of a nation.
>
> I am told that Lew always wondered why he was so blessed, and he was with family first, with business, with material things that come from running a business as well and in such a visionary way as he did. I know why he was blessed, and he did, too. He knew it came from above; it came from the Lord. But the world blessed Lew, because in a world obsessed by things where it would have been so easy for Lew to join the rest of the crowd and be just as obsessed by those things, he centered his life on people. He lived a life of love. It was at the center of his success and his blessings.

He is survived by his wife of thirty-nine years, Betty; sons Kent of Houston and Kevin, Craig, and Brian, all of Tulsa; his father, L. A. Ketchum; his grandmother, Bertha Ketchum; his brother, Dee Ketchum of Bartlesville; his sister, Pat Ketchum Donnell of Dewey; and nine grandchildren.

The following is by Dee Ketchum, brother of the late L. B. Ketchum: Our Delaware ancestry comes from both our mother and father.

The great-great-grandparents were among the families coming from Indiana to Kansas in the 1800s removal. The Ketchum name is found throughout that time. Captain Curleyhead was our mother's great-grandfather. His eight daughters and one son provided marriages into about every traditional Delaware family's history. After searching their family trees, people have been proud to discover they were related to their chief on either their mother's or father's side. This made Lewis B. Ketchum a very popular figure as chief of the Delawares.

Lewis A. Ketchum and Lillian Berry Ketchum were our parents. Lillian died in 1987. Lewis is living in Bartlesville today at age eighty-two [in 1996]. Our parents attended the Chiloco Indian Boarding School, where they met and married. Both had been raised on their parents' allotments and came from very similar backgrounds. My grandmother Ketchum is still living, and is 102 years old [in 1996]. Our family made its home in Bartlesville, Oklahoma. L. B. (as he was known by his family and childhood friends) was a high school athlete and leader. He lettered in three sports—football, basketball and track. He was recruited by Bacone Indian College to play football. After two years he transferred to Southwest Missouri State College on a football scholarship. During his senior year of college he married Betty Hahn of Winterset, Iowa.

After living in several states as an employee of Bethlehem Steel, L. B. and Betty came back to Tulsa, Oklahoma. It was there that he established Red Man Pipe and Supply Company. He also started his commitment to the tribe. He ran for tribal council and was elected. He served as assistant chief under the late Chief Henry Secondine, and completed Secondine's term as chief. Then L. B. ran for chief and served in that office for fourteen years. When the Delaware Trust Board was established in 1991, L. B. was elected chairman, and set this new entity on its course by his sound leadership.

L. B. was proud of his family and heritage. Each year at the Delaware Powwow at Copan, Oklahoma, he dressed in his traditional clothes and danced with his family and friends. He always encouraged me as I learned the traditional ceremonial ways of our People from our relative, Leonard Thompson, Delaware Ceremonial Chief, who selected me as his understudy. One of my pleasures was serving with my brother on the tribal council and trust board. We were close to the end.

Chief Ketchum was a man's man. He enjoyed golfing, skiing and boating. At his funeral, between 1,200 and 1,500 people attended. They were CEOs, business men, tribal chiefs, and life-long friends.

The tribute above is reprinted, in its entirety, by permission from an author who wishes to remain anonymous, from an obituary sent to Archeological Bulletin of New Jersey (which contains passages from an obituary published in Delaware Indian News, *Volume XVI, Issue IV, October 1995).*

FLOYD E. LEONARD

Miami

Chief, Miami Tribe of Oklahoma

Born September 19, 1925, west of Picher, Oklahoma

We lived in a very small house near Picher. I barely remember that. We moved to the farm. I remember very well living on the farm. We had cattle; we had to get up every morning and milk. Milk cows every afternoon, evening. Typical farm living. We had chickens, whatever. This was in the Depression years, so I remember very well the years that were hard times when there was the drought in Oklahoma and crops were bad.

Life today, from the time of my childhood, is completely different. I grew up on a farm where we had no electricity, no indoor plumbing. We lived off the land. We didn't have much, but we were very happy. We didn't realize we were poor because everyone was in the same kind of situation. We moved off the farm when I was in high school. I've never lived on a farm since then.

I started teaching in a one-room school in southwest Missouri. I taught there two years, all eight grades together. I used to have about twenty students. My third year of teaching I went to a fairly large school system in Joplin, Missouri, and stayed in that school system for the remainder of my career, except I spent nine years in a neighborhood school in Webb City, Missouri. I worked in the Joplin school system for twenty-four years. My elementary education was in Oklahoma. We moved to Missouri when I was a freshman. I graduated from high school in Carterville, Missouri. I went to college at Pittsburgh State University in Kansas.

My grandfather on my father's side lived until I was grown, so I got to know him very well. He was a typical Oklahoma farmer. He passed on when I was still in service in World War II, so he didn't get to see any

Floyd E. Leonard

Miami

Chief, Miami Tribe of Oklahoma

of his grandkids graduate from college. But I'm sure he would have been very proud, because he was a very proud man. He had a family of twelve children, and they all turned out pretty well.

As a young child in public schools we experienced prejudice for being Indian. Not bad, because mostly everyone was Indian. But we always wondered why they particularly wanted to know which tribe you belonged to, and so on, and your roll numbers, and these kinds of things in school. I found out later this was because the government was helping to pay for the education, but I didn't know that at the time.

I've always been very proud to be a member of my tribe. My parents were always interested in tribal affairs. One of my father's brothers, David Leonard, served on the business committee for many years. At his death I become involved and was elected to the business committee. That was in 1953, and I served for ten years. I was elected second chief in 1963 for ten years and chief from 1973 to 1983. I had a health problem so I resigned and was out of government until I was elected chief again in 1989. Chiefs are elected for three-year terms. Elections are at general council and elections are supervised by the Bureau of Indian Affairs.

If you go back far enough, Ray White, late chief of the Miami of Indiana, and I are cousins. My ancestry goes back to Tecumwah, who was the sister of Little Turtle. Tecumwah was married twice in her life. She was married first to Jean Baptiste Richardville, Pee-jee-wa-or, who was a chief. Then she was married a second time to a French trader named Bibianne. My ancestry comes through the second marriage. Ray White's ancestry came through the first marriage. The connection goes back to our great-great-great-great-grandmother.

There are old tribal books of minutes of councils that were held in Kansas before the tribe moved to Oklahoma. The tribe was first moved from the Indiana-Ohio area to the reservation in Kansas. When the tribe moved to Kansas, the chief at that time came to Kansas with the tribe and turned around and started back to Indiana, and died on the way. The tribe in Kansas immediately elected a new chief. We have a record of the chiefs from that time in Kansas. In 1936 the tribes in Oklahoma were allowed to organize under the Oklahoma Welfare Act and it is at that time that the tribes, with the help of the Bureau of Indian Affairs, worked out constitutions and governmental bylaws and things of this nature, and set up business committees. We do have records of the leadership of the tribe all the way back.

Tribal governance has changed since the constitution of 1938. Before that time, in the days of Indiana and Ohio, the leadership was different in that there were clan chiefs. Once we came to the reservation, there were no clan chiefs. There was a regular governmental organization with a chief, second chief, and three council people who run the government of the tribe. The general council, which is all The People, has the final say. The general council can change any kind of decision by the business committee. However, the business committee does have the authority, from the constitution, to make decisions for the operation of the tribe between one general council meeting and another. General council meets once a year.

In Miami history, after the arrival in Kansas, the Elders played a great part in the decisions made by the business committee or by the chiefs or by anyone else. Elders, particularly the female Elders, are very important to how the tribe functions. They are highly respected within the Miami Tribe. There are decisions I wouldn't think of making as a chief without consulting with some of those people.

Of course, traditions change as times change. For example, we always went to gatherings when I was a kid. We went to what we call dances, which are what people are more apt to call powwows. We had a lot of what we call Stomp Dancing, which is our style of dancing, and I can remember very well going to Devil's Promenade, which is a place close to here, for gatherings in the summer, all my life. I remember my father going, my mother, and the kids going, my aunt; we'd stay for several days. We ate, we visited, we talked. We did all the things you do as a group of people. Not only Miami Indians but all different tribes came to the same gatherings.

I remember some of the ceremonies which we always had when I was a kid, such as burial ceremonies. If someone died there was never any doubt that you were a Miami Indian. Some people spoke the language. But by now the language has gradually been lost. In my time as a youngster, quite a few people spoke the language. Older people spoke the language to each other. But it has faded away, and we are trying to get it back. I speak some. Not very much. I think the last person who spoke Miami fluently died about 1990.

We are working on a language project now through our librarians here in the tribal office. It was an oral language, not a written language, so we're trying to get it written down so it won't be forgotten for the future. The pronunciation guide is very important.

I did not attend tribal school. My father attended first a mission school that was a Catholic school at Quapaw, Oklahoma. Then later my father went to Seneca Indian School, which was operated by the Bureau of Indian Affairs, which is a little strange, in a sense, because in later years, as chief of the Miamis, I was an elected member of the Seneca Indian School Board, which is a board that advises the BIA on matters of the school. I was very proud of the school, and of serving, until the school closed. In our area, I could have gone to boarding schools. I didn't go. I went to regular public school.

When my father went to tribal school, they weren't allowed to speak anything but English. Tribal culture wasn't allowed. My father worked in the dairy as his job while he was at school. Everybody had their work to do. At that time they had a big dairy. They provided milk and butter for everyone who was at school. All I know about my father's experiences at school is what he told me. There were some very happy experiences and some very sad memories. The culture was not stressed at Indian schools at that time. In later years, they began to bring the culture back into tribal-operated schools, but at my father's time, no. The idea was assimilation, to assimilate the Indian into white culture.

Probably a lot of the traditions fade away because of the lack of the language. Some of the traditional mores of the tribe begin to fade away as the language is lost. Some of the identification, that "something" that identifies you as a Miami. Without the language it is hard sometimes to make the identification as to The People. The People are scattered. When it's not there, you don't know what you haven't got. When it's lost, you don't know what you've lost.

We try to keep people involved in the culture as much as we can. The tribe has classes in Indian crafts. We have a very good library in our complex here. We have computers available for our kids. We have a lot of genealogy material, a lot of old records. We try to encourage our young people to know where they come from. Sometimes it is a little difficult because at a young age we aren't much interested. Sometimes we have to wait until we get older to become interested in our background.

We offer a day care center. The tribe provides for day care for working mothers who cannot afford to hire an expensive baby sitter. We have at our center a food program for Indians of any tribe who are fifty-five years or over. We serve about 300 people every day. We have a child welfare program within our tribe. We have a tax commission within our tribe. We issue our own tribal license for tribal members for their cars. We get the tax money. Many tribes do this. It has become a way of providing services to The People, as well as the tribe making a little bit of money. The tribe does own a bus so we take our Elders on a lot of trips to various places. For example, they may go over to Kansas City to shop.

Miami are proud people. My father, even though he had never been there, referred to Fort Wayne, Indiana, as Ke-ki-ogo-gay all his life. That to him was the name of that town. Everyone always, I think, was very proud to be Indian. I am proud to be Miami. I think this is taught to the younger generation as part of growing up. I once heard a person ask a young lady in our tribe, "How does it feel to be an Indian?" The young woman's answer was, "I've always been an Indian, so I don't know." You try to raise your children with the idea, "Yes, you are Indian."

My family told me we were part of the Miami Nation, an active part of it, and that you should stay active in tribal affairs. I trace that back to my father's generation, my grandfather's generation, who passed this on.

When the tribe first moved to Oklahoma, there were missionaries among the tribe. I remember my father telling me about the priest who came around to visit him, in his buggy. Many Miamis are Catholic.

Trapping continued even when I was young. We sold trapped rabbits to a big market in town. We sold possum skins, particularly; coon skins. We did a lot of hunting. We hunted waterfowl in the winter time; ducks and geese, quail. I've eaten lots of rabbits in my time. In the winter we lived on ducks and geese. My father's family were all hunters. My family, we were all hunters. My son was always a hunter, but my grandchildren have not had that opportunity because of their location, which is urban. We were always taught, "You don't take any game you aren't going to use yourself, that you aren't going to eat." That's an important part of hunting.

If I could come back in a hundred years, I would like to see the tribe in a position to be more independent from the federal government. We're very dependent at the present time on the federal government. I would like to see not only the Miami but all tribes in a position through economic development to be more independent. Economic development is probably number one that we need to accomplish in the next few years. I would like to see a tribe that has maintained its heritage, maintained the spiritual, maintained the heredity coming down from the tribe and still being able to be independent. I have confidence and faith that this is going to happen.

We have an organization in our area, of all the tribes. We've gone together on some things that we couldn't do individually. One of those is an intertribal newspaper.

Each tribe's traditions and ceremonials are unique to that tribe. I'm sure every Woodland tribe has a burial ceremony. There are some differences, for example, in that some tribes feel that the spirit doesn't reach the end of its journey until all the remains are gone completely. Our tribe doesn't feel that way. Our tradition says it takes three days for the spirit to reach the place it's going. This is why at our burial ceremony we put a little white flag at the grave and leave it there for three days.

Within my lifetime, I think the biggest change is [from] the idea that it's not very good to be Indian, as it was in my younger days, to the time when it was good to be Indian, to now when it's great to be Indian. This has been a slow process that has been recurring. Part of this, I think, is due to the fact that the policy of the United States government has varied. The policy of assimilation, when I was young, was the government saying: "You're Indian, yes, but you're part of the rest of society, and you need to assimilate into that society to the point you'll be thought of as not being different in that society." The federal government has changed its policy a little, as time has gone by, to where now it's one of economic development, spiritual development, and of being proud you are Indian but still contributing to total society in any way you can. These changes I've watched through my life.

I can remember the days when you went to the Bureau and got a little piece of paper. You took this piece of paper to the store, and you got a pair of shoes, for example. I can remember feeling—well, this is a strange feeling. Now, with the economic development, you can see a self-determination which is important to us. We went from self-determination to dependence, and now we are going back to self-determination.

The importance of education is something we haven't realized until recently. We haven't really pushed our children to go further in education. To learn all they can learn and to be able to further the cause of the Indian in the big world outside, that we can't shrink into ourselves and stay that way. I think I've been particularly interested in advancing the education of our children and making it an important issue. A lot of our children now go to college. When I was a boy, it was not the "right" thing to go to college. You were kind of breaking the rule. I'm one of the first Miamis to have gone to college. But now it has become something you are expected to do. I think this is the salvation of the tribe, of tribal heritage. We need people who are educated, who understand the world to keep the tribe in shape financially and spiritually.

We have a very close relationship with Miami University in Oxford,

Ohio. The university has helped us by providing computers to work with our kids. We have people from the university visit quite regularly. We have students come spend several days with the tribe to learn more about us, and we can learn more about them. The university has developed an "Indian Room," with an exhibit of Miami clothing. Miami University is located on the site of a Miami Village from way back in 1809. My son is a teacher at Miami University, of which I am very, very proud. My grandson, at the present time, is a student there.

The advice I would give to young tribal members is, number one, be proud of your heritage. Number two, become involved in tribal developments at an early age. Advice to non-Indian people is just to be tolerant. Try to understand that we are a little different sometimes. And don't lump Indians into one big pot because Indians vary as much as other people vary. Please don't stereotype Indians, which is done so much. People get the idea that unless you have feathers, and clothing on from the 1870s, you're not Indian. Realize that we are people, proud people, and try to look upon us as friends and as co-workers.

> *From an oral history interview conducted December 12, 1994, at the headquarters building of the Miami Tribe of Oklahoma, Miami, Oklahoma.*

TOM MAULSON

Chippewa

President, Lac du Flambeau Band of Lake Superior Chippewa
Indians

Born December 7, 1941, in Hayward, Wisconsin

Tom Maulson

Chippewa

President, Lac du Flambeau Band of
Lake Superior Chippewa Indians

LOUIS E. MYERS

PEORIA/KASKASKIA

CHIEF, PEORIA INDIAN TRIBE OF OKLAHOMA, 1987-1994

BORN JANUARY 18, 1915

DIED APRIL 7, 1994

Mr. Myers was elected councilman when Guy Froman was chief (1947-1972). In 1959 Mr. Myers initiated work on the Peoria Cemetery. He described the unkempt area thus: "It was in the wilderness, with trees and brush, and cows were allowed to graze through the cemetery [where they] pushed over headstones." The result of efforts with his colleagues is a well-kept cemetery on the west bank of Spring River—"plotted, fenced, with flag-pole" and with an identifying monument. There on 30 May 1988 Chief Myers led the dedication of a monument to honor tribal members who served in the United States Armed Forces and who are buried in the Peoria Cemetery.

When the Inter-Tribal Council was organized, Mr. Myers was second chief. He represented the Inter-Tribal Council at the advisory board for an Indian hospital. The result of the board's work finally became the Indian hospital in Claremore.

Second Chief Myers' own words tell of work to push Peoria claims through the Indian Claims Commission: "Chief Froman and I were called to Washington to testify before the Senate sub-committee, which was introduced by Senator Harris. We testified on behalf of our tribe for its best interests. Then we were called back to the Congressional Sub-Committee on Indian Affairs. We testified before them and set aside $3,000 for the maintenance of our cemetery. Through former Congressman Edmondson, we put forth that all monies left over from the claims were to go back to the tribe for administrational purposes, because we didn't have any money at the time. This turned out to be a considerable sum of money."

Mr. Myers has spent many hours over the last forty-one years work-

Louis E. Myers

Peoria/Kaskaskia

Chief, Peoria Indian Tribe of Oklahoma, 1987-1994

ing to bring about better living conditions for the four tribes [Kaskaskia, Peoria, Piankashaw, and Wea].

He summed up his business life this way: "For fifty years I have been involved in upholstery, designing, plumbing and refrigeration supporting my family, although time was taken out for the United States Navy where I served in World War II on the Pacific Ocean aboard the USS *Haggard* destroyer. With an honorable discharge, I returned home to be with my family."

While reminiscing about World War II, he told about his ship being hit and the loss of life. He was not hurt so he began at once to save some of his buddies. He summed up the experience this way: At a time like that one doesn't think of personal danger.

After the death of Chief Rodney Arnette in September 1986, Second Chief Wallis O. McNaughton served as chief until the election in March 1987. At that time, Mr. Myers was elected to complete Chief Arnette's term. Then, in March of 1988, Mr. Myers was elected to a regular term as chief.

He married Doris Neal in 1959. The Myers have six children, two boys and four girls.

At the annual meeting in 1987, Chief Myers received a plaque which read: "In appreciation of the years of service you have given to the Peoria tribe as chairman of the Peoria Cemetery Committee. Peoria Indian Tribe of Oklahoma."

Another plaque of which Mr. Myers can be justly proud was received April 1989. It read: "In appreciation for your support of the Food Distribution Program designed to assist the needy and alleviate hunger among our Indian people. Inter-Tribal Council, Inc., Food Distribution Program 5th Anniversary March 28, 1984-March 28, 1989. FDP staff."

[During Chief Myers' term a new tribal headquarters building was built and the tribe published a 300-page history.]

The account above is reprinted by permission from The Peorias: A History of the Peoria Indian Tribe of Oklahoma, *edited by Dorris Valley and Mary M. Lembeke (Miami, OK: The Peoria Indian Tribe of Oklahoma, 1991), pp. 211-213.*

JOANNA J. NICHOL

Delaware

Elder, Delaware Tribe of Indians, Bartlesville, Oklahoma

Born September 12, 1919, in Hogshooter, Oklahoma

My mother was Josie Curleyhead, a Delaware. My father was Alex B. Pambogo. He was Potawatomi. He and my mother met at Chilocco Indian School. That's where a lot of our mixed tribes met because they were sent to Chilocco Indian School. And they got married, and as is the general rule with tribes, the man moves in with the wife's family.

My grandfather had two wives. The Delaware men used to have more than one wife that they would marry. Grandpa married Grandma Pomp, which is what he called her. Pom pa noc qua was her name. She couldn't speak English. She only spoke Delaware. When I was little, my dad had a stripped-down Model T Ford. The only one in the county, and Grandma Pomp loved to drive that car. She and I would tear across the field. There were no fences to speak of in those days, so we'd go tearing across the hills and through the fields to go see Aunt Kate. I always knew what she was saying, even though she was talking Delaware, and I didn't understand it. I'd been around her enough that I could get the gist of what she meant.

Momma could speak Delaware, but my daddy couldn't speak Potawatomi because his mother died when his sister was a baby. And my father's father spoke Potawatomi only when he was with his sister, my great-aunt Sing Oh. In Potawatomi that means Squirrel. Little Squirrel. She was a tiny woman. She and her husband used to get in their buggy and come down to visit us at Grandfather Pambogo's. This was an overnight journey. They'd sleep in the buggy one night coming down from Asher to Wanette; that's where Grandpa's farm was. It was always exciting for them to come because first the table was set, and

Joanna J. Nichol

Delaware

Elder, Delaware Tribe of Indians

they'd talk to Grandpa in Potawatomi, and then Uncle John would go hunting. First he would go down to the river and get turtles. He'd just take a bucket with him, and he'd go down to the river and get turtles and clean them and get the turtle meat and juice out. And then he'd go squirrel hunting and bring them in, and, and, oh, we would just feast the whole time they were there. They'd come down about once every two months, which is quite often for travel in those days.

We have better circumstances today but not really as much of a family feeling at all. Grandfather Pambogo built the home that we lived in. He was a carpenter. We lived there, '30, '31, and part of '32. During the Depression my Potawatomi grandfather invited us to move to Wanette because he had steady income. I enjoyed living there. The only thing was, I had to do all the work. And I wasn't big enough. I had to stand on a box to wash clothes. In Bartlesville, Oklahoma, Momma had had a washing machine. It was an old-fashioned one; it was one of those paddle kind. And we had electric lights, but down there all we had were kerosene lights.

One of the first things I noticed was the fence around Grandfather's house. He had built a beautiful cool house, where the well was and where we kept milk and things. It really stayed cool there, even on the hottest days. There was a fence enclosing all this. But it was a funny kind of fence. I had never seen a fence like that before. It had posts with wire running across the top. And I thought, that's not really a fence. That's not going to stop anything from coming and going, and I was studying about that. Well, I kept my mouth shut and went on about my business. When it got warm, Grandpa went out. Now Grandpa was about six foot two. He was a big man, and he was old. And here he came with his cane and a bag, and he goes out in the yard, and he sits down. It's quite difficult for him to get down on the ground, but he made it. He couldn't see well, but I could see where he would start feeling, and when he found grass, he'd pull it. He pulled up all the grass around him, and then he'd move over and pull up all the grass that he could feel. And he worked out there all afternoon. When he was through, he came in the house and he said, "Now I want you to sweep the yard." And I thought, "Sweep the yard! I never heard of anything like that."

And then he told me, "That's the old fashioned way. We always kept a clean area around our habitat. That way we always knew who came and who went, whether it be four footed or not."

He had a great respect for animals. When he built his house he had TB. He put screens on the kitchen and dining room, even between the dining room and living room, but all the rest of the house, the bedrooms and living room and stuff, no screens. And the doors were always open in the summertime. I was lucky. I got the input of two different Woodland tribes in growing up.

One day when I was cooking, Grandpa came into the kitchen and he said, "Come here, Sister."

Everybody called me Sister because I was the oldest, and all the families out there called the oldest "Sister" because she kind of took care of the youngest.

And he said, "Come here, Sister, I want you to do something for me."

I said, "All right." So we went into the living room, and he sat down in his chair.

He said, "Sit down. We had a friend come in, but I don't know where he went." And he said, "I want you to be very careful. Don't frighten him, and look for a snake."

And I thought, "Whoo, I don't know whether I'm going to like this or not." But I went looking, and I found him behind the front door. He had just come in out of the sun, and he got in behind the door where it was cooler.

And Grandpa said, "Now I want you to go back over there by the door. He won't move if you don't." And he said, "I want you to shut your eyes and inhale deeply because you'll remember that smell. Then, when you go walking in the woods, you'll smell him before you see him."

And so he made me stand there and inhale for about ten minutes. I wasn't afraid of the snake because it was a black snake, and I already knew that they weren't bad, although it still might be painful. And I did what he told me. And sure enough as I'm telling you, I could, even from the back of a horse, smell a snake. It's something that just gets burned into you, and there it is. So, once I got that down, he said, "Now get the broom, and use the brush end of the broom, and just guide him outside all the way so he can go under the porch where it is cool during the day." So I did. And I went back to the kitchen and back to work.

My dad and grandpa were very strict about learning. Grandpa used to write papers for the Kansas Historical Society. There are several articles written by John B. Pambogo. He would describe how they fixed their hair. The Potawatomi used to cut all their hair off, except for just the topknot. That goes back to when they had wars, and he said it was harder to scalp. You couldn't get ahold of their hair. He'd always end his articles with the words, "And now that the other people are here, we must go to their schools and learn everything so that we can better live with them, handle them, know what to do." So he sent his boys off to school—boarding schools. My father went to Catholic Mission in Shawnee. My sister and I went to St. Mary's Academy at Sacred Heart. After I got out of junior high I went to Chilocco, and my sister went to Chilocco. So that was our basic education.

The corn fields kept us alive during the Depression. We would dry corn on big white canvas sheets. If we had nothing else we had what they called hogback then and corn; you cooked it just like you cooked beans. We'd take the extra dry corn to the mill and get it ground up and have corn bread.

They'd bring the corn in by the wagon loads. They had tubs of boiling water out there, and they'd drop it in the tubs of water for about three minutes, not much longer. And then they'd bring it in from there, and this would be another thing for young folks. There would be a bunch of us young folks sitting around in circles around the clean wagon sheets, and this corn would be husked and cut. They would dump the corn out of the hot water in the middle. Then we took a spoon and, with the handle down, pressed down right between the rows. And we had whole kernel corn. We'd sit there and do this all day long. If we got a whole row out without it breaking, then we got to go around and get a kiss from whoever we wanted. We tried very hard, very carefully to get those long ones. That's totally different from the Delawares. Delawares cut their corn, and then they scrape the cob. The Potawatomis would do that, but only for a certain dish. But their regular, everyday corn, like beans that they kept, was always whole kernel. I don't know what they did with the cob or the husks. The only time I ever saw corncobs used for anything was when they were dry. Sometimes in the wintertime they would use them to start fires.

In Bartlesville I had a lot of Osage friends so I went out to make hominy with an Osage friend. We would carry hot hominy with lye in it back and forth. Boy, that was something. Quite a soup. But there wasn't a lot of food in those days. What we had we grew.

At Grandpa's the well was sixty feet deep. That's a lot of rope to pull to get a bucket of water up, and I had to water the stock. I was so little and skinny. I would climb up on the well casing, which was about four feet high, and hold the rope and jump down. I must have climbed up there tens of thousands of times. But I always got a watermelon in the summertime, and I put it in the trough and poured that cool water over the watermelon and had it for supper.

My Delaware grandfather and great-grandfather were the village heads. The Indians established villages. The village head was usually called captain. My great-grandfather was Captain Curleyhead. We never did know another name for him. He and Grandpa Albert came down to pick out where our family was going to have our allotment here in Indian territory. He picked out what's now Washington County, buying land from the Cherokees, who got it from the government.

I know more about the Potawatomi because I have all the treaties. My grandfather and great-grandfather and great-great-grandfather were all named Pambogo, and they all signed treaties because in the Potawatomis, if you didn't get each village to sign, only the villages that signed would move. The rest of them would stay because it didn't affect them. It took President Harrison, when he was governor of the Northwest Territory, to finally figure out that the way to get these Potawatomis out of there was to go around to every village and get a signature. I have copies of those treaties, and always on them is "as long as the grass grows, it's yours." It was a great big lie.

Most of my interests are in Bartlesville because Delawares are matrilineal. Matriarchal. In the Delawares, women always ran the tribe. I say "ran the tribe"; they ran from behind their husbands. They actually had a say about going to war with another tribe. They also had a great deal to say to husbands who were on the council because the women would get together. At times the men would ask the women together to give them their opinion, which they would do. Grandma ran the house from what I understand from Momma. And Momma ran our house. But she didn't do it obviously. It was done with quiet efficiency.

One thing Momma was very particular about. She wanted me to go to all the old ceremonies. She'd take me out of school to do this. So I got to go to a lot of things, but I didn't know what they were at the time, because I was so little. For instance, I was at the last doll dance. I didn't pay much attention to the ceremony itself because I was busy watching other things. They had a whole cow on a stick over a pit, and a whole pig, and there were two men out there, talking and enjoying each other's company and keeping that thing turning. And I thought that was quite interesting. There was a blanket put down on the ground; it had rocks on all four corners. As the people came the young ladies would drop a loaf of bread on that blanket, and I got interested in that because those were my sized loaves, being a little girl. So I watched these loaves of bread, and finally Momma came over and said, "We're going to eat pretty soon, but we are going to watch this." And I thought,

"Maybe I am going to get one of those little loaves," and I was excited. But four old ladies came, and they took ahold of the blanket corners, and they picked up those loaves, and all of the men were gathering around. And I noticed it was nothing but men, and they swung that blanket a couple of times, and then they snapped it so that loaves went in the air and flew every way. And the boys grabbed them, and the sign of the girl was on the bottom so they always knew who they were going to eat with.

Later in life, when I was in California and I was speaking to the school systems, I told them, I said, "The white people thought they invented bringing box lunches to church and pairing off the young folks with that. I guess they didn't know the Indians have been doing that for a long, long time before they got here."

I also got to take food to the graves for the burial ceremony. At the end of the certain number of days which it took the dead person to get to the happy hunting ground, we had a feast.

The Delawares believe that the dogs guard the Milky Way; the Milky Way was the way we were going to travel. So Momma and Daddy would always tell me, "Don't ever be mean to an animal, especially a dog, because you are going to have to get past a dog to get on the Milky Way, and I don't care how good you are down here, if you kicked a dog, you are on the bad side. You're on the list." They used to say it with a smile, but I knew they meant it.

There were a lot of beautiful beliefs. It was not unknown for us to have someone say, "I'm going to visit my ancestors and get counseled by them." They'd just go and talk to them.

My Potawatomi grandfather was born between Council Bluff, Iowa, and Kansas when the government was moving the Potawatomi west. Great-grandmother had to drop out and give birth and catch up with the rest of the tribe that night. The lucky thing for the Potawatomi, at the Hudson Bay Trading Post, they took up with the Catholic church and the priests, and they would never travel without a priest, so all of our travels are documented. The priests even kept a record of who died every day. They have that down in Shawnee, Oklahoma.

I didn't grow up speaking Delaware or Potawatomi. It was like you were born from an Italian and a Frenchman. You didn't speak it. My ear is "tuned" especially to Delaware. Except when Aunt Sing Oh came, and Grandpa talked Potawatomi with her, he'd sit in the outhouse and talk Potawatomi to himself. That's the only time we'd hear him talk. So my little sister and cousin, we'd go down there and listen. But when he got through—we knew when he got through—we'd get up and run because if he caught us down there listening, we'd get in trouble. But we never missed if we saw Grandpa heading that way. Grandpa was not a talker. He taught me, without saying anything, who was expected to do what. Whatever you decided to do, he expected you to do well. Not necessarily be the best, but always do your best. Always do well. That was something that was handed down to him, and evidently all the Pambogos were village heads.

My hopes for the future are just that my people have their sovereignty and continue to do as they have always done; take care of each other and themselves and be helpful to other people. I would like to see less infighting, but that happens in big families, too. We are a big family. Delawares don't have a name for cousin. The children of all siblings are brothers and sisters.

There's nothing in the world that makes me feel better than to see those little guys, those little itty-bitty guys, dancing, or seeing the momma sit there jumping her baby to the beat of the drum so that when he starts dancing he's got that rhythm automatically. An old-fashioned—or a new—spirit comes from the old days.

One of the nice things about being Indian, and this happens all over the country even in mixed tribes, when you go to a powwow you don't have to worry about your children, because no matter where they are playing or what they are doing some Elder is going to tell them right and wrong if they are doing something wrong. That is just something you automatically do, and I think that is one of the nicest things among all Indians—that we do that. We take care of the whole tribe as our immediate family. I've always been proud of that.

I adore children, and I like to see them given a good way to go, a good healthy tradition to carry along with them, make them better in the work force. Whatever makes them more secure. Give them a good, soft home—what I call soft is a lot of hugs.

Take care of the earth. Quit cutting trees. Don't start killing off animals because you think they are causing harm, because this world is balanced. The Creator made it that way. I read in the paper—of course, being Wolf Clan it made me mad—that the ranchers around Yellowstone Park want to kill wolves again. Wolves don't eat big animals unless they're sick or dying. They live mainly on mice and rodents. But you know the human failure of having to have somebody to blame. It's aggravating. I want the world to get wiser about that. Everyone. Indians. Non-Indians.

Keep your goals straight; try to keep your mind straight on what you want to achieve. You don't have to be the best, just the most honest. That's all. As long as you can face yourself every morning when you wash your face and look into the mirror without flinching, you've had a pretty good previous day. Those are words of wisdom from my dad. He said, "Never lie because if you try to lie, that's the hardest thing in the world to try to keep up. You've never worked so hard as you have to work if you've lied, 'cause just stop to think how many other lies you need to support that lie, and it gets wider and wider." My dad explained that to me when I was about five years old, and he kept on, and I kept envisioning this wider, wider, wider bunch of lies happening just to support that one lie.

From an oral history interview conducted December 14, 1994, at the headquarters building of the Delaware Tribe of Eastern Oklahoma, Bartlesville, Oklahoma.

MICHAEL PACE

DELAWARE

ASSISTANT CHIEF, DELAWARE TRIBE OF INDIANS, BARTLESVILLE,
OKLAHOMA

BORN LOS ANGELES, CALIFORNIA

My earliest remembrances, not history but tribally, began when I was very young. I remember when I was three years old, being at the Quapaw powwow, waking up next to the fire, and my aunt Anna, Anna Anderson, who is known as Anna Davis, was handing me my bowl and telling me to to get in line.

The history of our People I never really learned until I was an adult, but culturally things came naturally to me through my uncle Ray, Ray Elkhair. Ray was a tremendous Stomp Dance leader. He had spent many years learning songs. He would move around Oklahoma. He spent some time with the Shawnee, and he actually changed jobs to learn their songs. Then he would pack up, and he would move down to the Creeks, and he learned a lot of their songs.

We used to have a monthly event in our home. My mother would invite a lot of the people to come over and have Stomp Dances at our house. Those are the times when I learned about our history and the cultural things that we do and the customs that we have. I met with my own people, and I learned from them. Unfortunately, I guess, just because of the mobility that we all face today, we were forced to move away from the area for a while and probably lost three or four years there, and when we returned, even Uncle Ray was gone by that time. He had passed on. For some reason we were not able to carry on those events as we had done in the past. The Lead Dances, or Stomp Dances, were a great part of what we did. It's been real fortunate that within this last couple of years we have been able to bring our people back together and start doing those same things that we did when I was a child. Only this time, I think the difference

160

is that we are very, very interested in making sure the children know and that they learn, because no one forced me to learn these things. It was something that you asked to do, and you had to prove yourself worthy of doing it.

Today, when I hear some songs, I think of Uncle Ray singing that song. Because he loved those things so much, he wouldn't let anybody else lead; he would lead all of those songs, one right after another. Fortunately, we were able to capture a lot of his songs on tape. Unfortunately, he had recorded a lot on his own that have been lost.

As I went away to school and found my own way in life, I was away from the tribe for a long time. However, I never really lost that sense of who I was. I was always a Delaware. I grew up that way, and in that sense I did not have a loss of identity that a lot of our People have had. I was always proud of who I was, and I made sure everybody knew that. Culturally we kind of lost our way for quite some time, but I think the gains we have made in the last several years have been tremendous. And I envision that someday we will regain all of those things, and our children will know. We are telling these children, "It's up to you. We cannot miss this generation, because if we do, that will be the end of it."

When we started with our cultural preservation committee, we actually started with seven people. Now, when we have our meetings regularly every month, we're seeing sixty and seventy. We're drawing over to some of the other areas within what used to be the old boundaries of the Delaware allotments, and we're starting to branch out in other villages and bring those people back into touch with us. Eventually, we're going to go back to those times when Uncle Ray was leading those songs, and we met every month, and people couldn't wait to get there and have a good time. I want the tribe to come back culturally, to share the same things our ancestors a hundred years ago shared, because I see a tribal entity not as a federally recognized thing, or a group of people. I think of it more as a family that has the same interests, and they're bonded by their sharing of these songs. That to me is more important than federal recognition.

Even in Oklahoma there is still a curiosity about the Indian. It's kind of amazing, considering how many of us live there. I remember one particular event that we had at a little farm just south of Dewey, by Post Oak Creek, right next to the highway. We had built a large fire, and a lot of people had attended the meeting that night. We were all doing the Stomp Dance and having a wonderful time around the fire. A lot of cars were beginning to stop along the side of the road, just curious onlookers, probably wondering, "What are those people doing down there?" Although very few people came down to see what was happening, a lot of people were just sitting along the side of the road watching us. Uncle Ray said, "What are all those people sitting there for? Well, if they want to come, then let them come down and be part of what we are doing."

Probably twenty years ago was the last time we practiced all our dances in any great extent. Now we have a dance group learning our old Delaware social dances; the Raccoon Dance, the Go-Getum Dance, the Duck Dance, the Turkey Dance.

Lead, or Stomp, Dance is the most common social dance among the Delaware as well as among many of the tribes that originally came from the northeastern and southeastern coast of the United States. The Stomp Dance consists of a male song leader followed by a female shell shaker, who wears turtle shells, or tin cans, filled with various items to produce a rhythmic sound to accompany the song. The leader and shell shaker are followed by people in single file, and they circle the fire in a counterclockwise motion.

As the leader sings, he is seconded by the people, and, as they circle in step, a stomping sound is made as everyone is dancing in unison. There are many songs from many tribes, and these dances do not require any special wear or ceremonial regalia and are meant to be a social dance everyone can participate in. In Oklahoma, these dances are more common than powwows and have a big following of tribal members, most of whom prefer the Stomp Dance to intertribal powwows.

Social dances encompass many types of dances and are sung using a water drum and rattles. The water drum is a drum filled partially with water and covered with a skin that is tied in a ceremonial manner before the dance. Rattles today are usually bell-gourd rattles, but many turtle shell rattles are still popular and in common use. The songs are led by a head singer and several other singers with two to five being the usual. The most common dances among the Delawares are the Woman, Turkey, Go-Getum, Duck, Raccoon, and Cherokee. These dances are performed with the men and women dancing separately, but there are many variations. Two other dances, the Bean and the Alligator, are performed with a song leader using a rattle, who is followed single file by alternating man-woman-man.

Social dances vary among tribes. Some tribes treat these as ceremonials honoring certain totems, while among other tribes these are done as respect to traditional customs and honoring certain animals. Some dances are not public among some tribes unless you are invited. Other dances are open but limited participation may be enforced. For the most part, social dances are open to anyone who wishes to participate, but respect is requested at all times.

Social dances are making a comeback among many tribes, as [was] the intent of earlier times, to keep the tribal members together in a social atmosphere and create a common bond among tribal members. Today these dances are fulfilling their purpose by drawing back together tribal members who have desired to return to an earlier time to honor their traditions and honor their forefathers.

When we join with other tribes we do a Pan-Indian Dance; that's an intertribal Indian dance. We do the two steps or the round dance; most tribes have them. Those are friendship dances. Any time we deal with another tribe, we do so as brothers. We want to do it in their way, or they want to do it in our way, whichever we figure out. We always consult with them to find out if there's anything that we do that they do not do that they might find offensive, and they look at it in the same manner for us. Pan-Indian dances are accepted as being part of the powwow structure. It really doesn't have anything to do with our individual tribal custom dances.

Delaware Day is a fairly new special event held each year on Labor Day weekend in Bartlesville, Oklahoma, as an opportunity for Delawares to get together and enjoy a day of fun, games, good food, and social dancing. It is treated as a homecoming and a thanksgiving for tribal members. It is a way of introducing young people to their culture and the pride of being Delaware.

In 1992, when I first came to the Minnetrista Cultural Center in Muncie, Indiana, I thought that was a wonderful thing; they were recognizing that the Delawares were a part of what happened in Indiana. The Delaware arrived in Indiana in the late 1700s from lands in Ohio and through the cooperation of their brothers, the Miami. They had several villages in and around the White River, and one of those villages was under the leadership of Chief Anderson.

Chief Anderson was half-French and half-Delaware. He attained his leadership in his fifties. He was always a very well respected man within the Delaware tribe. His influence and integrity were respected among many of the villages, and he spoke for his people along with other chiefs in many treaty meetings with the U.S. government. He built a house and trading post in what is now Anderson, Indiana, after which the name remained. But the Delawares and the chief were removed again, first to Missouri and later to Kansas Territory. The legacy of the chief and the tribe remain a part of Indiana history, with several villages turning into cities and retaining the name, such as Anderson and Muncie. The chief lived to see his Delawares arrive in Kansas, where he passed away in the early 1820s.

The Delawares are proud of their legacy and history, which helped form the frontier in the early 1800s that today is the state of Indiana. There has been a renewal of the friendship and shared history between the Delaware and the people of Indiana in recent years, and the Delaware tribe hopes that bond will grow.

The thing I remember, leaving Muncie after the 1992 event to return to Oklahoma, was that I could not imagine my mother having to walk that distance. What would have happened to her had she been forced to walk to Oklahoma from Missouri? That really struck home with me, and I really didn't know what to think about coming back to Indiana the next time I was asked to return, because we cannot really be like our ancestors. We don't have the same make-up, and we did not have to suffer what they had to suffer in order to see that the tribe survived all the way to Oklahoma. I'm happy that people do recognize there was a wrong done, but I don't know that it can be righted, at least not in my mind, considering what the tribe had to suffer in order to survive. The fact that I'm even here today, because it could very well have been that I might not be here today, had the tribe not been as strong as they were and been able to travel that distance and survive. We do speak of it often—that we lived many places across this country and we had an effect on many events and many historical things that happened in this country, all the way from New Jersey to Oklahoma.

From 1991 to 1993 we have been welcomed "home" to four different states. I'm happy that those people are willing to acknowledge the Delawares were a part of their early history. New Jersey welcomed us back. We made a journey to Dover, Ohio. All four of the separated tribes from 220 years ago were brought back together and we had a meeting there.

In Kansas they were actually apologizing for the way they treated the Delawares. That was kind of a difference that I thought was nice, but I'm not so sure that I can forgive that, for being treated in that way.

What's important to me now is that I want to show those people that we are not gone; we are here; we did not lose everything. We came pretty close, and there's still a possibility we can lose it, but I think with the efforts we're making today, and with the help of the people we have, we will be able to restore a lot of what we have lost. It just takes time, and we have to work with a lot of people who want to do things correctly. We want to teach things correctly, and that is very difficult for us to do. Even when I'm trying to make an effort to help the young people, help my own people, sometimes I feel woefully inadequate. But at the same token, I also believe I must step forward. I must try to do the best I can do. And that, I think, is what we expect of everybody in the tribe. We want them to regain the pride they had, because we have a tremendous and very rich legacy that the Lenapes have passed down to us. I would hate for that to be lost. I would hate for that to be spoken of as being a past thing, a past history. I want it to be a present history, too.

I'm very proud to be a Delaware, and I hope that pride shows when we come back to Indiana to be a part of events we have been invited to participate in. I think it's important to educate the people in Indiana. By our actions we can show them that we are not stereotypes. We want to break those things down and show we are a very proud people. We were a Peacemaker. We were a Grandfather Tribe, and we had many other tribes looking to us for leadership. And they still do today. I want that to be passed on to our children and any of our tribal members who have lost their way.

Whatever situation the Delawares had to endure, whether by free will or being forced, we adapted to it. That's what we had to do in order to survive. The important thing about the Delaware tribe, the Lenapes, is that we made that transition from a Woodland tribe. Probably, by the time we left Indiana, we actually became a Plains tribe. We evolved to that because that's what we had to do. I don't know that my tribal People would agree with everything I have said about this, but I think we did things to help the tribe survive. Some things were very distasteful to us, and I can look back and see the leaders thinking in those terms because some things we had to do, we would not normally do. In our travels across the country we adapted. We still even joke today that we've become as technologically advanced as any other group. We make that remark, "Hey, you know, we're just using common sense. We're adapting to where we are." I think most of the Lenape have always been a very open

people. They've always been able to get along with everybody because we see it as the way we live. We don't want to live a harsh life;
we want to be able to work those things out. Perhaps that is why we
became known as "The Peacemakers." We were able to talk to both
sides in a calm manner and to clear the path for some sort of agreement.

I appreciate being asked to come out and participate in a lot of
things back East. There are some things I still might find offensive, but
I'm willing to sit down to talk about those things. And I am willing to
work things out and try to come to a solution where there's no injury
done to either side, but we can come to a compromise on some of those
issues.

My mother was one of those victims in the school system. When she
was twelve, they forced her into an Indian school, and they literally beat
the Delaware out of her. She lost a lot of her traditional ways, her
language. My aunt Anna Anderson, being much older, was able to
retain hers. So what I learned of our traditional things and customs I
learned from Aunt Anna, Anna Anderson Davis. She taught me little
songs, how to cook a lot of our foods. I learned to cook fry bread just as
well as she does. I do have some of the notebooks that I wrote whenever
she was telling me these things, in my scrawl of a twelve-year-old.

When we talk about fry bread, a lot of people think, "That's such a
wonderful thing." I say, "Well, actually fry bread was probably something we saw the French do, but we took it and we do it our own way."
There are many different ways to make fry bread. It's become so much
a part of our culture. When we see fry bread, we can tell you what tribe
made it, just because they stick to their traditional way of making fry
bread. The Delawares always did theirs in the diamond shape with a
slit in the middle, whereas you might see the Navaho have a much
bigger piece. And some of the Osage have a round piece, and they do
it in a certain way so it's kind of got a little bump in the middle. Fry
bread is probably the one food that we've talked about the most, but
it probably was not really an Indian thing. A lot of other traditional
foods are the same. We have two or three different ways to make up
several different recipes with corn. We have the regular real dried
corn, hard corn, where we make a corn soup from that. Then we have
corn where we scrape it off and let it kind of set, and it gets kind of a
milky color. You mix it and make a bread out of that. It's really, really
tasty. You wouldn't know it was corn. One particular kind of corn we
make a bread out of has a gritty texture. My cousin, Louise Dean,

improvised by using Fritos. You can use Fritos and make that bread in no time at all, whereas if you did it the old way, it would take a long time. We're able to adapt all sorts of things. It is one of our recipes in *The Lenape Cookbook* by Nora Dean that we sell. It is produced by Talking Leaves Trading Post.

> *From an oral history interview conducted September 21, 1993, in the "Delaware Room" at Conner Prairie in Fishers, Indiana.*

HELEN RAMERIZ

Shawnee

Elder, Absentee Shawnee Tribe of Oklahoma

Born 1935, thirteen miles west of Tecumseh, Oklahoma

My place of childhood is mostly [surrounded by] blackjack trees, post oak, cottonwood, wild berry vines, wild possum grapes, plums, and, yes, persimmons. We used to get the last batch of persimmons off the tree, which I used to make persimmon bread and sometimes a persimmon pie. We have a little creek that runs down through, runs off the farm, that we used to wade in and run up and down when we were children. This is my dad's land. I have a lifetime lease on five acres of land out there. Now we have a water well so we've got water out there. We're planning on getting a septic tank in. We do have an outhouse now.

One memory from childhood is of my grandfather. When we were small, all three of us—my brother John, myself, and my sister Alice—we always waited on my grandfather when we went to camp. He always brought us something. It might have been just one little old bag of peanuts, or maybe peppermint, or horehound candy. They were bittersweet, but they were good. But what I remember most about my early childhood is playing in the creek. It was just our creek because it ran right by our place. There were frogs, tadpoles, turtles. All kinds of little critters.

I remember when we were little, Dad used to set out rabbit traps, hand-made of wooden boxes that had a door that raised. And whenever a rabbit would go in it would shut, and that's the way he caught a rabbit. So we used to bundle up and go out there. Mamma used to put little gunny sacks on our feet because we didn't have overshoes. We used to go out and set the traps. My brother went to get them out if we got any rabbits. Sometimes we found two or three rabbits. We skinned them and cooked them. We didn't use the hide for anything.

168

We had squirrel. We had wild grapes that we used to make dump-lings out of in the fall. We had squash and corn that was cooked in all different ways, cooked with meat or cooked by itself just as hominy. Sometimes we'd make it into bread, pound it and make bread out of it. And fish. Sometimes we would go fishing and bring in tubs of fish. Sometimes they'd just throw them in the wagon, and they'd take them back. And they'd cook up the fish, and they'd cook the heads; have catfish heads. I remember those things so well. They just don't do that any more.

Now we live in a modern house; it has running water on the inside and gas and a restroom that's inside. All you have to do is just touch switches to have electricity and watch television. I've got a five-bedroom brick home, compared to the one little room that was divided into one corner for my grandfather and my brother and me. We slept on the floor. He slept on the west side of the heater stove, and I slept on the east side. My little sister had just a makeshift bed. Mom and Dad slept in the northeast corner of the house. We had a real nice setup. I liked the old ways.

Fry bread is part of my tradition. I'll make it any time they ask me. It's just made out of flour and salt and baking powder and warm water. Make a well in the mixture of flour, salt, and baking powder. Then put warm water in the well, stir it up, and keep on stirring until the flour is mixed in and the dough starts coming kind of thick. Then start knead-ing with your hands. Take a little ball of it, kind of flatten it like a biscuit, flop it back and forth between your hands, and make two slits before you drop it in the deep fat that's already hot, and you fry it. You make the slits right in the center, next to each other, like a button hole. Fry bread is particular to each tribe.

I have always been, and I always will be, proud to be Shawnee. When we went off to a boarding school, we weren't allowed to speak our language, and I was caught. They heard me talking to my brother, and the matron took me into the clothing room and put a piece of lye soap in my mouth. I could sing a high soprano. That soap, it burned me so. The blisters were just—. I don't know how bad they were, but I couldn't sing a word. I was like a little young rooster trying to crow. You know how they try in that little broken voice. I've never forgotten it. I'll never forget it. I remember it now. It's a memory I never forget. I always said from that day on, if I ever had children and if they had to go to a boarding school, I would not send them. I would do anything for them not to go to boarding school because I know what it was like. It was Pawnee Indian boarding school. The matron that did that to me was named Margret Walker. She's deceased now. There's no need for a human being doing that to another human being. And on top of that, she was Indian. I never could figure out how she could do something like that. I always spoke to the lady. I was kind to her even though what she did to me—because my grandfather, my dad's father, always told us, he taught us: "Be kind to people no matter what they do to you, because kindness will hurt them worse than if you're mean."

I always thought nobody could replace our chief. I always thought our chief was our leader. Then this governorship came in and lieutenant governor. I can't remember when we've had such, only our chief. The chief is supposed to be higher than the governor. The governor is supposed to go to the chief and ask his advice because he is the chief. The grandfather is the authority figure in the family. For the tribe, the chief is the authority figure. As far as I can remember, the chief is handed down.

My brother was speaker for ceremonial purposes. He spoke for the tribe when we had a traditional ceremony. My grandfather used to do that when we were children. It would be to speak within the tribe. He gets up and talks and prays. They are medicine men.

We don't say "Grandfather" like some other tribes do. We say "Creator." We call ourselves Absentee Shawnee. We have a story that was told to us that a turtle is holding up the world. That's where "People of the Turtle" comes from.

Traditional ways were practiced when I was a child. For the Stomp Dance, men get out there, and they lead, and the womenfolks have cans around their legs to make the sound for the rhythm all night long. The leader starts out, and the other men answer him. They dance all night long. They have different kinds of dances. One that's social dancing. We have a drum that goes along for the Stomp Dance, and we have different social dances that we do. The Stomp Dance is part of the intertribal dances. Traditionally, Stomp Dance belonged to the Shawnee. Now other tribes have taken on the Stomp Dance, too.

We used to have gatherings only at funerals, at full moon, at traditional ceremonies, and at Stomp Dances. These are our traditions.

I speak Shawnee. My daughter [Henryetta Blanchard Ellis] doesn't speak Shawnee. I am planning on putting our language on tape for my family. I think we lose quite a bit when we don't speak our language. It's not spoken quite as much as when I was a little girl. My grandfather used to talk the Native language to us all the time. My mother did, too, and so did Father. I just feel like now I'm lost, because it's very rare that you run into somebody who knows how to talk the Shawnee language. When I do run into someone who can speak it, I take advantage of it. Sometimes I even have to ask somebody about something I can't remember. And they'll say, "Well, you're old enough to know this." And I'll say, "Well, maybe I'm old enough to remember, but it just doesn't come back!"

Nowadays our kids are losing respect for Elders, and that makes us sad. We have a young generation now, a minority, that just makes fun of our Elders; the way they talk, the way they walk, and how they have done things. They are mean. We've got some Elders out there who are real educated. They really could help the tribe. You do not criticize your Elders. I have told my children over and over again, if there is an elderly person that can't get across the street or is having difficulty in a store finding things, make yourself useful to that person because God put us here to help our Elders, no matter what color they are. Elders are somebody to respect. Nowadays they don't. The ways of the Shawnee are changing.

When we went to Indiana and met Shawnees there, it amazed me. They don't look like Indians. Their skin is not like ours. The Shawnees have the oval face. I felt lost because I didn't feel like I was in Indian country. I felt like I was in white man's world. I feel sorry for people who try to copy the Indian ways and the way they dress. To me it's just a mockery for the Indian when they try to do that because they think it's right. But it's not.

I hope we never lose our traditional ways. I hope they will stay with us.

From an oral history interview conducted December 15, 1994, at Shawnee, Oklahoma.

DAN RAPP

Potawatomi (Pokagon Band)

Former chairman, Potawatomi Indian Nation, Inc. (Pokagon Band of Potawatomi Indians)

Born December 16, 1939, in Northport, Michigan

My father is an actual Pokagon Band member. My mother is an Ottawa, but everybody accepts her as part of the Pokagon Band because she has done so much down here. She's one of the old craftsmen. She is still making baskets. She's living on a reservation up in Mount Pleasant now and is taking care of her sister. She knows more about the culture than I do, the traditions. She remembers a lot about how it used to be.

My father, on the other hand, wasn't taught too much about the culture except the language. My father died about eight years ago. It was sad to see him pass away because all of a sudden it changed my life. I knew that this generation was going to take over. But as long as my mother is alive, I can always go to her. Agnes is my mother's name, and Michael was my father's name.

My mother teaches basketry. She started doing that after she first started getting into the culture. I think that late in her life she has done a lot of things. Of course, earlier in her life she did a lot of things, too, raising us. But late in life she got involved in the culture and the traditions. And she's had a heck of a time, I would say, because she was always at home, and all of a sudden she is traveling around the country now. She is giving demonstrations all over. It's pretty interesting. I used to help her out years ago to go to the demonstrations. I would introduce her and her group and the people in her group, and then they would take over. It was a lot of fun back then. It was her and Julia Wesaw. She is still active, and she will remain active as long as she is alive. She's at the age where nothing bothers her.

My childhood home started out up north, but then we came south to

172

Dan Rapp

Potawatomi (Pokagon Band)

Former chairman, Potawatomi Indian Nation, Inc.

Benton Harbor. It appears that's where all the jobs were back then in the '40s. The war was still going on then. From Benton Harbor we migrated, moving from DeSoto to Eau Claire to Dowagiac. I moved to Dowagiac because I met my wife here, settled down here myself.

I went to school in a mostly all-white school. There were only three people in that whole school that were of a different color, and that was my brother, me, and I believe my other brother. That wasn't unusual; I didn't think it was. You just grew up in it.

Then I went from that school to a ninety-percent black school, and that was a heck of a change. There is probably where I began to learn about prejudice. I ran around with the black people, and I picked up on the culture, the way they talk and the way everything goes. And the neighbors, which were just down the road, didn't like the people that I played with. They resented that, and then they resented us.

I grew up as a Native American, and in high school I began to realize that there are people who are prejudiced against us, just automatically. I've learned to live with it. You could see how the whites were treating the blacks back then. In my own mind, I could see that they would treat me the same way. So the thing to do is just not associate with those type of people. You just stay away from them.

We didn't do the traditional thing as far as Native American traditions were concerned back then. But we were a traditional family. They taught us not to lie, not to steal. The traditional Indian ways I never picked up on until about fifteen years ago.

Our generation before us had not practiced the traditional culture in ways that we do now. If I look back, I would say that Tom [Topash] was the catalyst of what happened to bring the traditional ways back as far as Native Americans are concerned in this area. There were traditional ways going on, but not many people knew about it.

I am so glad that we are practicing right now. It's really a fulfilling thing for me. I picked up on different ideas and prejudices and biases. I feel like right now I've made great strides in my life because I've learned to respect a lot of things that I never did before.

I am learning how to speak the Native language. My parents, they mixed them both [the Potawatomi and Ottawa languages]. They could talk either one. After a while they couldn't tell what was Potawatomi and what was Ottawa. They are almost similar. Why should they teach us? English was my first and primary language.

We found several tapes that were made in Wisconsin. These tapes were located in Canada. Right now we are trying to figure out adverbs, adjectives, and other things, and how to pronounce them and where they come in. You have to have a different mind set when you go into the class because it's not English.

To put it another way, some of the non-Indians expect the Indians to speak Indian, but they don't understand it's not like this Hollywood version of "How" and "We come" or something like that, which I grew up with, too. I always thought Indians talked like that. It's important that you have your Native language because it is part of the Native American life. The English language, I find, is pretty rough compared to the Native American, which is, I would say, beautiful. It takes into account all the things that are around us. Not the buildings here or there, cement. It takes account of what was here before, like the woods and the trees and the animals and the swamps and anything else other than what we have now. There are a lot of words, we are finding out, that were put in afterwards, slang words that just don't fit into the original language.

I only knew one great-grandfather for a short time, but one of the things he passed on to me as far as I can remember was that the life you live doesn't have to be complicated. All you need are the simple things in life to survive. They built their own sleds; they built their own skis; they built their own snowshoes. These were things that were enjoyed, whereas now, I enjoy a four-wheeler. Compare that to what he had back then. That was my great-grandfather. I remember him, John. He died in an auto accident. It cut everything short. And I think about this a whole lot. It cut me short, too, because he knew more than my dad did about culture and traditions. I used to like to listen to him talk because he had a nice way of saying things. He had a really large family. Most of that part of the family are gone, almost.

My dad could go out into the woods and pick out the medicines and herbs to use for what discomforted him, just him. That was one thing that I really was interested in but never pursued. Every once in a while he would give it to us, us kids. But other than that, nobody picked up on that.

I say Native American, Potawatomi, Pokagon Band. It all depends on who I'm talking to. But if you want to call me one or the other, I would just as soon be called Anishnabe. I am Anishnabe from the Pokagon Band.

In twenty years the Pokagon Band should be pretty well settled and have a reservation. They should have another generation started. In twenty years they should have a band government formed. We've been thinking about this for the last three or four years, saying, "In five years we should have this and this." But twenty years is not a very long time; it's a short time. One hundred years is a short time, too, but in twenty years a lot of things should be done, settled. In twenty years the generation born now should be grown up and in the government of the band. I want to know how that person feels, how this person looks upon the Pokagon Band. Since we are just starting, we are just now wondering if we are going to go through what all the other tribes went through, all the bad times in order to obtain all the good things. We have to be prepared for the bad things and straighten them out. We're doing a lot of preventive talking right now, trying to steer away from those bad things happening. When you say "modern-day reservations," they have housing and a center and schools. That should be done in that twenty years. I'd want to see how they are governing themselves and how they have grown.

What I've run into now is that all of a sudden I am an Elder, and they think that I am wise and have all kinds of information that they can use. Well, this has been hard to adjust to because I have always looked up at my mother or father for guidance there. But now all of a sudden it's been left on some of us who are in this generation, and it is expected of us that we furnish the guidance. It's been an adjustment that we have to assume. We have to do what I've learned in the past, and my "past" only goes back fifteen years. I've learned to listen to the Elders. You take care of the smaller ones, as my teachers have taught me. Be fair and as honest as you can. The teachers have taught me, and I do practice a lot of things that nobody else does. I listen to what the Creator has given me out there. I listen to the animals, the birds, and the bees and the trees. I don't take these for granted any more. I've turned into an environmentalist. I don't hunt or fish any more unless I think that I have to survive from this. My views have changed. Right now I would just as soon be out alone in the woods rather than in the city.

I like it when we practice the traditions. There's not that many of us that practice this, but there are a lot more that know about us now because we have made an impact on people of the tribe. A lot of us go to church plus practice this religion, and that's where I've never had any trouble. My wife has some trouble. She doesn't totally understand the way I practice my religion because she's a devout Catholic, and I respect her for that.

We had a bishop that picked up on the Native American traditions, and I made reference to that a long time ago. It seemed that burning the sage was the same as burning the incense. And the sprinkling of the water I always associated with our water ceremonies. When you refer to the fire, that is the candles. I could see where maybe the Native people way back when looked upon this as a way they did things. I picked up on it. I said, "Well, that's true. There is a similarity there."

From an interview conducted October 28, 1995, at Dowagiac, Michigan.

CHRIS SCHENKEL

Miami/Sauk and Fox

Honorary member of each, given the name of Mo-nun (Speaker Who Loves All People)

Born August 21, 1923, in Wabash County, Indiana

I was born in northern Indiana on a farm one and a half miles from Bippus. I was one of six children. When I was only a few months old my dad moved to a farm on the north side of Bippus. I am proud of my Wabash heritage because as I got older the Wabash River became very important in my life. My mother was Theresa Sell. She married Phillip Robert Schenkel. They lived to 82 and 83 years of age. They had a good life. I married Fran Page on January 1, 1955. We have three children and three grandchildren. I was in World War II and discharged as a first lieutenant in the infantry.

Growing up on the farm was really one of the best things that happened to me because you really learn how to work. My dad ran a grain and feed—an elevator operation, a lumber yard—and insisted that we always live on a farm and work it. We did it with horses. He refused to buy a tractor. But then eventually when he retired and sold out, he bought a tractor. It's a Ford Ferguson that I have now. I still use it. So we finally got the tractor. But I learned how to work. When it rained, I unloaded cement, coal, whatever came in, from railroad cars. So I just learned how to get along with brothers and sisters, neighbors.

There were only eleven in my graduating class from high school. Most of them were relatives, either on my mother's or dad's side, and the little town was filled with Swiss and German people. Some were Schenkel cousins who became very big dairy operators in Indiana, Ohio, and Michigan. My Schenkel cousins grew up on a farm just down the road. We were like brothers. My dad raised beef cattle, and their dad, my dad's brother, was a dairy cattle man. My dad just loved cows, but not dairy cows. My uncle was right. He made more money than my dad did.

Chris Schenkel

Miami/Sauk and Fox

*Honorary member of each, given the name of
Mo-nun (Speaker-Who Loves All People)*

The elevator where they stored the grain was a huge concrete structure out on the plains of Indiana; one hundred feet tall. We put a Christmas tree on top every year. You could see it for miles. But it had to be repaired, or painted, and there was always a company from Chicago that would come and do it. My dad would hire them, and it was rather dangerous work. There was one black worker on the crew. Some of the farmers had probably never seen a black person. They were starting to ridicule him. My dad tore into them. That always impressed me because he just said to them, "Look, he's one of God's children. Come on, you guys obviously don't even know him, and you hate him. Dislike his ways if that will make it better for you."

So I learned never to hate anybody. I first learned about discrimination there. The discrimination lesson stood me in good stead later on because I met others who were discriminated against.

Not too far from the farm we could go walking, ride our bikes. I started finding [Miami Indian] arrowheads. I was intrigued. I wanted to find out about the Miami Indians, but Bippus High School didn't have any books about the Miami Indians. None. So I started searching for whatever I could find on the Miami Indians, and it took a lot of years to put together [my own library]. I think I have every book that has been published on them. As a result, it got me a tremendous rare book library.

I grew up with children of the Owens family and got to learn the heritage first-hand all through the years. Bob Owens, who is one of my best friends, was the "classic-looking" Miami Indian, although he was not full-blooded. Indian ways, and everything about him, were wonderful. Great golfer. So I learned a lot about how they were sometimes looked down upon in Huntington County, but not by the Schenkel family.

My dad didn't think much of golf, so I didn't start playing it until I was sixteen. The high school coach just sneaked me through the golf course. Dad just thought it was a waste of time.

I became friends of the Miamis in Huntington County, in particular, and then as I traveled around the country I got to know more people, like Jack Thorpe, Jim Thorpe's son. Well, all of Jim Thorpe's children, because he was my original athletic hero. So I started collecting things on him, books especially. Of course, there weren't many on him, either. He sort of paralleled the Miamis in that way. He was Sauk and Fox. Eventually, I was made an honorary Sauk and Fox chief. I hold my breath every day that a letter will come in the mail that they are taking it away from me. I am so honored by that. As long as a Thorpe is alive, I know they won't take it away.

Jim Thorpe won two medals in the 1912 games [in the decathlon and pentathlon events], and they were taken away from him [in 1913] because he made five or six dollars in some baseball game. This was a terrible thing. It was discrimination at its finest. The Olympic committee in 1913 went against its own rules since the complaint against Thorpe came after the designated period to register such complaints. Avery Brundage was the president of the International Olympic Committee [1952-1972] responsible for refusing to reinstate Jim Thorpe on the Olympic record books through 1972, and to return the medals to Jim during his lifetime. Jim Thorpe's daughter, Grace Thorpe, had asked Jack Kelly, Grace Kelly's brother, who was a member of the American Olympic Committee, to intercede for the Thorpe family at the gathering of the American Athletic Union. Later, President Gerald Ford acted on behalf of the Thorpe family.

Brundage was in the same decathlon with Jim Thorpe, and Jim was first, the gold medal winner. Avery Brundage was fifth, and it is well known he didn't like Jim from that day in 1912 on, and it seemed to a lot of people he just ruined the man's life. Brundage has since passed away, too. [He died May 8, 1975.] This issue was again raised at the Montreal Olympics in 1976. Bill [William E.] Simon, who was our secretary of the treasury [under President Ronald Reagan] and head of the U.S. Olympic Committee for a while [1976-1982], and I used to talk about it. He said, "Well, I'll just get back to Lord Killanin," when he was the international president, but Lord Killanin tabled the issue when it came up in 1976 after discussions with President Ford. Then, in 1982, Bill Simon talked newly elected International Olympics Committee President Juan Antonio Samaranch into pushing the matter through. The ceremony was held in 1983. Gail and Bill Thorpe, two of Jim Thorpe's children, accepted the silver medal replacements [the originals were gold] on behalf of the Thorpe family and donated them to the State of Oklahoma. They're now on display in the State House in Oklahoma, where they should be. All seven children received silver replicas of the medals.

Bill just kept working and working and working on the International Committee and finally one day IOC president Samaranch got tired of Bill and all of us harping on it, and they had copies made. The originals were given to the runners-up in 1913. The trophies Jim Thorpe got are reportedly in Lausanne, Switzerland. The gold medals have since disappeared, according to Grace Thorpe. Those were gorgeous medals. But just getting the duplicates made the family very happy. Grace Thorpe is now seeking to restore her father's honorable past.

I liked Mr. Brundage. He was the world's greatest jade collector. A very wealthy man from Chicago who could be a wonderful guy to talk to. He was at the Munich games [in 1972] where I was the anchor man [for ABC-TV sports coverage]. That was his last. He made a lot of tough decisions there. I give him a lot of credit for continuing the games regardless of the tragedy. [Terrorists killed members of the Israeli Olympic team.] [Brundage said,] "Don't let this interrupt things." A lot of people would have stopped. He said, "We will go on," and he had a memorial service before [the games] went on. So you know, I'm just telling a fact. It's strictly a fact about the Jim Thorpe medals.

I did get to meet Jim Thorpe. I came to New York in 1952 to do [broadcast] the New York Football Giants games. I wasn't paid very much money so I could afford only a small room. It was in the Parkmont Dome Apartment complex on West 57th Street. In the corner of the building there was a bar. It was owned by Willie Pet, a great boxing champion. I'd go in and sit down, and Willy was tending bar. [This time] he gave me the head movement like "look to your left." I did, and there was Jim Thorpe sitting right next to me. The reason I didn't recognize him was that he was so thin. He was ill. But I introduced myself, and I asked him how long he was going to be here. I bought him a beer. He said, "Why?" I told him, "In my room, I live in this building, I have a picture of you. Would you autograph it?" I ran and got it, and he autographed it. It may be one of the last autographs because it was in 1953, and he died that year. But his hands are in it [the photograph]. He had these marvelous hands. He didn't want to talk necessarily about Native Americans; he wanted to talk about the Giants when he found out I was the new Giants announcer because the Giants had all these contracts of his when he'd come to do an exhibition of drop kicking, and all these things. I'd try to tell him, "You don't need all these contracts. Chris needs them for his library." But he saw through this. [The Giants' organization] knew I wanted to collect them. They still have them. They gave me copies. I said, "Some day, if you ever do give the originals back to Oklahoma or the Thorpe family, it would be great because they'd get a charge out of seeing that he signed up for $500 in those days for an exhibition." I'm talking the 1940s, hey, and he was a real star, Jim Thorpe.

My favorite Miami chief was a man called William F. Hale [Chief Mon-gon-zah], who had fought in five wars. He was born in an army barracks. That's where they put the Miamis in Marion, Indiana. They were the Meshingomesia Clan members. He was so good at disseminating information on the culture of the Native Americans, on all tribes. He was a fantastic man who lived to be eighty-seven. We were friends for, I don't know how many years. I used to have to defend him among some of his own tribal members because they thought he was sort of a buffoon. But what they didn't realize was that he was the only one pushing their culture forward, trying to teach them to preserve their heritage. They had been so pressed down that they didn't think, "We'd better preserve this heritage."

Chief Mon-gon-zah had a great ceremony at "The Appeal to the Great Spirit" in Muncie, where I gave him an Indian peace medal, one from my collection, and he gave me a war bonnet. Having that honor was just incredible because Chief Mon-gon-zah had worn the bonnet he gave me. "The Appeal" is a 1929 bronze cast replica of the original Cyrus E. Dallin statue. The original was made in 1904 and rests in the Boston Museum of Fine Arts. This statue shows an Indian chief on a horse, arms extended in appeal, pouring forth his troubles in prayer. It is the fourth and last of Dallin's Indian statues. The replica of Dallin's statue was donated to the city of Muncie, Indiana, by the E. B. Ball family in memory of E. B. Ball, father of the present E. F. (Ed) Ball, who has been instrumental in building the Minnetrista Cultural Center. The statue is actual horse and man size.

Chief Mon-gon-zah never got into the type of tribal affairs that the Miamis have had now for quite a few years [to bring back the heritage]. It is just too bad Chief Mon-gon-zah can't be alive to see what progress has been done and be able to enjoy the progress. I think it's been phenomenal.

[Several years ago] I got a call from the athletic director [at Haskell Institute] just out of the blue. He said, "Will you speak for our athletic banquet." You know, I would have walked there because I just couldn't wait to get there and see more and learn more. So I spoke at the banquet, and they sort of adopted me. I threw it open to questions and answers. I had said, during the talk, "If we could adopt an Indian child, Fran and I, we certainly would." A lady in the audience asked me, "Now, if you had the luxury to adopt an Indian child, what would you teach the child?" And just like that it came; it was my sincere answer. "To teach him or her to be proud of their heritage." It was the right thing to say, in her mind. From that moment on they sort of adopted me. I'd go back every chance I had, and pretty soon they started a foundation board, and I became a board member and tried to raise funds for them. In more recent years I've been able to raise a little more with friends like Mike Shinkle and everybody else kicking in.

Haskell was a trade school, which was necessary because students came off the reservation. They still do. So they learned to be a carpenter, learned to be a mechanic. And if they had artistic talent, Haskell had a heck of an art department way back, and to this day, so it was a great opportunity. The first year I was there 103 tribes were represented on that campus. The president [of Haskell] invited me to a graduation ceremony some years back. I was never so impressed in my life because they wore their beautiful native dress—all of them, whether they were graduating or not. Oh, it was incredible. But strangely enough, now they put students in caps and gowns. To me, it's rude; that's in reverse. I guess the board of regents maybe thought it would get them closer to the Bureau of Indian Affairs or some other ridiculousness. Who knows?

Now, may I offer a very special salute to a very special person who has been on my mind and who is often on my mind. The person is Lora Siders. She has been a consistent glue that has held the Miami People in Indiana together through many difficult times and years. There is no one who would come to your assistance quicker than Lora, should you need help or have a problem, whether you were Miami or not. A phone call would get her there, and if that wasn't necessary, she would go about in her own way, finding the right people to help you out. And that's why she has been, and is, such a pillar in the Miami Nation. She epitomizes the word "Elder" in any tribe. When I think of her wisdom I am awed. I have often asked Lora questions when I did not know the answer. She always thought it out. She thinks about her answer before she answers you. She has always been to me the Peru Miami's version of Bob Owens of the Huntington Miamis. She is considered "It" from all along the Wabash River to Oklahoma. Both of these people act the part, have felt the part, and both have been very proud to be descendants of the great First Americans. These people have so much to do with this part of the country I grew up in, along the great Wabash River. I grew up in Miami country, and I've had an opportunity to see it all "up close and personal," as they say it at ABC Sports. There is no person I admire more than Lora Siders. Lora is a friend. I love her. I can't say enough good about her, a pillar, just like the sacred rock pillars on the Wabash which the Miamis hold so dear. She's that strong in everything she does, and it is always in such a consistent Miami way.

Other Miamis have been important in my life, like Sue Strass and her daughters, Angela and Katrina. They are descendants of Chief Lafontaine and Chief Little Turtle. Sue is a niece of Robert Owen. She is fierce in her loyalties and beliefs. She is a fine historian. All members of the Strass family are my cherished friends.

From an oral history interview conducted February 18, 1995, at Peoria, Illinois.

FRANCIS M. SHOEMAKER

MIAMI

RETIRED PRINCIPAL CHIEF, MIAMI NATION OF INDIANS OF THE STATE
OF INDIANA
BORN NOVEMBER 13, 1912, IN WABASH, INDIANA

I was born November 13 at five-thirty in the morning. Five or six minutes later my twin brother was born. His name was Charles but everyone called him Chas. I came from a poor family. My mother was Indian [Lillie Marks Shoemaker, granddaughter of Chief Chapendoceoh]. My father was of German descent. Three children are left; my brother Clarence, my sister Helen, and myself. Two brothers died, including my twin.

When I first got on the Miami Nation Council [1937] my grandfather used to beat my legs with his cane. He'd say, "Now is the time to sue the government for recognition." He weighed something like 350 pounds. He was a big man. Nearly beat my shins off.

Back in those days they [his grandfather's generation] wouldn't learn to speak or write English. He worked hard, but when the paper mill burned down in Marion, where he lived and worked, he couldn't get another job. That was uncalled for. It was his own stubbornness about English.

For us, his grandchildren, we went to public school. Junior high and all the way through high school. My brother Clarence went to work for Ford Motor Company in Detroit. My other brothers [Curtis and Charles] and I continued to live and work in Wabash, Indiana. We grew up among blacks and Catholics. I worked as a conductor with the Big Four Railroad until I retired.

We used to go to the Indiana State Fair [in Indianapolis]. They gave us space—a booth—to put up a display to show what Indian People had done. It was supposed to be intertribal but it turned out the Miamis did it all. We had photographs and artifacts, such as arrowheads and stone

186

Francis M. Shoemaker

Miami

*Late Principal Chief, Miami Nation of
Indians of the State of Indiana*

of a tomahawk, things like that. Then they ran out of space so we stopped going. We used to go down and stay all day. Once, when we went, a man gave me an amulet of tobacco. I still have it.

I have two traditional suits. One is of buckskin, the other of cloth. They were cut out and made by Miami women. I wore them for traditional events.

In the 1980s Huntington [Indiana] honored me during their parade. My sister Helen and her children have been living there. We used to ride in a lot of parades. We won first prize for our float in Peru [Indiana] in the summertime Circus City Parade. In Roann [Indiana] we won the novelty award in their falltime parade.

We went to Miami, Oklahoma, where Chief Leonard honored me. The government split families [during removal] so some are living here and some are in Oklahoma. Families here and there are the Stitt family, the Avelines, the Mongosas. We also went to Oklahoma before Chief Leonard's time. We went with Bob Mongosa and Carmen Marks, Lora Siders' sister.

Things happened so long ago, you tend to forget. My dad taught my twin brother and me to box. Back in those days we did exhibition boxing at the armory to help Dad out. People came and paid to see Charlie and me box. We played basketball. Later on I was in the National Guard for twelve years.

My grandfather was active in tribal affairs. So was my brother Curtis. My mother spoke Miami. My grandfather wouldn't teach me. He said, "Everybody will be talking the white language." I heard Miami spoken, but he never would teach me. He never taught any of us. I disagreed with him. But he wouldn't teach us.

When I was growing up my family did traditional things. We canned things for the winter. We ate the traditional way. Elders ate first, children ate last. We had good gardens. All our food came from there. My grandfather gave the prayer in the Miami language.

My grandfather told stories about Indian-white fights.

When I was chief I wore a Miami headdress of turkey feathers. That's what we wore. Turkey feathers. The feathers stand straight up around your head. The more we did, the more feathers we had coming down our back. You got a feather to add on a string coming down your back. Fifty-four years of tribal service. That's a lot of service. Now, no one knows me. The younger ones don't know me.

If I were still chief I'd go talk to the governor—to Bayh; and I'd talk to President Clinton. In the old days you had to fight your way in to government offices. We would send people to Washington but if they didn't know the protocol they couldn't get in to see the right people. They'd run out of money before they got to see anybody. Might have to borrow money to come back to Indiana. Now, you also have to know the paperwork.

One time I gave Governor Otis Bowen [Indiana, 1973-1981] a tomahawk and tobacco. The governor gave us a promise that went like the treaties. Everything turned out to be a lie. He promised state recognition. The Miamis need recognition for our kids' welfare; for health, for schooling, to start with. There is no law in Indiana where we could apply for state recognition. We need to start with a law. Birch Bayh, when he was senator for Indiana, used to do so much for the Miami Indians. Evan Bayh is another thing. We need to get with whoever is the next governor. Before I pass on I would like to see President Clinton about recognition. You have to keep going. Every time you stop you're in trouble.

We got the old school building [at Sixth and Miami Streets in Peru, Indiana] for a tribal complex. It happened this way. One day a school board member told us we should bid thirty-seven dollars and a string of beads for the abandoned school building, and call it "the Manhattan compact." But we decided to bid one hundred dollars. No one else put in a bid so we got it. Soon after that one of our members asked if anyone put up the hundred dollars we had bid. We said, "no." So he gave us a hundred-dollar bill. We took it to a bank, deposited it. That's how we got a building to benefit the tribe [used for social services including child and elder care, youth programming, and cultural activities]. They're naming the cultural center "Little Fox," after my Indian name, Pa-pa-quan.

From an oral history interview conducted March 11, 1995,
at Miller's Merry Manor [Nursing Home] in Peru, Indiana.

LORA MARKS SIDERS

MIAMI

ELDER, MIAMI NATION OF INDIANS OF THE STATE OF INDIANA

BORN MAY 3, 1919, IN WABASH, INDIANA

I am part of two clans. I think most of us have become so mixed up, we take in several clans. I'm from the Menqousa clan that takes in Richardville and Godfroy, which makes us Loon and Turtle. My Indian name is Monqua, which means Loon—the sacred bird of the Miamis.

We lived in a house high on a hill, south of Wabash. I remember visiting neighbors. They had a long porch that was up high, and you could look out over the river. This lady always made cookies. My father wasn't much to visit any place, but he would go down and visit those neighbors. I can remember him carrying me up the hill, up the steps to the orchard, through the orchard. I was probably three and four years old at that time.

When I was five years old, we moved to a farm where we had what we called a garden and a truck patch. We had cows, we had pigs, we had guineas, we had chickens, we had geese. I can remember having donkeys on the farm, so we had everything we needed to survive. Later years, after my mother died and my father died and I had to come to town, I found out what hardship was when it comes to food and surviving. No place for a garden. You had to purchase every bite of food that went into your mouth.

I can remember paying off for a bed. I can remember paying off for tires, at sometimes fifty cents a week. Fifty cents. If I raised it to a dollar, I was really proud of myself. But I would save my tips until I had at least fifty cents, and I would make a payment.

My father was not Indian. However, he was raised among the Indians, and his best buddy was Indian. He went to an Indian school. He

Lora Marks Siders

Miami

Elder, Miami Nation of Indians of the State of Indiana

wasn't one to talk a lot about anything to anybody. He was kind of a quiet man, and if you got him to talk it was rare. But he understood the Miami language fluently. When we would go to reunions, the men would stand around and would talk in Miami. And Mom would say, "What did they say, Pop? What did they say, Pop?" And he'd say, "I'll tell you when we get home."

I didn't learn till years later they were telling dirty jokes. Some of the women understood it, and you'd see them grinning over at the side. But a lot of them didn't understand. My mother didn't understand Miami because her mother told them when they went to school and learned the white man's language they would no longer speak the Miami language in their home because they had to live in the white man's world. She was afraid they would get mixed up or wouldn't speak English properly if they talked the Miami language in the home. So, as her children went to school, they were told not to speak Miami at home. However, Uncle Joe did. Talked Miami pretty fluently. I have an idea when he was away from his mom he probably kept on using Miami. Besides, he ran around with boys who used Miami. But most of the girls were taught not to use the Miami language after they started school. Not just my family, but the others my mother would have run around with. So we did lose our language that way.

My father was a kind man; he was the breadwinner. He worked on the interurban for the Interurban Company besides farming. Mom got out and farmed with the horses and the plows. Of course, all of us kids had to get out and pull weeds and hoe, when we got big enough to handle a hoe. We hand-pulled weeds away from the corn so the corn plow could go down the rows.

Between the two of them, my mother and my father, if anybody didn't have a home, they had one. My mom was a midwife. She was allowed by the state to have three unwed mothers a year come into our house. She never took that many a year, but they came. And they stayed with us. I blame my bad memory on this because Mom would tell these girls when they came, "You don't have to give us your full name; you just give us something to call you." But when they live with you, pretty soon they begin to tell you things about themselves. And we were cautioned, "Don't tell anybody." I would say I forget, and I got so I really did forget. It was during the Depression. We lived on the farm, and I didn't know you could can anything in less than a hundred, hundred in quantity. Usually two or three hundred. I just thought that's what you're supposed to do. All winter long people would come every night. Different families would come to our home, and Mom would give them a can of green beans, can of tomatoes, can of peaches, can of pears, a big basket of canned goods. And she would say, "The only thing I want is bring this basket back." And, of course, milk and homemade bread and eggs, anything they needed. I thought, "Mom, why do you push this stuff off on these people?" I didn't realize these people needed that much. I had to grow up and learn what that need was.

I would say our tribal law and positions of authority are pretty much the same now as from the time before. We've kept that pretty solid. We've changed some. It's been a necessity. But basically we're still the same. I notice that these younger ones who argued with me are now agreeing that it's good to keep the old ways.

The mother has been the predominant authority figure. In our family Mom was predominant. That's probably why, when I got married, I had such a hard time because I wanted to be boss and so did he.

When I was a child we had what we called powwows. I can remember sitting cross-legged; I can remember having the ceremonial pipe, which was one with the tomahawk. There was a tomahawk on one end and a pipe on the other, and the men passed that. The women didn't sit in the circle; they sat back of the circle. However, since I was a child, I sat wherever I wanted, and sometimes I sat on the ground in the circle. Sometimes I sat on these different men's laps because they were all like extended fathers to me.

At the same time, some of the women would be cooking things in these big iron pots. That was our summertime meetings. In the wintertime we did go in the house and, if there were enough chairs in whoever's home the meeting was, we sat on chairs. And if there wasn't, some of them sat on the floor. But we continued to have meetings winter and summer. I didn't know what they were about. I just knew we met, and I always went with Mom to these meetings. White people were not allowed in an Indian meeting. Up until, oh, I'd say twenty years ago, you still didn't. The white people still did not come to the meeting unless they had a part, like an attorney or a state senator or a federal senator might. Those kinds were all that were allowed who were not Indian. The doors were monitored. It's just been in the last twenty or twenty-five years that we've allowed spouses and other white people to come in. Now, recently, our council meeting is a closed council. We began to have some problems; some white people wanting to make changes that we are not ready to make yet. I'm not saying they might not be good changes; I am just saying we are not ready for them. So our council is a closed council. However, our general meetings are reunions; all of these are open to all of the families.

My mother made us very aware that we were Miami Indians. She also made us very aware that if someone we knew who was Miami didn't want the outside world to know they were Miami, we didn't tell, because it wasn't popular to be Indian. I knew I could have cousins that were, and I could have cousins that were not wanting to be known as Miami. This is one of the things that I was taught from way back. Mom told me a lot of stories about Grandma. Mom must have lived Grandma's life practically over again because Grandma always took anybody in and kept them, took care of them. Grandpa was a medical doctor, but he was also a herb doctor.

Things Mom told me had come from her parents. My great-great-grandfather was the principal chief, and she told me all about Chief White Wolf and Bets, and Betsy's sister, Mary Godfroy. Some of this is in history books now, but a lot of this is not written down any place. There was a woman chief when the Wea were coming back from the Wisconsin area to what is now Kankakee, Illinois. There the Wea group of Miamis got so large they decided they would have to divide. They divided into four sections, the Wea, the Piankashaw, the Kaskaskia, and the Illini. This had to be back in the early 1700s or maybe even before. Chief White Wolf was a descendant of this woman chief.

Mom told us about where different ones in our family were up around what is now Chicago, which means "little onions." And she told a lot of the stories about the beginning. We have the same story of Jesus walking and being here that is in the Bible. That he was here and walked around Lake Michigan. This always puzzled me because, well, I thought, how did he get up there? These stories come from when I was little. As I have read the Bible, there are so many things that compare with our language. One of the songs, the only song I can remember— Mom used to sing a lot of Indian songs—but the only one I can remember was "Yahweh, yahweh, yahweh hey; ana dia ana yahweh; yahweh, yahweh hey; ana dia ana; yahweh, yahweh, yahweh, hey; ana, dia, ana, yahweh; adia, yahweh, yahweh, yahweh, yahweh, yahweh, he ada." That's as much as I remember, but I asked my sister before she died. I said, "Carmen, what did the words of that song mean? I can remember Mom singing it, and I can remember how she sang it." Oh, Momma had such a beautiful voice. Carmen said, "It's a prayer. It's a prayer for a little boy to live or a young man to live." How many times do you read in the Old Testament "yahweh"?

Many of our People were converted. And the missionaries said the reasons why the Miamis were so easy to convert was that about the only thing they changed was what we called the Great Spirit, and they called it God. One of my uncles was converted, and he spoke. And they would go from one place to the other. They didn't always have a specific church, but they did have a number of churches built—not like the churches that are here now. They were kind of like longhouses. They were a meeting place for God then. It was the language; they dropped the Great Spirit. However, I kind of go back to the Great Spirit because to me that says it all; the Great Spirit says more than God.

When the Native language is not spoken, a lot of family closeness, I think, is lost. It seems as though we kind of go in waves to and from family, because some of the families get so destitute they have to go someplace else to work. So they get lost from us. Then, as they get older, they get this inner yearning. It's something inside people, to come back. That's our greatest loss; we lose each other.

We've been having classes. Language is where we're working with others to write it down. J. P. Dunn had written it down on three-by-five cards. Now a young man from Berkeley, California, is working on the language. Chief Floyd Leonard of the Miami of Oklahoma and I were at a symposium in Huntington, Indiana, probably back in 1983, and I heard him speak. They say the same words we do, but it's like the North and the South. You have a different way of saying it. He said some words his way, and it took a minute for me to remember what they were. And I told him, and he said, "You do understand Miami." And then I told him how we say those words. We still use the same words, but it's a little different accent to it.

We have craft classes. Part of our group in Huntington or in South Bend are having thirty people coming to those classes. So many of our people went up there a number of years ago because of the Studebaker plant, Bendix employment. There was nothing here in Peru for them, and that's how our people got spread. They had to go where there was work. They worked one place, and if they closed, they worked at the other place. They practically migrated a whole family from the Muncie-Anderson area to up there.

What I'm trying to bring to my own family is that they need to take care of themselves and their families first. And second is the church, and third is the Miami Indian tribe. I want us to be educated in both ways, I want the Indian education, and I want a white education so that they can be able to live and not know poverty the way of some of our Elders, who died as paupers. It wasn't because they were lazy. They were energetic, they were good people. But they didn't have the education to take them out of poverty. I want education for our people.

The people in the photograph on my wall, the Elders who have passed on, I can remember conversations with them. I can see them dance. All I have to do is just close my eyes, and I can see each one. No two dance the same. That's the point of Miami, of Indian, dancing. You start from within your heart. This is where the dance starts. It starts in your heart. This chief in this picture, Chief Godfroy, was my kidhack [school bus] driver when I first started to school.

I've been asked by teachers to come and talk about the Cherokee. And I tell them, "No. If you want someone to talk about Cherokees, you get a Cherokee Indian to talk to you." And they're dumbfounded when I say we're not the same. "But you're Indian." Because you're Indian, they think you ought to know everything about all Indians. And I explain to them, "You look at the continent of Europe. You've got France, and you've got Spain, Portugal, Holland, Italy." And I said, "that covers less area than what we do. That's how different the Indians are."

From an oral history interview conducted July 22, 1992, at the headquarters building of the Miami Nation of Indians of the State of Indiana, Peru, Indiana.

BILLIE SMITH

SHAWNEE

ELDER, LOYAL SHAWNEE TRIBE OF OKLAHOMA

BORN SPRING, 1924, IN CRAIG COUNTY, OKLAHOMA, ABOUT THREE MILES
WEST OF WHITE OAK

It was during the spring that I was born. They were camped in at the ceremonial grounds. My dad was ceremonial chief then. He walked towards the ladies. They were in the woods picking leaves, and they said, "Oh, see our chief coming. We'll know soon, huh, what cheer, what new person we're going to have to help us." When he told them it was a girl, then they said, "We have a new member." And they gave names out there, where they were picking leaves. My Indian name explains that I would be a Coon Clan. We are named after animals. We use raccoons in our ceremonials. It was a real joyful time out there for everybody.

When I became a teenager and got married and had children, I moved away with my husband, where he had to work. During those years I was away from this area. We would come back, but we lived in California. Then, when the kids got all grown, we came back. That's when I started with the tribe again. You don't forget, especially when you have a mother and father who spoke Shawnee. That's all they spoke. They were full-bloods.

I still have my dad's allotment, which is my grandmother's allotment. Land that has never exchanged hands. Never has been sold. This goes back to when they had the Indians come to Oklahoma.

My mother's father, Samuel Perry, was one of the children that the government came and grabbed up with the Indian children and took them off to government school. He had long hair. They cut his hair off. They told him he couldn't talk Shawnee any more, and they taught him Christianity. So that's where he learned to become a Christian. He was not allowed to practice our traditional ways. When he came back, and

Billie Smith

Shawnee

Elder, Loyal Shawnee Tribe

when he got children, when my mother was born, he taught her that, the Christian ways. They couldn't teach the traditional ways. The government wouldn't allow it. You had to follow Christianity. So that's why I was brought up in a Christian-taught way.

They never did catch my dad. He was faster or something. They had been practicing the traditions when they came from Ohio. They moved from Kansas to this area in Oklahoma. That's when the government gave them allotments. My dad's mother's maiden name was Susan White. She was married two or three times. When they allotted her land she was married to James Bigknife.

They had a little one-room schoolhouse, which was just about a mile from our house. We had to walk to school. Before we went to school we did not have English, so I was about six before I spoke English. When we went to high school the school bus came to our corner, but we had to pay tuition, which was, I think, $2.75 a month. I was not eligible for government school because I lived too close to a public school. We had it rough all the way around. This was back in the hard times. My parents said, "We just can't pay for your tuition." Nothing to do but to drop out. That's one reason why most of the area children dropped out.

My parents stayed together; they didn't divorce. A lot of these Indian kids that have education, their parents broke up. The government school would take a child from a broken home. It still breaks up families because you can get better advantages if you separate. That's one thing my husband and I didn't do.

I don't remember too much about my childhood, outside of what my mother told me. She told me, "You know, you were raised up in a hammock." And I'd say, "No, I didn't know. Tell me." She said, "We always had a hammock. We didn't have baby beds."

In the corner of the house, from one side of the wall to the other, they put a rope crossways and a stick to hold it apart, just like a hammock. Then the blankets were rolled over it, and that's where she put me, when I would fuss. And I would swing there, and I was content. She said, "You were ready to walk by the time you got up out of there."

I remember—now we call them mobiles—hanging right above there by the hammock. She left it there a long time because my brother is younger than I am, and he used the same thing, so I remember him looking at it.

Dad raised corn. And he went out to the cornfield in the fall, and he would get corn stalks. And he would fashion a bird's body out of corn stalks, and he fixed it so the wings came out of the center. And he fixed it so there was a beak and the little feet and the tail feathers. And he stuck a pin in the middle of it, and that was on a string over our hammock. When the wind circulated in the house, it made it move. Well, naturally we were content.

For the longest time, Dad at Christmastime or at wintertime would make ornaments like that. I don't make these things now. There are too many commercial things. Too many conveniences to be making our own. I remember that as being our first toy. It did keep us quiet. When we were toddlers we had them on a stick and carried them. I remember so many things, at different times. They don't all come back to me at once.

My very favorite friend during those early years was an elderly woman. She was really old, or so I thought. Her name was Susan Flint; she was an invalid. She taught us ways. She had no children. She was a tiny woman; she walked on crutches. We would go get her, my little brother and I. He had a little wagon. She would sit inside it. We would pull her from her house to our house. And on the way she would tell us, "You see this medicine here, this weed here, and this good medicine."

On the way—we would travel maybe half a mile—we would stop and rest. We were, I'd say, seven and ten years old, around that age. We would take her to our house and keep her two or three days. During the night she told us stories. That's why we liked her so well. She would sit with us. Our mother and dad would go to church, so while we stayed home she would tell us Indian stories. Well, there were so many we enjoyed, we would just have her repeat them over and over again. They were stories from back in Ohio, and then things she learned as a child. We had wintertime stories, and we had summertime stories. They could be told only in certain seasons. I've told these stories to my children. We really enjoyed her company. She was the one we were closest to. She had no granddaughters. She had three grandsons. She called them her grandsons; they were her niece's children. You always claim relation to somebody. We called her our aunt. We called her Na-na. That means aunt in Shawnee. And we talked Shawnee to her. We tried to teach her English. She was something. She is buried here in the cemetery at White Oak.

The other Elders, the friends of my mother, would come to the house, and they would spend time with us. And they would go over the stories, so we heard them many times. We had our favorites. I feel like these stories taught us different things. We studied the animals. We could understand them better. We try not to mistreat them. If there were animals that we were going to use, they taught us to give thanks for those before we were going to eat this animal. That is the same way with our medicine. There are so many things which will be lost unless there is someone who is really interested. We have a certain site where we use the cedar. When we take it from the tree, we have a certain ritual that we go through.

We have our traditional beliefs. I know the prayers. But there are changes in the ceremonial dances. I think that's the biggest change from the old way.

From an oral history interview conducted December 13, 1994, at the headquarters building of the Loyal Shawnee Tribe of Oklahoma, White Oak, Oklahoma.

DAVID LEE SMITH

WINNEBAGO

TRIBAL HISTORIAN AND CULTURAL PRESERVATION OFFICER, WINNEBAGO
TRIBE OF NEBRASKA

BORN MAY 24, 1950, ON THE WINNEBAGO INDIAN RESERVATION

I was never proud to be an Indian at the beginning because
Indians were looked down on. We were taught that cowboys were
better than Indians. So when I was going to school, I always wanted to
be a cowboy, not an Indian. It wasn't until I was thirty-one years old and
I was going to Morningside College in Iowa that I was proud to be an
Indian, because I went through all kinds of racism and that stuff.

When I was growing up, I went to St. Augustine Mission. There was
racism against Indians on all sides. I never experienced that so much as
when I was in high school, when we used to go around the area and beat
athletic teams in football, track, and basketball. They hated us; they
warwhooped; they called our girls squaws.

When I attended Morningside College my sister Pat and I were
warwhooped and [they] were calling my sister a squaw, laughed at us.
In our terminology squaw means whore. I couldn't take any more, so I
went up there and wiped two of them out. They were going to expel me
from school, kick me out of college. But me and my buddy, Bob Conley,
who was director of Indian Studies, were going to Channel 9. [School
officials] got wind of it, and they called up a big meeting of all the R.A.'s,
and they laid new ground rules: "Anybody that says any prejudiced
remarks on either side will be dismissed from school." During that time
they put me on probation. They put one of those other football players
on probation, too, and kicked two of them out. After that, every time I
walked into the dining room, the whole dining room shut up because of
what I did.

I was proud when the American Indian Movement started its organization. I was proud to be an Indian because at least someone was

202

David Lee Smith

Winnebago

*Tribal historian and Cultural Preservation
Officer, Winnebago Tribe of Nebraska*

defending our identity. Before that, no one wanted to be Indian; now everybody wants to be Indian.

I was never so proud as when my Grandmother Lucy said it's better to be an Indian than any other race. And I agree with her today. The Creator made us different, and we are different. Damn proud of what we are. We would never want to be anything else.

When the tribe moved from Wisconsin to the Winnebago Reservation in 1863, we were ruled by what we call a clan system. It was twelve clans. There was the Air Division and the Earth Division. The Air had four clans, and the Earth had eight.

In the Air was the Thunder, the Eagle, the Hawk, and the Pigeon. On the Earth was the Buffalo, the Bear, the Wolf, the Deer, the Elk, the Water Spirit, the Fish, and the Snake. Each one participated in tribal affairs. For instance, the leaders come out of the Thunder Clan. Besides making Thunder Clan leaders chiefs, the Thunder Clan also had important functions connected with the preservation of peace. The Bear Clan, next to the Thunder Clan, was the most important in the tribe. Its functions included regulating the hunt, broad disciplinary powers, and they effected the orders of the Thunder Clan chief.

The Hawk Clan concerned itself mostly with warfare. It was authorized to make life and death decisions when captives were taken in war. Its name later changed from Hawk to the War Clan. The Eagle and the Pigeon probably had responsibilities of supplying soldiers in warfare but otherwise performed less significant roles. The Pigeon Clan became extinct in the second decade of the eighteenth century, but it came back today in Wisconsin. The Wolf Clan possessed powers of considerable importance. Clansmen were called minor soldiers and were closely linked with Bear Clan members. Their functions resembled those of the Bear people, and they probably assisted the latter. They also performed social welfare roles regarding public health and safety. Observers described them as specialists in the area of health. They monitored the quality of water used by people as well as by animals.

The functions of the Water Spirit Clan weren't said to be important. Some say they had a rivalry with the Bear Clan that served as chiefs of the lower division. Others claimed that the Water Spirit people originally ruled over the entire tribe, but were usurped by the Thunder Clan. Water was very sacred to the Water Spirit Clan, as it was to the Wolf Clan. The Elk Clan had certain functions relative to the distribution of fire throughout the village, the hunt, and the pursuit of war. Limited information indicates that the Deer Clan had responsibilities that dealt with environment and weather.

The Buffalo Clan acted as town criers to the chief, announcing the report to the village every morning. They also acted as intermediaries between the chief and the people. To be admitted as a member of this group in the Buffalo, a warrior had to count coup four times. The small Fish and Snake clans were of late origin. There is little information on the Snake People and practically none on the Fish Clan. Besides supplying clansmen for warfare, their main function was sanitation. That is, they performed jobs around the village that no one else wanted to do. In warfare, they formed the first line of defense. They always located their lodges on the outer perimeters of the village, and they acted as listening posts for intruders.

We also have what we call friendship clans. All clans are patrilineal. The friendship clans were arranged so that the Thunder Clan's friendship clan was the Warrior; the Eagle, the Pigeon; the Bear, the Wolf; the Buffalo, the Water Spirit; the Deer, the Elk; and the Fish, the Snake. This arrangement provided for services between friendship clans on four different occasions. Number one, if a member of one clan visited his friend clan, the friend clan was obliged to perform various services such as supplying him or her with food and shelter for the night. Secondly, clans sought revenge for injustices committed against a friendship clan. Third, the friend clan could be called upon to lend a clan name to an individual being honored in a Naming Feast. Finally, clans always arranged a burial of members of a friend clan. When members die, a friend clan always dressed and painted a body according to clan specifications. The wake lasted four nights, and the achievements of the individual were recounted. This way, clan affiliates assisted a soul on its journey to the next world. After the burial, the friend clan sponsored a feast for the relatives and friends of the deceased.

When the Winnebagos moved to the reservation in 1863, the clan system broke up. When we lived on the Missouri River bottom, we tried to bring it back. There was fourteen villages, all clan villages. But there was no more warfare. And our clan system was built around warfare and religion. When they tried to take our religion away, that shattered the last remnants of the clan system.

Around 1670 there was a chief of the Thunder Clan which we know as just Thunder—Chief Thunder. He died in 1728. When a chief dies, he usually names his brother's eldest son to succeed him. In this case, he had no son. He had no brothers either. He only had one daughter. Her name was Hopoe-kaw, which translates into Glory of the Morning. So the twelve clans got together in 1728 and debated for three days what to do. Who should succeed Chief Thunder as chief?

Hopoe-kaw married a Frenchman called SaGrevoir DeKaree in 1729. Out of that union she had three half-breeds. The first boy was called Spoon—Chou-k-ke-ka; the second boy was called White Breast Deer—Chah-monk-sha-ga; and the girl was called Oak Leaf.

There were ten kids born to Spoon, so a lot of the DeCorah names go under that. White Breast Deer had three boys. The first of his boys died. The second boy was called One-Eyed DeCorah. The third boy was called Waukonhaga, or Waukon DeCorah. That's the line I came out of.

Waukonhaga fought with Miami Chief Little Turtle in the border wars of the 1790s, along with Naw-kaw, Hu-jop-ga or Four Legs, and White War Eagle. All of them fought with Tecumseh and The Prophet in the War of 1812. Waukonhaga's first family got killed on the Mississippi. He married again and had two kids. One was Chief John Waukon and the other was a girl called Mrs. Henry Big Fire.

The DeCorah family is pretty big. On my side, we are descendants of chiefs, but you don't go by chiefs any more. One of the well-known DeCorahs was Chief Little DeCorah. He had a boy named David Too Tall DeCorah, who had a daughter called Angel DeCorah, who was the first Winnebago educator and artist. She graduated from Hampton School, studied under Howard Pyle; graduated from Smith College; and later went on to Drexel Institute and taught at Carlisle [Indian School].

Some of the traditional things that were still practiced when I was a child were our powwows—our celebrations. We started our first celebration in 1866 in honor of Chief Little Priest who was killed fighting the Sioux. So we have the oldest traditional powwow in the United States.

The Medicine Dance—our traditional religion—was still practiced, but when Paul DeCorah died in 1956, the religion went back to Wisconsin, to the Wisconsin Winnebagos. The Bear Clan tried to bring part of it back in 1988, called the Medicine War Bundle. It is still practiced here by a small group of Winnebagos. Most of the Nebraska Winnebago people today are members of the Native American Church. Half of the tribe believes in that religion.

Our clan system doesn't function any more, just naming ceremonies. A lot of it is done through the Native American Church. Sometimes I give names to my own people, to my own family. We have a dinner, and we give names. We also have Coming Out of the Mourning Ceremony. When you lose someone important, you are supposed to mourn for four years. They don't mourn those four years any more. But some do, like

my sister did when my dad died four years ago. She went into mourning; didn't dance for four years. Some do it for one year; some don't
mourn at all.

Of the twelve hundred people on our reservation, only about sixty of
them are fluent Winnebago language speakers. There's over one hundred who can speak it somewhat. Most of the language was beaten out
of us during the boarding school era of the late 1800s and the early
1900s. If you spoke your language you were beaten. I remember when
I was going to school from 1955 to 1963 at St. Augustine. Sometimes if
a person spoke the language, they had to eat soap until they threw up.
That's how a lot of people lost their language.

I think when you lose the Native language, you lose your culture. A
lot of our cultural traditions are not being practiced. There are ceremonies that are not being practiced. One of our major ceremonies was the
Green Corn Dance. The Winnebagos are hardly farmers any more, so
we don't practice that. At our annual powwow we once had traditional
dances. They don't do that any more either.

We are bringing our language back. We had a woman come from the
Southwest to put language curriculum in our institutions—our high
school, grade school, Head Start, and college. We started a language
program four years ago. We put the language into a computer system so
that it's now ready to go in Head Start and into grades one through six.
So each month, they try something different. I hope a lot of the students
pick it up so they can be fluent speakers by the time they are in high
school. That's the goal, and I help any way I can.

When I went to school in Winnebago public school from 1965 to 1969,
there was nothing in the curriculum that told us about Indians. Nothing
about our own people, the Winnebagos. I knew what everybody else
knew—that we come from Wisconsin—and that's it. Nothing else. Today there are only two Indian teachers in our whole school system, and
they're both in lower grades. Most of the Caucasian teachers don't like
to take college classes about Indians. I think that's stupid. If I went to
Spain I'd study the Basques, I'd have to know Basque culture. If they
come here and teach here, they should know a little bit about our culture
because each culture is different. Each Indian tribe is different.

Grandma Lucy's stepmother took care of both her and her sister. She
used to tell my grandma that she was in the massacre of Wounded Knee,
and she would always cry. She said that they were running from the
field when she heard a gunshot and felt her whole shoulder go numb
and was bloody. She turned around to get her baby, and the baby had a

big hole in it. And the baby fell off her back. She kept running, went back looking for it but couldn't find it.

Dad used to tell me a story about Chief Little Priest. In 1866 Chief Little Priest formed a group called Company A, Omaha Scouts, to fight the Sioux. It went against his heart to fight his own people, but he was tired of being moved around so much—from Wisconsin to Iowa to Minnesota to South Dakota and to here. He wanted to bring peace to the Winnebagos after so long. So he joined the Cavalry as a scout. He fought in South Dakota, North Dakota, Wyoming, Montana. In 1866 he journeyed west to Fort Kearney, to Julesburg, and had a running fight with Red Cloud's Oglala Lakota, Northern Cheyennes, and Northern Arapahoes at Powder River. Two months later he also had a fight with some Oglalas and Northern Cheyennes at Tongue River. It was at Tongue River that Little Priest got shot four times.

The Lakotas used to have a song honoring him. In that song it says that Little Priest stood behind a rock and fired. Every now and then he'd show himself and fire again. But every time he showed himself, he turned into a bear, and they couldn't kill him. Finally, his medicine wore out, and they were able to kill him. But he didn't die. His group of Winnebagos arrived and rescued him. This scared the Sioux. His medicine was powerful. The Winnebagos brought him back to the reservation here, and he died of his wounds that year.

Chief Gray Wolf called a council of all the clans, and they decided to honor him and all veterans. This is why we have our annual powwow today, in honor of Chief Little Priest and all veterans.

There are no tribal healers today on our reservation. Some people know stuff like I do, though. Certain herbs out there; certain plants that we use for medicine. We're having a class this week on tribal healing, herbs for medicine, and foods.

We believe in spirit beings. We believe that when a person dies, they journey to the spirit land, and it takes four years.

There's a story that I treasure. It's called "A Chief Journeys into the Spirit World to Bring Back His Wife." This story explains to our younger generation why we have a four-year memorial feast and a four-year wake when somebody dies. It explains where the spirit goes and what happens to it if we were good or if we were bad. It used to be told at wakes. We have a four-day wake when the family goes into mourning. The family usually doesn't have to spend much money because the whole reservation donates for food and tries to make the people happy. We sit with the body, and on the last night they play games. On the last morning, one of the Elders hollers, and it releases the soul on its journey. Then we bury the body, and for four years afterwards the family puts on a feast to thank everyone for what they did. That's the Winnebago way.

If I come back in a hundred years, I would like to see the Winnebago tribe as it is today. I mean, I would like to see the Indians looking Indian, with brown, bronze, reddish skin. Also I'd like to see our people speaking our own language, singing our own songs, and practicing some of our traditional beliefs.

I'm in the process now of trying to write the tribal history from the beginning to 1816, Book One. Then I would like to have Book Two, 1817 to today. These would explain the culture of the Winnebagos. See, we were at war ever since the Winnebagos met Samuel de Champlain at Lake Superior in 1614. It was in 1634 that we met Jean Nicolet. Our tribe was 25,000. Three massive epidemics in the 1630s reduced us to only 125 people in 1640. The other Winnebago people at that time—the Otos, Iowas, Missouris—migrated onto the plains in 1638. They were once Winnebago people, too. They took the new names when they left Wisconsin in 1638. But they have their oral traditions; they have their oral beliefs; and they still remember that they were once part of the Winnebago Nation. That's why today they call us their grandfathers.

Those are some of the things I'd like the future generations to look at when I'm gone. Look at my books. Look at mythology. Look at the history. Be proud of what we did. We didn't want to fight, but we had no choice in the matter. We were forced into it. As my grandpa always believed, "It is better to die than to cry."

All the people here don't like to be called Native American, because everybody is native to this country. If they call us Indians, it still has that derogatory slang to it. So if non-Indian people want to call us something, call us by our tribal name, which is Ho-Chunk. That's what our name is, Ho-Chunk. That means People of the parent speech—the first voice.

Winnebago isn't our name at all. It comes from a Potawatomi word winpyeko, meaning people of the filthy water. The French called us Puants, people of the stinking water. The Objibwa called us Una-bu-gay-oshu, meaning people of the filthy water.

We lived along the Fox River in Wisconsin, and every year it stunk up the high heavens with dead fish. And that's how we got our names. But our real name is Ho-Chunk. The Wisconsin branch of Winnebagos is changing their name back to Ho-Chunk. The Winnebagos here today go by the name Winnebago. But a lot of things are named Ho-Chunk. I started and founded the Ho-Chunk Historical Society to promote tribal culture. I founded it last year with three Winnebago women, some outsiders, and some of the people from the community college.

We have a tribal business called Ho-Chunk Incorporated, which generates revenue coming off the reservation to our tribal coffers. For instance, I am a board member, and our company buys businesses, make businesses, and buys real estate off the reservation so we don't have to rely on the casino so much.

A lot of Winnebago Woodland cultural traditions were lost in 1640 when we were almost wiped out by diseases and warfare with the Illinois people. We kept a lot of our beliefs. Most of our belief systems were Siouan, like the Santee Sioux. But we've changed our political and social structure to that resembling Algonquins. If anybody wonders about traditional culture, that's when we lost it.

Today on the reservation some of our traditions resemble [those of] the Plains [Indians]. We still have Woodland patterns to our dress; we still have the floral designs in beadwork and in quilt work. What made us unique as a Woodland tribe was that we were a horticultural people. Even during the fur trade [era], we were horticultural people. We never suffered as other tribes did that followed the fur trade, who hunted for the pelts. When the pelts weren't there, a lot of them starved.

The turtle plays a most important part in our mythology. He was the one that created the world. He was the one that got The People on the right path of life. So he is important. The Winnebagos have built hundreds, even thousands, of turtle mounds to honor him. See, the white people at that time never asked the Winnebagos who built them or why they built them. They always have to have some scientific explanation for them. But that's what makes us different from other Woodland tribes, even though we fought with other Woodland tribes. We did join them when we knew that the only way to unite and beat the white man was to have a group. But there weren't too many of us then, and we got beat.

We have our culture—solstice ceremonies, equinox ceremonies. We're bringing back our language. We believe in sticking together. The whole town, even though they fight politically, when someone dies they get together and help each other. We're glad of that, and we have our Native American Church, which unites families. We lost most of our land during the Indian Allotment Act. Three-quarters of our reservation was allotted out, so we're trying to buy our land back today.

The biggest change that our tribe has experienced today is in the field of education. There're more and more Indians getting a degree. Back when I was growing up there was hardly anybody with a degree or advanced degree. Most of our tribal leaders had no education whatsoever. But today we have lawyers; we have teachers; we have educators; we have doctors. So now we can fight the white man on his own ground, which is law.

If I had a chance to speak to future Winnebagos, I would tell them the stories of my life, the hardships that I went through, the poverty I was brought up with. We were a large family, and we lived in a three-room house. We slept maybe four or five to a bed, but we were happy.

One thing I'd like to say is that alcoholism is wrong. A lot of us experienced it. A lot of us quit. Some of us didn't quit. A lot of us died. That is wrong. I would like this young generation to stay away from that. And also to try to regain the spirituality that was lost, that was forced out of us. I was telling some white girl a while back that our priest in the Catholic church prays with an eagle feather. He uses cedar in his ceremonies, also holy water. He wears beadwork on his vestments, and in the church there is a carved eagle. And she said, "There is no way we'll ever use an eagle feather." That's our belief. We believe in the eagle. They have their own beliefs.

People wonder why we never leave the reservation. It's because it is our home. We were born here; our people live here; our people are buried here. We have ties to the land. Our architecture isn't that good; our homes aren't $100,000 to $200,000 homes. But it's our home. Our little gardens are small, but they're our gardens. We still practice traditional horticulture methods.

Even now, you see a lot of people going to wakes. Even though they have jobs, they go to wakes and support. Even eating with the family that is in mourning helps out, and that's what I see happening today. There's a rebirth of this culture, but I would like to see the younger generation look at themselves and like themselves inside.

Our child welfare program is doing pretty well. We have a good director who is doing an excellent job. He is trying to cut juvenile delinquency down. Before, they took kids off the reservation and placed them in white foster homes out East or out someplace. In older years, they lost their culture completely.

The Indian Child Welfare Act says that no Indian child shall be taken off the reservation any more. If they take a kid away from parents that are bad, the child is usually given to one of the parents' parents—the grandparents, the mother or father, or one of the brothers or sisters. Second choice goes down the line to the cousins, and another choice is to an Indian family on the reservation. If they go off the reservation, they can go to an Indian family off the reservation. They try to keep the Indian culture of the kid intact.

We had bingo to start with, but we don't have it any more on our reservation. The Winnebagos' casino took over about four years ago. It generated a lot of help to the reservation. Before the casino came, our tribal council worked for nothing. There was no money for education or anything else. The whole town was going to hell.

Casino revenues put more money into education. They started Ho-Chunk Incorporated to buy real estate and hotels to bring in revenue to the tribe. They started new programs on our reservation, like Healthy Start, the Diabetes Project and Drug Dependence Unit, and Land and Water Management. We're buying land back. We support the college, the high school system, and we're reinvesting money.

I see the attitudes changing toward the elderly. A lot of the elderly are sent away to old folks homes, sent to bordertown old folks homes. But our tribe is in the process now of building an old folks home on our reservation here, which is a very good idea, because when I get old I want to be here among The People, not someplace else with other people. I want to be with the people I know; the people I grew up with. And when I die here, I want to be buried here among The People so my spirit can roam.

We don't have too many sacred sites on our reservation, but we do consider wherever we bury people as a sacred site. Today the Ho-Chunk Historical Society is in the process of fencing these sites off, so farmers won't bury them under their plows. People's graves are sacred to us. Most of our sacred sites are in Wisconsin and in northeastern Iowa. We don't believe in digging up people.

I think that as our tribe approaches the twenty-first century, we are better off than we were when we were approaching the nineteenth century. At least, we are better educated now. We know what is going on. We could fight for our survival all over again in courts. That's what I like the best about it. We won't be looked down on any more because we are Indian. Every one of us is proud to be an Indian. I can speak for the whole tribe.

From a self-recorded oral history interview conducted June 5, 1995, at the headquarters building of the Winnebago Tribe of Nebraska, Winnebago, Nebraska.

NICKY GLENN SMITH

Shawnee

Member, Loyal Shawnee Tribe of Oklahoma

Born August 17, 1951, at Claremore, Oklahoma

My dad was part-Indian of the Peoria tribe, but back in his time that was the period when it wasn't good to be Indian. Everyone tried to cover up their Indian blood because of the persecution by the white people. So his family never did pursue his ancestry to find out how much Peoria he was. My mother is full-blood Shawnee. My grandmother's grandfather was a ceremonial chief, and he is the one that officiated at the funeral of Black Hoof. My grandfather was Amos White, Sr., who was ceremonial chief, and he had a son, Amos White, Jr., who was also a ceremonial chief. We always called them by their Indian names, Summaka and Jimmo. They're both full-blood Loyal Shawnee. My Shawnee name is Nickesimmo.

When my father married my mother, his family disowned him because he married "one of them damn Indians." His family came from Missouri originally and moved up around Chelsea, Oklahoma. I believe he was in Chelsea when he met and married my mom. He never talked about his family, and I never met any of them. They disowned him, and he disowned them as well.

I was not born on an Indian reservation. My first recollection is of a three-room house on allotted land. The government allotted the Shawnees' property for each head of the household, and it was on my grandfather's property. When he passed away, it went to my grandmother. It was allotted land as opposed to a reservation. Allotted land wasn't under tribal jurisdiction; it was rather an individual allotment of land by the federal government.

If my family had just moved away after my grandfather died, the land would have remained in trust. Nobody could have done anything

213

Nicky Glenn Smith

Shawnee

Member, Loyal Shawnee Tribe

with it. It wouldn't have gone back to the tribe. It never was tribal property. It was allotted to the individual head of the household and remained in that person's name in trust by the federal government. So we still own that property. If we moved off and left that property for a hundred years, it would still be our property.

Before I was big enough to carry a rifle, I'd get to go hunting with my uncle. We'd go hunting in the woods, shooting squirrel. He wouldn't let me shoot until I got a lot older. When I was eleven or twelve, they gave me my own rifle, a single shot 22. And I'd get to go hunting by myself; I'd take off in the morning and go squirrel hunting. I might come back for lunch, might not. Just the solitude in the woods.

And there was the time they chose me for the Buffalo Dance. I was just a kid; they'd use little kids in there. Sometimes we had trouble finding enough men to be there for the whole dance, and so they'd indoctrinate younger kids into the Buffalo Dance. And we would wear our paint, come back up out of the woods and partake in this ritual. It was special to me. We'd wear a clay paint on our bodies and war paint— ceremonial paint—on our faces. Our clothes, usually it was jeans and tennis shoes or jeans and boots, but with no top.

I was always proud of being an Indian. At one point I remember in school we spent a year in Parsons, Kansas. My dad found work up there in a refrigeration plant building refrigerated trucks. I went to school in Parsons, Kansas, for a year. It was a little old public school, and I remember there were all white kids in there. There were no Indians at all. I looked around and saw this dark-headed kid, and he might be Oriental. I looked at him and asked him what tribe he was. He said, "I'm Japanese."

We were playing on the playground, and this one little girl for some reason or other got irritated with me. I was playing with these other little boys and gettin' rough with them, and she called me "one of those damn Indians." The tears just welled up in my eyes, and I looked at her, and I says, "Yeah?" And then I realized there is prejudice against Indians still. The little girl was just reflecting the views of her parents. I thought, "Yeah, so what? I'm proud of it."

When we came back to White Oak I was aware of prejudice, but that really brought it home after that. We rode a school bus back and forth to school, and there was some vandalism on the school bus. And I know who this little boy was that did it; it was a white boy. But the first person the principal would come talk to would be us Indian boys. He said, "We know you did this." He said, "You better confess right now or I'm gonna paddle you, or talk to your parents."

We'd say, "But we didn't do it."

I never did tell on that white boy for doing it, though. The principal was unsure that we did it, or didn't do it. But we were the first ones he came to, to ask if we did it or not.

Grandmother always said that Indian children didn't cry. It would be a life-threatening situation for Indian children to cry. It would give away their location. The soldiers would come—she'd call them pony soldiers—and they would kill us.

My uncle Jimmo and my grandfather Summaka were both ceremonial chiefs. Any Elder could be the namer, the ones who gave the babies their names. It wasn't specifically one person. They were to keep the traditions, to make sure when it came time for our ceremonies that they followed an exact and precise course, an exact way of doing things. There were no shortcuts. It was a prescribed, set ritual that you went through for every aspect of our dance from the day we first camped to the last day. On that day after the dance, there was a performance, a ritual, and it was to go just like beadwork, just one after the other. And if you get the beads out of sequence, the pattern of the beadwork would change, and we weren't supposed to change these things.

There was an even distribution of power between the women and the men in terms of tribal government. A woman was never referred to as a chief; she was just what we called the Head Old Lady. Old Lady was a term translated into English from the Shawnee language. It means an Elder, one who is supposed to be old enough to know all our traditions. On the other side was the Head Old Man. There was an equal distribution of power, and the seat of power would change according to the seasons. The Elder women or the Elder men would determine when our dances would be. The Council of Elders was chosen from people who knew our traditions, knew how they were done in the past, had been around it all their lives, knew the correct ways.

I don't speak my Native language fluently. I can speak it. When I'd come back from public school, or I'd get out of school, I'd spend summers with my grandmother, my grandfather, my uncle—they all spoke fluent Shawnee. And I'd stay the summer with them, and my grandmother rarely spoke English. She could read and write English. My grandfather could speak just very little English, and he could write his name. My uncle was fluent in English and Shawnee. So whenever they're telling you to go get something, to go do something, and they're speaking in Shawnee, well, it's easy to catch on. I'd respond to them in Shawnee.

If you wanted to learn Cherokee, you could go in any gift shop and buy a complete manuscript on Cherokee. We're more a secluded private life. Our rituals shouldn't be made public. It's not like a game or a pageant or something for the general viewing public. This is held sacred to us. We don't want people to come in there and video it, or take snapshots of it, or recordings of it.

The only distinction among the Shawnee tribes is the name put on us by the United States government. Whichever agency we registered at, then we became the Loyal Shawnee, or the Eastern Shawnee, or the Absentee Shawnee. We're all Shawnees. The purpose of the government was assimilation, to divide us up. Some of our tribal members didn't feel like we should be put on reservations, put within a prison camp, which is basically what it was. And they would take off when they were still fighting, and they'd go fight in other portions of the war. Some of our old and our sick couldn't go; they had to stay at the main camp. The main camp would be moved to another state. We were all Shawnees, all the same tribe; we all spoke the same language.

Band was another white term they put on us. I'd say tribe. We, the Loyal Shawnee, are not on a reservation now. The Loyal Shawnee had the distinction of being placed on allotted land within the Cherokee Nation. The Shawnee Nation was whole at one time. Then, depending upon which moniker they wanted to put on you, you became a tribe, or band, or nation. If you were going to talk about Shawnees, then it would be the Shawnee Nation. [Each Nation is] distinct in culture, distinct in our language, distinct in religious ceremonies. That [is what] places us as a Nation. Nation is a federal term—U.S.A. term.

I'd like to see that our dance is still going on a hundred years from now. It's our religion. It's the way we believe. It's supposed to be what governs our everyday life—to help one another, not attack one another, or spite somebody. And to give thanks for our very existence. Each dance has a different name, but each one is a part of our religious ceremonies. It's the way we give thanks to the Creator.

In the springtime, we have what we call a Spring Bread Dance, and we bake loaves of bread similar to the Christian offering of unleavened bread. The Bread Dance was to give thanks to our Creator for our survival through the winter. We have a thanksgiving dance called a Green Corn Dance in midsummer that was to thank our Creator. We used only the purest and cleanest things that we have to build our things that we use as—I guess you could call them offerings—that we offer to the Creator for His help in producing these things for us, for letting them grow. Then there was a Fall Bread Dance that was to thank Him again. It was always for thanks, to pray for help, help for our crops, help for our ill, help for our Elders, help to find the right way, for His guidance, to give thanks for everything that He provided for our very existence here.

And there's yet a fourth dance that is handed down from generation to generation, always in the same family. It was given to us through a vision to one of our tribal members. It's called the Buffalo Dance. And it has been going on as long as there have been Shawnees. It can be held in the midsummer to late fall. The harvest of our crops used to determine all that, and the moon does figure into it. There are four ceremonial dances each year. The Buffalo Dance wasn't participated in by the entire tribe, just the people of that clan—the descendants of this person who got the vision. It's up to those families to carry on.

As to my preference for the term Indian, or Native American, personally, I prefer to be called Shawnee. I'm not from India, and I was a Shawnee before I was an American. Before I realized that America existed, I knew I was Shawnee.

The biggest change that the Loyal Shawnee have gone through during my lifetime is, I think, overexposure to the general public. The resurgence of the interest in Native Americans has brought us much, far too much, exposure to our religious ceremonies, which should have been kept private, kept within the tribe. Now we have people come down there who we don't even know; what tribal affiliation, what race, or what their interest is. Just to observe; just tourists.

I'd like to be remembered by future family members as one who was totally involved in our ceremonies, that I gave one hundred percent of myself, that I was there to help out in whatever capacity I could. I feel like that's my responsibility—to do whatever it takes to help this dance go on, whether it be to carry water, cut wood, mow grass, help put up tents, take care of our religious functions. I wanted to help in any way I could.

From an oral history interview conducted June 12, 1995, at the Minnetrista Cultural Center, Muncie, Indiana.

LAWRENCE FRANK SNAKE

DELAWARE

PRESIDENT, DELAWARE TRIBE OF WESTERN OKLAHOMA

BORN 1955, IN OKLAHOMA CITY

My Indian name is Peponah Gitomen. My grandmother gave me that name, and it means little boy always on the move or always running, always moving around. My sister has two different names. One of them is Waylopamah, and the other one is Ninemokway. One's Shawnee, and one's Delaware. But they both mean pretty girl or pretty little girl. My dad's Indian name is Kuskahkakwah. It means little pig, or pig, so I have to watch the way I say his name. His English name is Lawrence Snake, and he is former president of the Delaware of Western Oklahoma.

People have asked me about the origin of the name Snake. There's two or three stories on how that started. One of them was that a young boy—a little bitty guy—was always running around hissing and making snake noises, crawling up over the logs. So they started calling him Snake Man. My grandfather took the Man off of it and just had Snake.

The Eastern Delawares—Cherokee Delawares—use the title of chief when referring to the tribal leader. Why some Delawares tribes use the term president and others use chief, I don't know. I guess we just took our constitution when we made it and modeled it more after the United States Constitution, which is kind of ironic because the United States took the Indians' way of life back in the 1700s and modeled the United States Constitution after it. It's kind of one of those full-circle deals, where you come back around again.

The Algonquin tribes and the Iroquois Confederacy, all up in the eastern part of the United States, all have the same type of government, the same form, which was a three-tier government in which they had checks and balances. And Thomas Jefferson and Benjamin Franklin thought it was quite unique. They spent a lot of time with the Indians learning it. This is one of the things that kind of struck me as odd being in junior high and high school in an American history class. And the way that the books taught us, it was like one weekend these guys decided to sit down and write a constitution. You know, hey, let's get together and do this. But in reality, once you start checking into it, you find out they had spent a lot of time with the Indians finding out their culture and how they worked the system itself and that they did have the forms of government set up.

What also strikes me as interesting, or different, is that they take our form of government and form the United States government with it, and we're supposed to be savages, heathens, primitives who don't know anything. And yet they, they take ours and mold it into their own.

As for our tribe's future goals, we would like to set up a whole lot of social programs. We would like to have our own hospital, our own elderly center, retirement/community center, and dental clinic. We're looking also into trying to buy up and establish a reservation because our land that we have now is this ten acres on which we sit right here. We have joint tenancy on about 1,500 acres back there behind us with the Wichitas and Caddos. That's called WCD—Wichita, Caddo, Delaware. You have to get all three tribes to concur on anything, and that's next to impossible. We're the smallest tribe with about 1,340 members. The Wichitas have about 1,800, and the Caddos have roughly 5,000. So the Caddos want everything paid per capita or by population, and the Wichita and the Delawares want it paid in thirds.

The Delawares were allotted lands under the Wichitas. A few got allotted under the Caddos, but most of the Delawares got allotted under the Wichitas, and so the Wichitas claimed that this was all their property in the first place and that the Caddos and Delawares were here just because the government put us here.

But we're not underneath the Wichitas; we're not under anyone. We're totally three separate nations over here. We have our own government. We're federally recognized, the Wichitas are, and the Caddos are. We would like to buy private land around here and have nothing to do with the other two tribes.

My mother's name is Dorothy Alene Hildebrand Snake. She is, I think, half or three-quarters Cherokee and German, hence the name Hildebrand. On my father's side, my grandfather was Frank Snake. Frank got killed by lightning back when my dad was probably about eight years old. The story goes that my grandmother, after the burial, came into town looking for my grandfather, actually his brother, Willie. Came in looking for him because it was the old way where the brother took the brother's widow as his wife. She came into town and said, "Come on, we're going home."

My childhood home was like any one of the number of block houses along the street in Midwest City, a suburb of Oklahoma City. I first realized that I was an Indian when I was real little. We used to go to dances when I was little, probably three, four years old. And we used to go to ceremonies. From where I lived in Midwest City, Shawnee, Oklahoma, was closer than coming down here. Also, my great-grandparents had some Shawnee in them, as well as Delaware. They used to travel back from here to Shawnee, which is approximately seventy-five miles. We used to go over there to the Green Corn Dance, Squirrel Dance, and other dances when I was little.

These were ceremonial dances. It was kind of like praying for a good crop. Then later on during the year you harvest the crop. Then you pray to give thanks for a bountiful harvest.

Typically, I did not dress in ceremonial dress when I went to the dances, at least not very often. I was out running around. I was a little kid. The first time I wore a ceremonial dress was when I was probably about four years old, and I had a mohawk, and I was down here at the Indian fair. I had on a bustle and leggings, and I was in the parade. I was standing in front of our '55 Chevy. That was in downtown Anadarko at the Indian fair. As to whether or not I was proud to be an Indian, I couldn't say. I was a kid. I don't know. All I remember was standing up there smiling at the cameras and waving.

There was a whole lot of prejudice while I was growing up all the way through from when I was real little, and it still goes on every once in awhile. We got hassled by the police one time because of being an Indian, and they kind of picked me out because I was with a group of non-Indians. What was strange was that there were white and black both, but they came and grabbed me and yelled, "Come here, Chief," and this kind of stuff. And the whole time I was laughing. I told them, "I'm not a chief." They didn't understand what I told them. So even growing up in grade school, junior high, and high school, there'd be a group of two or three that would start picking on you because you were Indian.

I learned how to fight when I was little, probably just six or seven years old. And I was really good at it. I was real athletic, and there was not a sport I couldn't play. And that made a lot of the white kids mad. I was very good at anything that I did, so they were always calling me "little squaw" and this kind of stuff. Like I said, I learned how to fight when I was real little and through that fighting gained a lot of respect. I learned how to win. The winner of the fight is the one who walks off. And that was always my philosophy. I was always going to be the one to get up and walk off.

There were different words used that offended me, words such as squaw, blanket ass, just about anything you could think of. These were mainly white male protagonists and older than I was. For a while I didn't want to be an Indian. I couldn't change it. My skin color is dark. At that time it was a lot darker than most people because I stayed outside all the time. I played from sunup to sundown; I was outside roaming around. So there were times when I would pray and every-thing else not to be recognized as an Indian.

It hurt. But through the fighting of it, I showed that I was better than they were. My grandfather on my mother's side was a preacher, a Nazarene preacher, so in the home I grew up in, you turn the other cheek, you walk away, be a better man. I couldn't do that. I couldn't walk away. I could walk away after the fight, but I wasn't one to turn around and just walk off. My mom and my dad were that way; they both just kind of gulp down, turn around, and take off. I see now, the way that things happened, and the respect they had from others, [their way] was good. But me growing up, I wasn't going to put up with it. And I didn't.

It's hard to say when I was proudest to be an Indian because I was always proud of my identity, although at times I wished I wasn't an Indian. But a lot of my self-esteem came through sports, knowing I was usually the only Indian kid out there. I always made first team; I'd always been a starter and I wouldn't accept anything less than that for myself. That made me very proud. I kept thinking about Jim Thorpe the whole time, and if that guy can do it, maybe that will give me something to keep going on.

I guess the one time when I was the most proud to be an Indian was when I was voted the football king or football beau in ninth grade, and I didn't know anything about it. I mean I knew that the cheerleaders were all getting together; they do the voting. I was probably more surprised than anybody when they called my name to go up. And that was one of the times that I thought, "Here I am an Indian doing these things that I've seen all these others do and never thought I'd be able to do it."

I graduated from high school but never learned my tribal language. I know a few little words, and that's about it. They have a language class now that is instrumental in getting going again. They started a program the fall of 1994. I've heard that there's two students there that are real exceptional. One of them's a girl named Crystal Silverhorn, and the other one's a young man by the name Mick Loden. They've gotten to where they can pray in the Delaware language. It's great. And then we have Crystal's grandmother and my aunt who teach. There's very few fluent Delaware speakers left down here, and my grandmother's one of them. She's ninety-eight [in 1994]; she's not going to be here too much longer. We're hoping another twenty years, but that's not going to happen. Other than that, there's maybe only two or three that speak fluently.

That's on my father's side. My aunt Gladys grew up around my grandmother and my great-grandmother. My great-grandmother, Duncsee or Tennessee Thomas—a little bitty woman—spoke nothing but Indian. She spoke Delaware, Shawnee, Comanche, Apache. And my grandfather Willie, my grandpa Frank, and my great-grandpa Willie Thomas, who was the last Delaware chief, all spoke several different Indian languages. People think of them as just Indian languages, but I'm talking separate total languages. It would be just like talking Russian, French, German, Portuguese, but they are talking Delaware, Caddo, Wichita, Kiowa, and Comanche.

My parents did not speak Delaware. We did use certain phrases— little things such as meetis, that means come and eat, or food's on the table. It's just an expression. Havuptzi which means hurry up, get over here, hurry. When my dad and my aunts and uncles were growing up, in order to go to school, they had to go to boarding school over at Riverside. They got beat with a rod for speaking the Indian language, so they had to learn English. Then when they would go home, the kids would all talk English, and they'd get beat up for not speaking their Native tongue. My grandparents started picking English up so we lost the language because of the boarding schools. Most of the Indian tribes around here were Kiowas, Comanches, Apaches, Wichitas, Delawares, and Caddos. Plus there were some Choctaws, Chickasaw, Cherokees, Sauk and Fox, and a variety of the others. They all got severely punished for speaking in their own language.

When the Native language is not spoken and cultural traditions are not practiced, everything is lost. Everything. When I was real little, we used to sit around on Sundays when we'd get tired—most times we were outside playing—we'd come in and sit down and listen to the Elders talk. And Grandfather Willie was telling a story that he'd been told by his grandfather that once the Lenape (or the Delawares) totally lose their language that's the end of the world.

That's similar to the Book of Revelation in the back of the Bible; when certain things happen it's going to be the end of the world as we know it. That's the same way with the Indian way. To me, language and culture are the same thing. We could probably go on without our Native language by still talking English and still having part of our culture. But, to me, language is the culture. That's what separates us from the rest; that's what makes our group here unique. That would be the same as what would happen to all the Germans or Japanese if they lost their language. When you lose your language identity, you lose that little thing that separates you from the rest. If I were to die tonight and were to come back a hundred years from now, I'd like to see that my people have brought back a lot of our old culture—a lot more of the language, mainly the old ways that we lived.

I see non-Indians trying to buy in, trying to be an Indian. There's a lot of people back East that are running sweats—sweat lodge ceremonies— and charging $1,000 for people to go in. There was one man back there that was claiming to be Lenape or Delaware. For women he charged an additional $2,000 to impregnate them, so they would have a fully Delaware baby. This is just a crazy way for someone to make a living.

There's a lot of ill-respect or no respect for Elders right now that I see in children that we didn't have back then. We had respect. This goes way back. A girl and her dad called me—she's doing a report on the women Lenape. Seven years old and she wanted to know what they're doing now. They were from Georgia. They called up, and they were on two different phones. She asked me: "What about your culture? And why do Indians respect the Elders as much as they do?"

I said, "Well, the thing was, a long time ago the Elders were the ones that taught the children. The Elders stayed at the camp, and then they took care of the kids. They were the ones that taught the children; they were the ones that explained the culture to the children; they were the ones that taught them the religion of the tribe. The Elders were the ones that taught. They were the ones that gave them love. They were the ones that hugged them, because the parents were out working."

That's what I would like to see in a hundred years. Get back to the old part of it. As for the message that I would like to leave for the non-Indian population, my very first thought was that we would have better immigration laws next time. The reason I say that is we were the ones that made the first treaty back in the 1600s with William Penn. I've heard other tribes say that Lenapes or Delawares were responsible for all of this. Could be or could not be. We're all basically people; there's no doubt about that. There's certain values in life that I think are not exactly unique to the Indians. It's mainly respect for each other. To me, the Elders and the children are very special.

Aunt Martha's Prayer is real long. The old folks used to tell us, "The longer the prayer, the better." They used to pray for everything—each blade of grass, each little ant. This prayer is a lot longer than what they've translated, but its title is Aunt Martha's Prayer. It says:

> Now my father, I've got to say good words. Let us find ourselves alive with the morning light. The true words will come to us. When we wake up this day, welcome. When we see daylight in the world of ours, we are thankful, Father. We are thankful for letting us live this long—letting it cover everybody. I pray about the birds and the bees; they realize they have another day to live. Now you made this world round and put it here. This world you put us in and you're giving us this message and I hope it affects everyone, no matter what you look like as long as you have heart. Even the beasts and the birds and the little birds have another day. They begin to sing and make noise because they know it's becoming daylight, for we live on this earth. Even after daylight they fly around; and they can also find food. We're glad when we get to see the morning. Thank you Father for not forgetting us; [for] the light of the sun. Father, there is no end to your thinking. One of these days that's the way it'll be. You have shown us, Father, everything you have done, like a flowing river you have shown us the way. What you say never ends. Thank you for everything on behalf of the whole world; I thank you for every way of life. Now we are sitting around this table, and we are poor. We have lost everything, our Delaware language and our ways. No one older than us can carry on our traditional way. The people [who] know the culture best have been picked by you and are gone. If you can, grant us our wishes, whatever we beg for as a group. We pray no disease will hit us. We are all like our brother and sister since so much blood runs in us. Now this white person who is related to us are all kin, but that is the way of our blood flow. This is the reason I am making this prayer talk. Help us in our cultural preservation. Give the Delawares wisdom, I am begging you, that you give me another day and that I'll walk again. Watch over us; it is daylight. Take care of us and guide us on the path that we are going, holding our hands, Father, for we do not know what is ahead of us, and we don't know how to get that corner of us. Do you hear me, Father? I am repeating, praying for the days I've come. I want to believe and follow. To love and help one another.

I am praying as I sit here. I am thankful for the honor of praying. Give me good words. If I am asked to talk I will not hesitate because I am living that life. I have embraced this speaking. That is the reason I hold the hands of my children and grandchildren. I pray for the mothers and the fathers because they are not teaching the young people. How their lives are pitiful—our young boys and girls. Give me the knowledge to teach them so this religion will continue. Now I'm begging that as I sit here, Father, to you, too, Jesus. Hold our hands so we can follow this one road. Now, that's all I have. Amen.

That's a prayer from my aunt Martha. We called her Aunt Martha. It's an Indian name. But this whole thing was a lot longer than this, but what I'm saying is they pray for everything, everybody. The people that are here, the ones overseas, the soldiers, the service people, the people who are working, bless the family. Then they usually go into the people who are bereaving, the people that are shut-ins in the hospitals, the people that are in the prisons, the people that are not able to go out anywhere. They pray for everything, everybody.

> *From an interview conducted December 15, 1994, at the headquarters building of the Delaware Tribe of Western Oklahoma, Anadarko, Oklahoma.*

RICHARD SNAKE

Delaware

Deputy Grand Chief of the Delaware Nation Grand Council of
North America; Retired Chief of the Moraviantown Delaware of
Ontario, Canada

Born January 31, 1938, in Chatham, Ontario

I can remember living at home with my mother because Dad
was in the Second World War. Just she and I were home pretty all alone
all the time, and we used to go visiting. We took the walk through the
woods. There were paths through the woods at the time because mostly
everybody walked. There was no other mode of transportation, not too
many cars around. The woods and, I imagine, the paths are still there,
but they're probably grown over, because nobody walks any more. You
drive around with a car now. There were trails through the woods
where people walked to different houses. There was nothing special
going through the woods. It was normal life, day-to-day living. Nowadays, people just go for a walk to enjoy the sights, but at that time it was
just a normal thing.

This was back in about the 1950s before we ever got our first hydro in.
Otherwise we had been using lamp lights—kerosene or coal oil. And we
used coal oil stoves during the summer so you wouldn't heat up the
house with your wood stove to cook. Mostly our heat was done through
the wood stove, cooking and heating. Stoves had reservoirs on them for
hot water. If you wanted really hot water, you had to put the kettle on.
Nowadays, everybody goes camping, and they're living like we lived
back then. Today's campout was comfortable living for us every day
back then.

We don't have tribal laws; we just update federal laws as our laws as
each year, each day, goes by. You can't live in the past. You have to
continue on and live. Things have to be changed. The only tribal law is
what they call band elections, custom regulations where the Department of Indian Affairs doesn't have any jurisdiction over our election

Richard Snake

Delaware

Deputy Grand Chief, Delaware Nation Grand Council of North America; Retired Chief, Delaware Nation Council, Moravian of the Thames Band

regulations. The people at a general meeting do that. I know a lot of politicians in our non-Native society wish it was that way, where they could throw their politicians out by just having a meeting. This happens on our reserve. If you become corrupt and the majority says you're out, you're out.

We have band elections every two years, but it can be done shorter so you've got to walk a narrow and straight path or else you're out. You've got to have a different standard; you've got to live a higher level for council service. For civil elections, you're stuck for the full term.

All the reserves have to come under the Indian Act, the Department of Indian Affairs in Canada. It is the Bureau of Indian Affairs in the U.S.

My father was in the First and Second World Wars. He was a blacksmith by trade, so he shoed horses and repaired wagons and machinery. My mother worked out in the surrounding area, Thamesville and Ridgetown, doing housework.

My mother told me the way it was supposed to be when you become chief of the reserve. You're supposed to be looked up to; you're not supposed to be intoxicated; you're not supposed to be fighting. You're there to help your people no matter what, no matter if they don't like you, because they want help. That's the reason I was twenty-eight years in politics, I guess.

Sometimes I wondered, when I was driving down the highway at three or four o'clock in the morning when I could have been home, in bed sleeping, instead of representing my people. My opposition didn't see it that way. They thought it was a gravy job. My mother told me that tradition-wise you had to have certain items in order to run for council. You used to have to have a farm in the past because that was the only way you could survive; a little farm so you could grow your own vegetables and everything else to eat. Ways have changed in such a short time.

In 1965 I got in as a councillor; my first time into politics. I learned from the Elder councillors. In 1969 I was elected chief. My mom told me, when I became chief, in the history of our reserve I was the youngest one ever. Usually you have to be decrepit and have white hair, like what I have now, before you are wise enough to be chief. At the time I was growing up, I thought chief was the worst job anybody could ever have. I would never try that. Well, it is, but somebody's got to do it, I guess.

While I was in office I was a founding member of several groups. One is the Native organization in Ontario, the Union of Ontario Indians. Another is the Chiefs of Ontario. And ARISE, an Indian-owned corporation for economic development to lend money to Native people. Here's a little background on why we started that up. We can't go to the bank as a Native to borrow money because our land can't be collateral. We can't borrow money on our land because it can't be taken away from us. If we forfeit on a loan, they can't come in and say "this is for sale."

The other group I helped found is Indian Agricultural for Native Farmers. They couldn't borrow money either, so we started that organization to help Native farmers. Then I was on the board of directors of Skanahdoht. That's a reconstruction of a neutral Indian village situated about five or six miles from the Munsee-Delaware Nation Reserve, on Number 2 highway. It's open daily for tours.

Native Horizon is another thing I helped start up. It's an alcohol and drug abuse center located in New Credit Reserve, which is the Brantford-Oshweken-Hagersville area. And still another is the Southern Ontario Secretariat. It's a tribal council for this area. Nobody wants a tribal council, but they'll call it something else. And they railroaded me as the lifetime member of the Minnetrista Council for Great Lakes Native American Studies.

I've been a tribal councillor, a band administrator, a welfare administrator. I also worked as a local government advisor for the Association of Iroquois and Allied Indians; that's AIAI. Two other organizations way up north, in northern Ontario, are Treaty Three and Treaty Nine.

There's also a Delaware Nation Grand Council of America for all the Delawares. You read in the history that we were the ones with the Moravian missionaries, with the Bible. That's the reason we separated from other Delawares. So our Delaware tradition has died out. Some of our families use other tribal traditions. People have married into other tribes, and they've got their traditions that they brought with them. So while it's not our Delaware tradition, there is tribal tradition coming back. It is the same Creator, no matter what tribe.

We're getting a lot of traditions back from the Delaware of Eastern Oklahoma and the Smithsonian. This is where we got our patterns for our costumes, or what the wife calls "regalia." We didn't keep our traditions. We have to go out and find them again.

There are two different dialects of the Delaware language. In this area we use the Munsee dialect. In Oklahoma, the Eastern Delaware and Western Delaware use the Unami dialect. It is the same language but, for instance, when you say "thank you," we here say anishiik. For the Oklahoma Delawares it's wanishiik. It's close, but it's a little different. Even so, you still know what it is.

My dad went to the Moravian church before the missionaries left to go back to the States. The Moravian church died out, but the Delawares stayed. The reserve we're living on now had been put in trust of Moravian missionaries, so when they left they just gave it back to the remaining Delawares. They left everything here. The Moravian church is still being used but by another church now, the United church. It's a historical landmark; it's been renovated. It still belongs to us.

The land here is not so different from the land the tribe came from in what is now Ohio. New Philadelphia, Schonbrunn, Gnadenhutten, and Newcomerstown—we walked along the river in Ohio, and it is identical to where we're situated now in Ontario. You think you're in the same place. It looks as if our ancestors were looking for an identical home to move to in Ontario that they had in Ohio.

According to some of the papers the Reverend Zeisberger had, the Delawares still were picking berries at certain times of the year, and harvesting the fish at certain times of the year, and harvesting the corn. That kind of tradition still stayed on. But I don't know of any Delaware religion traditional things. We have to get ours from the Delaware in Eastern Oklahoma because they kept them. They carried theirs on. We're still in the process of learning. But the Eastern Delaware lost the Big House during the 1920s. Everybody has to try to get back something.

The only thing we've got left from the past is a doll. The Department of History of the Presbyterian Church (USA) is repatriating a sacred health guardian doll to the Delaware Indian tribe. The doll represents and guards the health of the tribe and is highly valued as an integral part of the spiritual well-being of the community. A part of the Department of History holdings since the last quarter of the nineteenth century, the doll was donated by the daughter of a Presbyterian missionary, Cutting Marsh. The Reverend Marsh had obtained the doll from a Delaware named Big Deer when he converted to Christianity in 1838. The doll is believed to date to the mid-eighteenth century.

My first language is Delaware. When I went to school, they sent me home again. I couldn't speak English. So they had to send me home to learn English. Now I'm starting to forget Delaware because I've got nobody to talk to. The thing I can't do is count in Delaware. People ask me, "Why can't you count?" I tell them, "In my younger days, I didn't have anything to count." They think that's funny, but it was the truth. Why learn? No material things to count, so you never did learn how to count.

When Delaware is not spoken, you lose your Indian ways; you really can't say you're a Native if you can't speak the language. You lose your sovereignty if you cannot speak your own language. Now we have only about sixteen people in the world who speak the Delaware language. That's including Oklahoma people.

One of the things I was glad to do while I was chief was to get the people involved in knowing that there is another world out there with Delawares in it—in Oklahoma and New Jersey and Ohio—that we aren't the only ones around. And try to get them back to their roots, to the traditional ways.

There was no TV when I was smaller. The Elders used to come over. Dad also used to cut hair, so he sat there, the Elders sat there, they told stories, what went on. And being the young person at that time, it just goes in one ear and out the other. Now I know my ears should have listened, and my eyes should have seen what was going on, what was happening.

My mother's dad's name was William Noah. He was the first Royal Canadian Mounted Police Native officer. His jurisdiction was the entire Dominion of Canada. My mom used to tell me about it because he also had the first telephone on the reserve. He had red hair, and he didn't look Native. Red mustache and red hair. We never did go to family trees. He never checked back, but my mom told me that we had German or French ancestry some place back.

From an oral history interview conducted July 24, 1993, at Bateman's Inn, Ridgetown, Ontario, Canada.

EDWARD LEONARD THOMPSON

DELAWARE

CEREMONIAL CHIEF, DELAWARE TRIBE OF INDIANS (BARTLESVILLE, OKLAHOMA)

BORN 1904, NEAR BARTLESVILLE, OKLAHOMA, INDIAN TERRITORY

On my birth certificate, a Cherokee Indian roll, my name was Edward, and that's all. Army papers also say Edward. The Leonard part of my name was given to me when I was about eight years old by the United States Marshall. That was in the Indian Territory days; it wasn't Oklahoma then. And this marshall was a friend of my folks. And there was an outlaw named Leonard Trainer, but this officer kind of liked this Trainer. He said they accused him of things he didn't do. Said, "I'm going to name you Leonard after Leonard Trainer."

I was born about twelve miles east of Bartlesville, Oklahoma, Indian Territory, Coowescoowee District.

My first ancestor that come to Oklahoma was my father's father. They came to Indian Territory from up close to Lawrence, Kansas. That was a Delaware reservation then. I don't know the year they came here, but it was before 1906 because the folks already had a home, a big two-story house.

When I was a boy, I'd say about six years old, I went off from the house about a couple of hundred yards. There was an old tree that fell over, leaned over. And I was walking along, going down, just walking around. I got close to that old tree, I'd say about fifty feet or more, and I looked up, and there sat an old Indian man on that log. And it must have been springtime, because he had buckskin pants on, buckskin clothes, and the feather in his hair tied with buckskin string. That's the way it is worn if there is no hat. That feather blew like that [waves hand] in the wind.

I stood there a little while, looked at him, and then I got frightened, ran to the house, and told my folks about just what I'd seen. They said, "That was the one that would have given you power throughout life. If

233

Edward Leonard Thompson

Delaware

Ceremonial Chief, Delaware Tribe of Indians

you'd just stayed a little longer, he'd have told you something. Then you could have told what you had seen in that old Delaware Indian church, your vision."

And about forty years later, or maybe about thirty years later, I was in a peyote meeting. Well, I was in there. I was looking at that peyote and praying to make myself well, to feel better and have good health. That's what I went in for. And I was looking at what I call the chief in the middle of the tipi. There sat that old man again. I saw him again. And I think, well, "I see you again." So I told my folks about it. Dad said, "When you're in trouble or something, you'll see him again." But I never saw him any more after that.

My dad said he was just a vision-like. What all Indian boys strive to get. It's something like a guardian angel, you know, through life to be with you. He said, "If you'd stayed, he'd have probably told you something." Well, I ran. I ran to the house. But my dad told me, "If you're ever in battle, you'll see him again in battle."

But, fortunately, I didn't have to get into battle. I was drafted in the Air Force during World War II when I was forty-five years old. We shipped stuff by airplane out into Burma and China. We were at war with Japan. We were stationed in Karachi, India, and in Pakistan.

When I was young, we traveled around in a wagon made by Studebaker Wagon Company. And we also went in a buggy, and we had a two-seated thing they called a hack. It had a top on it. That's the way we went different places. 'Course, when we were traveling thirty, forty miles, that was a long ways. Papa fixed a covered wagon. From here to Vinita, we had to camp before we got there. We didn't go over ten miles an hour in a wagon. We made it a little faster in a buggy or a hack. Maybe the horses would trot, go about fifteen miles per hour.

Papa bought kind of a canvas that we covered the wagon with. It just fits over a wagon and bows over the top. It's like an automobile. You can close it and sleep in there. Of course, they cooked meals out on the ground. Make rocks around and put a kettle on whatever it was and cook on the rocks that would fit a pot or a frying pan.

My father raised hogs and cows and planted lots of corn. We'd sell that produce off of what we farmed, and that's where we got our money to buy things when I was little. And the government was still paying us some money. We'd go to Coffeyville [Kansas] every fall. Go up there and each adult person on the Roll would get about $100 or $75 from the United States government [to compensate for ceded land]. That was a lot of money then.

Old Man Charlie Elkhair was one that came down to Oklahoma [during removal]. He said that sometimes they wouldn't give them time to bury the sick ones who died [along the way]. The ground was frozen; they couldn't dig anyway. They'd make scaffolds to keep the animals from getting the bodies.

The Delawares moved about ten different times between here and the Atlantic Coast. We'd get a piece of land, and the government would say, "This is yours." Well, got too many Caucasians in there, and they took over, so we had to move again. Just moved every time like that until we got down in Kansas—in 1867, I believe. We were the last ones up here by Lawrence, Kansas, Delaware reservation. They liked it. Well, the railroad company got to wanting to have nice trees—forests. They wanted those trees to make railroad ties out of. And the people [railroad workers] would come in and put a house up right on the reservation. The government couldn't keep them out if they wanted to, but they didn't want to. So, eventually, they moved us down here to Indian Territory. We sold that land up there in Kansas and came down here and bought land. The Cherokees were already here, and so we bought land from the Cherokees here in Washington County now. And that is where we settled. The government gave each adult person 160 acres wherever you wanted to file for that 160 acres.

When the Delawares went out there to Coffeyville, Kansas, the first time, they didn't have English names. So the government, or the government clerks, gave them names. A fellow could name himself. I know of one man papa said come through there and heard the name Machine. And [the clerk] says, "What would you like for your name to be?" He says, "My name's Machine, John Machine." All right, they put it down there. He must have never had any children. I never saw any of them since that time that was named Machine.

I guess I was really proud to be an Indian when I got to go to school. Then the government paid ten cents for a pupil a day for each Indian in elementary school. The ten cents was ten cents a day for the teacher. I went to school in a little one-room schoolhouse to the eighth grade. There were white kids in that school, too. They never made fun of me for being an Indian. Nobody said a word. Nothing.

I guess I was seven or eight or nine years old before I first thought of myself as being an Indian. I knew we were different, and our People ourselves called us Lenape. That's what we called ourselves—Delawares. We talked different languages. We had had different beliefs in religion and different ways of getting married. They got married by the old Indian way. But they got married later by a justice of the peace or a judge.

In our religion when I was a boy, we just worshipped the Creator, our Creator in heaven. We called him the Great Spirit. There was a church about half a mile from my home, a schoolhouse. And they'd have services in that schoolhouse. They used to scare me, them old preachers, when they talked about the Holy Ghost, which I would misinterpret. I was afraid of ghosts, and I was scared.

Back when I was a boy, all my people spoke the Delaware language. Then, after awhile, they'd mix it up with English. Well, they'd say tani hach hta, or there might be one who would say, "Where you going?" or something like that and they'd just kind of mix it up. My mother and father both spoke English. Papa went to the fifth grade. He went to the Quapaw Mission over by Miami, Oklahoma.

I can't remember any prejudice in the one-room school, but when I was older I could see they gave more preference to the white kids than they would me. And even in the army, I could outshoot a lot of them fellows and do drills as good as any of them, but they would give somebody else the rank before me. I could see that as plain as daylight. But, generally, everybody treated me good. Most of the fellows that were in this outfit, this squadron I was in, they were from up around the East and New York state, and Kentucky. I was the only Indian in that squadron. They called me "chief" but said it in a good way.

A long time ago among the Delawares, the woman ruled everything. She took care of the house, and everything went through her side of the house if there was a falling out. If she wanted to get a divorce from the fellow, she just tossed his stuff out of the house, and that was it.

They didn't live in those little tipis like Western Indians or Plain Indians. We built little houses out of reeds, like [those that] grow in the lakes. And the women built them while the men hunted. They'd go in the water and get the reeds. Fix them to overlap on the roof so they wouldn't leak. For furniture they had maybe logs or something to sit on, and they had boards like benches more or less. Later they'd sleep on them little benches, and they had the fire in the middle of that reed house.

I became ceremonial chief about 1980. I used to talk at the ceremonies. We were supposed to talk in Delaware at the ceremonies. And that's when I got to be the ceremonial chief. Now, I still perform things at funerals. And name givings, I give Delaware names to anybody. I'm Name Giver.

People might want to know about name-giving. Well, if it was a boy who needed a name, I'd go out by myself and ask God to help me in choosing a name. You can't name a baby with the same name of somebody that's passed away or some man whose name is already living. You have to give an altogether different name. So it's a difficult assignment.

I have prayed to the Creator, "Give me a clue to name this child." An example of this is a Delaware woman who had a grandson and wanted me to name the new grandson. So I went out to my old place, and I said, "Now, what shall I name that little boy?" So I sat out there at the old place and talked to the Creator, "What shall I name him?"

I was sitting under an old walnut tree. And there was a woodpecker up there, "peck, peck, peck, peck." I sat there about an hour, and he was pecking around up there. And pretty soon he flew off. And he didn't fly over twelve or fourteen foot off the ground, and he got about forty feet away from me, and a feather came out of it. It's one of these woodpeckers we call golden wing woodpeckers. Real pretty. And a feather came out of him. I went over there and picked up that little feather. "Oh, what a pretty feather," I just told him that. It dawned on me. I told the Creator, now you've given me a clue—a good feather, a pretty feather. And I named that little boy Oolequin, or "Pretty Feather."

Old Man Charlie Elkhair was the last ceremonial chief. But he inherited that, I guess. He was the one that came with The People from the East. I heard him talk many a time at funerals. He sure could talk English, but when he talked Delaware, he went in order. He'd talk about going back to the beginning, and he'd bring everything right up—cultural beliefs. I try to follow in his footsteps as much as I can. It's my decision as to who will replace me. And I'm training him now, as best I can, to take my place when I'm gone from this world. His name is Dee Ketchum, and he will be the ceremonial chief.

I stopped speaking the Delaware language when I went to school. I had to talk English. In high school they wanted me to have a foreign language. I told them, "I'm studying a foreign language, now." Made the principal mad. He got kind of vexed.

When our people ceased to speak our language, we lost our religion. In the old church, I could feel familiar. Abraham had kind of a temple. It was similar to that. Faced east. And some of the ceremonies—if I read the Bible right—coincided like with our church. We had three clans in there—the Turkey and the Wolf and Turtle clans—and they sat in different parts of the church. When you were a young boy you were sent out away from home to go into the forest to get some spirit, someone to talk to you, give you a vision. And he could relay, or tell what he had seen, in this church.

When I was a boy, it lasted almost all night. It got to where it'd only last till about midnight. No more. Now they can't do that with little kids five years old. Parents can't send them out to get a vision. They have to go to school. If they don't, they'll have their parents arrested. But they got vision now—television.

Back then, they'd put charcoal on their faces so that if they went to some neighbor's house or friends to get something to eat, they wouldn't let them eat. They'd tell them, "Go on back into the woods." Finally, I guess the spirits would feel bad about him. Maybe it was a bird, maybe it was a wolf or something, would talk to him through, they claimed, through the Creator. They couldn't directly talk to the Creator, so they had to talk through some animal, or bird.

Back when I was a little boy, maybe a teenage boy, us kids and our parents sat around at night and told stories. But when we had company back in those days that would come and stay overnight, then the old people sat around, and the kids would sit over in the corner on the floor—but didn't say anything, the kids didn't. They sat, and they listened to the old people tell stories. The old men would smoke, them that did. The women would just talk. Sometimes they'd tell witch stories, or ghost stories. Oh, I'd be so scared I wouldn't go outside in the dark.

The kids sat over in the corner and listened while the adults told stories. They told us to keep still. We weren't like kids now. That's the reason lots of times if we'd ask questions, "Shut up, let the old people talk."

The old people also told stories about other things as well. They talked about the removal of our people from back East and other things way, way, way back. And they talked about witchery. With us, that was a real thing. But the white man, the way he talks about witches, he just doesn't hit it. He calls it black magic. Well, I guess there is kind of an evil to that, whatever it is. But in our day, I've seen witches when I was a boy.

Once, when my brother was real sick (he was fifteen years old), we had a doctor from Ramona, Oklahoma, come up to him. There weren't any hospitals near. The doctor came up to our place. My brother must have had appendicitis. The doctor wanted to operate, but they were scared to death of operations then. So they didn't operate. And one night we were sitting in our old big house there in the breezeway. It was just getting evening, dusk. My aunt and her children and Papa and Mama were all sitting on the porch. We looked out on the yard on the northeast side, and my aunt all at once said, "Look there!"

It was a big old hog coming along. And we knew what it was. It was a person that looked like a hog. And he'd come to make my brother more sick. That's absolutely the truth. Of course, you can't tell people that, for they won't believe you. But, my half-brother ran in and got his deer rifle. Was going to shoot him. Well, don't you know, my aunt and mama wouldn't let him shoot him. But if it had been now, you know what I'd have done; bang, bang, bang. The Bible says in the Old Testament to "suffer not a witch to live."

But a witch will live one year after you shoot him. And when you shoot one like that hog, or maybe it was a dog or something, well, fire will fly out of it at night. That's blood. And he'll live one year. And he smells like a skunk, but it's not really like a skunk. It's a little different smell than a skunk. It's similar to a skunk smell. And sometimes it can be in the form of a dog—a witch—or it can be in the form of a bird or even a duck.

If I could come back a hundred years from now, I would like to hear the Delaware people speaking our own language. And I especially want my descendants to remember that I could speak my Delaware language and that I know about the culture, too. That's what we try to tell them about now, our culture and our religion, just so they'll know it.

As for our people's powwows, they didn't call them powwows then. Now, like the Shawnees, we have a Bread Dance and a Green Corn Dance; they are religious dances. Of course, after religious dances they have what they call social dances. And lead dances are where a man leads a song like he says a chant and leads them around a fire at night, and they all answer him. And the woman—if she wants to dance with a man—dances right behind him. That's the way it was back then and still is.

The women wear shells—turtle shells—on their legs below the knees, six on each leg. They would shuffle. Now they wear cans to keep time. Dee Ketchum's wife is good at it.

We got that from the Creeks. The first time I ever saw the Creeks, I was down around Okmulgee [Oklahoma] when I was seventeen or eighteen years old. I saw the Creeks have a dance. That's all they had all night long, that lead dance. They had turtle shells on their legs, the women did, held on with buckskin strapped around their legs. And they'd keep time with the turtle shells. That was religion-like for them.

Just at sundown—dusk—they'd get the women and the turtle shells and put them in a little row facing east. They'd talk to them [the shells]. They'd say, "We didn't kill you for nothing, brother. We killed you so we would use you in these religious dances. That's why we got you to use. We didn't kill you for nothing. And I'm going to give you a drink." And they'd pour water on them. Pretty near all the Indians, when they killed the animals, like they killed a deer or a bear, they'd go up and tell him, "I didn't kill you just to be killing you for sport. I killed you because we needed food."

The Delawares had war dances that had a water drum. It's made out of a little keg, like a five-gallon keg, about one-fourth full of water. You put a buckskin over it real tight with little ropes. And that was what they used for a drum. I'm talking about Delawares, now. They sing songs like the ones they call Cherokee Dance now. We don't know why they call it Cherokee Dance. And they have a Bean Dance and different dances like that, and they use that drum: "bum, bum, bum, bum bum." They would be chanting a few words as they danced around the fire counterclockwise with their shells and cans.

The fellows behind the lead singer sing, and the women keep time. I could lead, but I can't do it now because of my sore throat. But with the Creek women, not all of them, sometimes when they're shaking shells for you, they got a kind of a power. It must be the shells. You can feel it right here in the chest. It is a kind of a vibration. You could feel it. But you can't feel it with these cans they got now, I don't think. But they sound good.

We have war dances, and we use a water drum, too. One man sings war dances and uses a coconut shell or gourd rattle. And one takes sometimes those little bells they got now. He keeps time with it. They danced everywhere out there all around. They have buckskin clothes on and sometimes just a breechcloth. And the war dancers—Delaware— have a tomahawk in their hand. Sometimes the dancers would go up there and stop that drum. It stops. Then a dancer explains that he'd been in battle. He'd tell about it. He would say, ""When I was in battle . . ."

Then he'd stop a little bit, and that drummer would hit that drum. Then he'd go on again and tell them what all he'd done. The dancers would do this. Any of them that had been in combat. Yeah, he'd come up there and put his hand on that drum and it would stop. And he'd talk. He'd say, "I was in battle at a certain place and this and that."

They'd have a pause; then they'd hit their drum, "Boom." And they'd commence again. I know Old Man George Falleaf, he was with some scouts, and he'd tell about being in battle. And he'd hit that drum and tell them what he'd done. He must have been a scout for the U.S. Army at Fort Sill.

The Big House church was, I'd say, eighty-foot long and about forty-five feet wide, made out of logs. Used to be they didn't use nails. But later on they put some boards on it with nails. And the shingles were clapboards. They had two big square holes about half as big as this table, two of them over the building, where the smoke could go out. They had two fires. These fellows that maybe had a vision, whatever spirit talked to him, he just sat there right by the door, and he'd start that turtle rattle. He'd pick that turtle shell up, and he'd start his story. I'll tell you about Old Man Charlie Elkhair.

"When I was a boy," he'd say. "When I lived on the Kansas River, my brother—I loved my brother, my older brother—he died. And I was walking in the forest, and I was just sure grieving. I wanted to die. What am I living for? I want to die."

And all at once while he was thinking that, he said something hit the ground by him. "Bam." And he said that. And that's the story he's telling. And he said they told him, "You mustn't think that way. Think about you going to live a long time. And you're going to live to tell about when you talked through the Creator to this hawk."

And then the next man, that turtle rattle goes to the next man. He tells his story. And he has the option of dancing or not dancing. I call a road counterclockwise like the road to heaven.

The upright had a face on it, carved out of wood on this post, to hold the roof up. The carved face was red on the right side, black on the left side. This represented the spirit that took care of the game animals and watched over it, for the game was where we made our living, where foodstuff come from. He was the spirit that takes care of the game. Sometimes he'd scare the game towards the hunters. It also portrayed the good and bad in life, black and red. And it goes for twelve nights and days; on the ninth night they make two different fires. They make two fires, and women take the ashes out and throw them out the west side. And they build a new fire.

Then they use sticks that we call prayer sticks. The Delaware word for these prayer sticks was mahtahikan. They sing a song. They go around; there's twelve of them prayer sticks. Put it down, and if it falls in front of you, you take that stick up and use it the last three nights in there. When he's telling stories, you take that stick and keep time with it. And when they pray, Uh-h-h-h-h-h, we didn't talk. You hold that stick up.

Now for the drum, they got a buckskin about one-half foot wide and three feet long with slats over it and stuffed with deer hair. And it's got four hickory slats. It's what they used for drumming. The drumsticks are flat. It's got a man pictured on one stick, on the top, and the woman on the other. That's the way we use them on the ninth night. That's the way we started from, man and woman. The man tells his story and sings his song. Like that when they danced, too.

I believe the fourth day, they send the hunters out to go hunt game (deer mostly). There weren't as many deer here as there is now. But they'd get them with their bows or rifles. Finally, there were four of the hunters. They'd go up there to the Head Man. Old Man Elkhair was there then, and he'd pray for them. They'd lay their guns down—bows, they used bows before they had guns. And then they'd send them out to hunt. As they went out, these drummers sing a song they called the going-out song. The hunters went out. When they came back, if they killed two deer they'd whoop twice, "whoop, whoop!"

Well, these drummers sat there all the time, ready all day long. When [the hunters] come in, they start that hunting song, coming in song, welcoming them in. They'd come in, lay that game down there, and the families mostly would partake of that deer meat.

Elkhair's nephew can sing the coming-in song. I know he sings it; he's got a drum. That's the only one we've got now. But he's got a drum almost exactly like it [the old ones]. He made it from a picture. On the twelfth day at high noon, everybody faced east all in a row. Faced east and prayed twelve times, and that was the end of the meeting. Everybody went home.

They boarded up the church house. And when they quit, that old building fell down.

From an oral history interview conducted December 14, 1994, at the headquarters building of the Delaware Tribe of Indians, Bartlesville, Oklahoma.

GRACE THORPE

Sauk and Fox

Tribal District Court Judge, Sauk and Fox Nation

Born 1921, in Yale, Oklahoma, near Tulsa

I was named after my aunt Grace. My Indian name is the same as my great-grandmother's, Notenoquah, which means "A woman who has the power of the wind before a big storm hits." It's Thunder Clan. My name is shortened to Wind Woman. My brothers call me Big Windy Woman.

This gold medal [I'm holding] is [a duplicate of] the one that my dad, Jim Thorpe, won in the 1912 Olympics. He won the Decathlon, the Independent Decathlon [and the pentathlon]. The International Olympic Committee gave two medals to our family [in 1983], and this is on display now with Dad's bigger-than-life-size portrait in the rotunda at Oklahoma City.

My dad's Indian name was Wathohuck, or Bright Path. He was actually from four different Indian tribes but enrolled in the Sauk and Fox Tribe. He was also Potawatomi, Kickapoo, Menominee, and French and Irish. He met my mom at the old Carlisle Indian School in Carlisle, Pennsylvania. They were married there shortly after the Olympics.

Dad's grandfather on one side was Irish, and his great-great-great-grandfather was French—a French fur trader, whose name was Jacques Vieux. He opened up the first trading post in Green Bay, Wisconsin, and in Racine, Wisconsin. He is considered one of the founding fathers of the state of Wisconsin. His son, Louie Vieux, was the head man or chief of the Potawatomi after the removal of the Potawatomis from the Wisconsin and Michigan area. They went over into Iowa; that's where he was head man. That was about 1837.

The Potawatomi used head man instead of chief. All the tribes use different names for their leader. Some are governor, some are chairman,

244

Grace Thorpe

Sauk and Fox

Tribal District Court Judge, Sauk and Fox Nation

some are president, some are chief. In our case, that is, the Sauk and Fox, we use the terms principal chief and second chief.

I grew up away from the Indian people. I went off to Haskell, a boarding school in Lawrence, Kansas, when I was six. That was the standard procedure then for Indians my age. As to what it felt like as a six-year-old leaving home to go to a boarding school, I didn't think anything about it. That was just the accepted way of doing things.

Some of my special memories of childhood have to do with my father because he was an athlete. A very special memory goes back to the time I was at Haskell Institute. I remember Dad kicking a football from center field there in Haskell's stadium over one goal post, then turning around and doing it the other way. So that's one of my very first memories. Dad was in his middle thirties when I was born. So he was forty by then.

I recall that it was always fun to see him. He traveled a lot, so he wasn't around the house all the time. So I remember how glad I was to see him. I'd run, and he'd pick me up and throw me up about ten feet in the air and catch me. So I remember how big and strong he was and what kind of fun it was.

My mother was pretty much Anglo, but she grew up in Indian boarding schools also. Her mother passed on when she was five years old, so her father was left with six children. He probably did not have the resources to take care of the family, to keep the family together. And so they were sent to Indian boarding schools. My uncle Earl, who was my mother's older brother, and Aunt Grace and Uncle Clyde all went to Chilocco Indian School.

Even as a little girl, I always thought of myself as an Indian. I used to get challenged quite a bit. I can recall that because of my fair skin and green eyes, when I was in Indian schools. But when they did that I'd fight. I'd go right at them. "What do you mean I'm white?" I'd say.

I was proud to be an Indian, even then. Today I hear people say they were ashamed. They didn't want anybody to know they were Indian. But I never ran across anybody like that back then or now. Everybody I knew that had Indian blood was always very proud. I don't know where all this stuff comes from that I hear people saying. So there was no particular time in my life when I was proudest to be an Indian. That's just something you take for granted. You don't go around saying something. You're just who you are, I guess.

I never personally experienced prejudice, thanks to my background. I had a very famous father. He's still a very famous father. So when I go to gatherings, whether they be Indian or non-Indian, I can still see every now and then somebody nudge somebody and say, "She's Jim Thorpe's daughter." So I've never experienced any prejudice personally.

I'm sure that some of my friends did experience prejudice. It seems to me that the closer you get to the Indian communities and the closer you get to the Indian reservations the more prejudice there is. And in some cases that I've overheard, the people didn't realize then that I was Indian. They'd say that Indians have a preferred status, a special status, super status, as opposed to the rest of the citizens. They don't bear in mind, of course, that we've given up all our land, and that many of our treaties—the Sauk and Fox treaties, in particular—that provided teachers for us as part of the deal. "You give up the land and we'll give you teachers; we'll give you doctors; take care of you if you move to other areas." That was just part of the deal, part of the contract for giving up the land.

I think a lot of the non-Indian people that live around these Indian communities are not taught this in their history books. They are not taught this in their libraries. They're not taught this by their parents. But if they were, they would realize that the Indians are a special people because of these treaties, because of our particular status of being here when the Europeans and the Asiatics and the others came into the area.

Insofar as the importance of my ancestors is concerned, I guess you could start chronologically, probably with Chief Black Hawk and the Black Hawk War of 1832. Incidentally, the Sauk and Fox were the last tribe of Indians to fight for their land east of the Mississippi. The tribe was almost killed off then. It was sent off into Iowa.

Black Hawk wasn't a part of my ancestral family, but he's in the same Thunder Clan, and that is a loose relationship. Dad made the statement once that he was prouder of being in the same clan as Black Hawk than he was in winning at the Olympics in 1912. That gives you an idea of the stature that Chief Black Hawk has with me and with many other members of the Sauk and Fox Tribe.

Louie Vieux, my great-great-grandfather, was the head man of the Potawatomi. He was considered one of the founding fathers of the state of Kansas. He had a drawbridge built to go across the Vermillion River, and the people on the Oregon Trail paid him a dollar a day to go across his bridge. In some of the history books, it shows he made as much as $350 a day from people on the Oregon Trail.

I recall visiting here in Oklahoma many times with Dad. I remember us being with Aunt Mary. Her land was right near a creek, and I remember sleeping out on the porch, and Dad slept inside. I recall waking up just as it was getting dawn and watching him go through the trees with his gun. He shot squirrels out of the trees, out of the pecan groves, and then he'd bring them back, and we'd have fried squirrel and biscuits for breakfast.

I left the community here when I was about twelve, and I really didn't live here any more. I was off in boarding school. So, in the case of Indians, things probably started changing when the Indians were sent off into boarding schools in the late 1800s. They were pulling so many of them off the reservations and sending them away. In the case of Dad, thousands of miles away to boarding schools. Grandpa Thorpe [in 1904] had to sign a statement that Dad would stay at Carlisle for five years and not return. Dad was not even to return for the summer, return for holidays, nothing. Had to stay there for five years. The idea was, if the Indians were away for five years, they would become assimilated. If they kept going back and forth, they would not.

A lot of the Indians went to Carlisle. Now, I have met many of them. I remember meeting a fellow in Pennsylvania that was in his eighties. I think he was Santee Sioux, from right on the Nebraska and South Dakota line. He was sent there to Carlisle. He married a Pennsylvania Dutch lady. He told me he never returned to the reservation. He left there about 1915; I met him about 1975. He didn't want to go back.

Dad went off to the Sauk and Fox School, which was right across the street here, when he was six. It was a boarding school. He didn't like it then. He used to keep running away from there. And his twin died. Dad was a twin. His twin died when he was about nine, and then Dad kept running away even more. And so Grandpa signed this statement and sent him off to Haskell for three years around the turn of the century [1899]. My father never talked about having to go to Carlisle and stay away for five years. That was just an accepted way of doing things.

I never learned to speak our Native language. And Dad didn't speak it at home. Mother would not have understood. I don't know who he talked to. He'd have to sit there and talk to himself, except when he had visitors and relatives that would visit from time to time. When I was in my teens in Stockton, California, Dad was working for the motion picture industry as a casting director for Indians. During that period of time, I can recall many of our Sauk and Fox people coming to visit. And Dad and them would go back and forth all the time. Then when I'd come here to visit in Oklahoma with Dad, they would be speaking Sauk and Fox. But he just never spoke it with us at home, I'm sorry to say. I wish he had.

When the Native language is no longer spoken, I feel that the thinking of the people in cultural terms is weakened. I suppose if you can speak your language, you are thinking in the language. It seems like it would change your whole thinking; the old way of life would soon be diminished. Fortunately, here with the Sauk and Fox, we do have language classes now. We did not have them when I came back here in 1976. So there has been a kind of renaissance and attempt to return to— to relearn—some of our old customs from some of the older people. There seems to be a resurgence of interest, maybe a continuation of interest, among early middle age to middle age people who are really trying to get hold of our cultural heritage. Perhaps they see more of the importance of it as they become mature adults.

In addition to the language classes here, craft courses have been going on for quite a while, especially beading. And we used to do a lot of weaving of the grass mats to put around our dwellings back 100 to 150 years ago. There was a class in that not too long ago that a Kickapoo lady taught. And there are classes in ribbonwork. Our tribe is known for the beautiful ribbonwork that they do.

I learned after I retired in 1976 how to make baskets, how to gather materials like buckbrush and honeysuckle to make baskets. I've also learned how to work with clay in order to do pottery in the old-time coil method and throwing pots on the wheel. I've also done some beadwork, but I'm not doing beadwork now. The beads are quite little, so it's hard to see the beads.

It's sad to see that we have less and less Sauk and Fox blood within our members as times goes on, because we have a small tribe, and people are marrying out into others. Out of five members of our elected tribal council here, there's not a one of their grandchildren that has a quarter Sauk and Fox blood in order to get on the rolls. That's a very sad situation. So, eventually, what will have to be done is reduce our blood requirements in order to have a tribe. Eventually we'll just go out of existence, because there won't be enough here with one-quarter Sauk and Fox blood.

During the Black Hawk War of 1832, prior to that there was a large community—a large Sauk and Fox village in the area called Saukenuk [in present-day Illinois]. Today it's called Rock Island. It's set up on a cliff overlooking the Mississippi River. I'd just really like to see how everybody lived then. That would be a wonderful thing. The Sauk and Fox had big houses that were similar to the Iroquois longhouses. It would be fascinating to see the kind of life it was then. We'd be going back to the late 1700s and the early 1800s.

I imagine that through the stories that they told back then, they were trying to teach character to their children, to teach them a way of life, things that were expected of them—character things such as generosity, courtesy, and, in the case of warriors, probably the tenacity, fierceness, not being afraid. I suppose it would differ with boys than what it was with girls. I can imagine stories that were about a way of life, the things that would be expected of children as they became adults.

About three years ago [1991], just about this time [December], here in Oklahoma I read in the *Daily Oklahoman* that my tribe had put in for a $100,000 grant to study the feasibility of putting nuclear waste on our Indian lands. I was horrified, especially when I thought about the Sauk and Fox being the last tribe of Indians to fight for their land in Saukenuk in Illinois, and wondered what had happened to the past generations since 1832 that our tribe would even contemplate such a thing.

I didn't know much about nuclear energy, nuclear waste, so I started studying on it. I found that it's a very complicated subject. But when I found that you couldn't read and you couldn't feel, you couldn't smell, you couldn't taste radioactivity, but that it was the most lethal poison known in the history of mankind, I didn't figure I needed to know anything else. So I started to take action. I read our tribe's constitution to find out what we had to do in order to withdraw from this program. I learned that it was necessary to get fifty people on a petition, stating they wanted this special meeting on the issue. So, we very quickly were able to get the petition signed and a special meeting called.

I made a motion that we withdraw from what was called the D.O.E's M.R.S. Program—Department of Energy's Monitor Retrieval Storage Program—of nuclear waste. There were seventy-five votes, and seventy of the tribal members voted to withdraw from it. The only ones that were for it were the five elected officials. And in all fairness to the elected officials, one of their jobs is to keep money coming into the tribe. Since then I found out that it really doesn't bring any money into the tribe. The great majority of the money goes to the consultants and to the lawyers.

So I won my battle with the tribe about the nuclear waste. After that, I just started getting calls from all over the United States from other tribal members and universities asking me to be a keynote speaker. For the last three years about all I've been doing is going around and talking to various Indian and other environmental groups. We had eleven tribes here in Oklahoma that put in for these nuclear waste grants. We were able to get every one of them to withdraw. The last one just went in August, the Tonkowas. So I have gone and been around attending rallies with the Mescaleros, the Fort McDermott Paiutes, Goshute Paiutes, and the Prairie Island Sioux in Minnesota, as well as California groups.

The thrust of my presentation at the Indian Sovereignty Program was that we are sovereign as Indian Nations at the whim of the government because right now the government wants us to take the nuclear waste which they are responsible for by law. Indians are sovereign, so they can bypass the state and county environmental laws. But, in the case of Oklahoma here, we want to put in a gambling casino. "Oh, no, no, you're not sovereign now. You can't do that. You have to go through and get an approval from state authorities." So sovereignty is, and I say it again, at the whim of the government. It's a joke.

Presently, I am an elected tribal district court judge. In order to qualify according to our constitution, you have to have a law degree, or you have to have a paralegal degree. I have a paralegal degree. I used to be called to serve as judge until I got involved in the nuclear waste issue. Now I haven't been called to serve for over two years. I still got re-elected as tribal judge. The people reelected me a couple of months ago, but I haven't been called in over two years.

Probably ninety percent of our budget is federal money. So I'm very much concerned right now about this transition with the Republicans. Though, I must say, Richard Nixon wrote some very good legislation as far as Indians were concerned. But I have an idea that the federal government is trying to rid themselves of the so-called Indian problem, as they call it. So this is of great concern to me right now. I have seen in the last twenty-five years many things that young people take for granted, such as scholarships at universities. They didn't have those back then. Back then you had to have a three-point grade average in order to get a scholarship. You could get one from the BIA if you had a high grade average. But you had to pay it back. There were no such things as grants and scholarships then.

If this were my last chance to speak a word to future tribal generations, I would say to them, "Hang on to the land. Hang on to the land. Don't give it up. Keep the land clean and as healthy as possible."

From an oral history interview conducted December 16, 1994, at the Sauk and Fox National Library, Stroud, Oklahoma.

BEULAH TIMOTHY

DELAWARE

ELDER, DELAWARE NATION COUNCIL, MORAVIAN OF THE THAMES BAND,
ONTARIO, CANADA

BORN 1916, MORAVIAN RESERVE

We were fairly isolated. We never went into town much because it was with horse and buggy. We had no electricity. We had wood stoves, and we had outside water wells and outhouses. We walked to school. Fortunately, I didn't have far to go. My school was where that red brick building is now that's the school on the reserve. There was a house there where the teacher lived. He also served as the United church minister. But he taught. Everybody liked him. It was one-room, and he taught grades one to eight. It was never used for grades above eighth.

My parents' home was on the church road. The house isn't there now, but it was a two-story frame house. It had two rooms downstairs and two rooms upstairs. There was a shed built onto the back. That's where my father kept his boards so they would be dry in the winter time. Also his shovels and things like that. That's where my brother Herb's house is now.

In those days, everybody had enough; you stored enough stuff to last you through the winter. My father always bought one-hundred-pound bags of flour. He'd buy them, and he'd have them kept in town. He'd bring one home, and my mother would bake what we called light bread. We always grew enough potatoes to last all winter. My mother canned all kinds of berries and everything like that, so we didn't have to buy things except like sugar. Most of the time we had a cow, and we milked her. My mother made butter, and we kept chickens so we had eggs.

In those days it was a treat to get a loaf of bread from town. It was different. I used to get tired of homemade bread. Now I'm glad to get it. My daughter makes bread all the time now. Two of my daughters work

Beulah Timothy

Delaware

*Elder, Delaware Nation Council,
Moravian of the Thames Band*

in London [Ontario]. They have an apartment there, but they are here every weekend. They come home Friday nights and then go back Sunday. Janet is a breadmaker. She makes about six loaves every time. They take one back and freeze the rest. But when my mother made bread, the yeast was different. They were little squares. She'd cook potatoes, mash them, and use the potato water. I think she put lard in it and the yeast. She'd wrap it all up and keep it warm overnight, then use it the next day. I guess she was doing that to activate the yeast.

It was just my brother Herbert and me who lived in that house with our parents at that time because my brother Richard was not born yet. I was twenty-one, and I was gone [when he was born]. That was during the war years, and my dad was gone a lot. My brother Herbert was in the army, too. So when Richard was born I stayed over at my mother's for a while because my husband did some farming, and then he'd go to Detroit, and he'd work there up into March. Then he'd come home. There were no jobs here. My oldest boy is three years younger than my brother Richard [Snake].

I started to school [on the reserve] when I was seven. At this school we learned the Indian language first. I was eight when I went away to school in Brantford. My parents sent me to Brantford because they felt I would get better teachers there. When I started to this school I couldn't speak English very well, but I didn't feel out of place because there were lots of other kids like that. But I had to speak English because there was hardly anyone else there who could speak my language—really just my mother's sister and me, just the two of us. There were two or three other girls from here, but they didn't speak Delaware. My husband couldn't speak Delaware. His mother and father spoke it, but they thought their children would learn faster, get along better in school, if they just spoke English. At Brantford the other children came from Quebec and Six Nations. I think the ones from Quebec were Mohawks, and the Six Nations are all different so there are six different languages. If my aunt and I got together and spoke our Delaware language, we weren't punished. When we are together now, we speak our language. She's in our nursing home in Brantford.

I was there until I was fourteen. This was a residential school. Our summer holiday started the first of July, and we went home until the end of August. We never came home for Christmas. When we'd come home for the summer, for the first few days you forget some of your language. I remember once talking to my grandmother—my mother's mother—and I said one wrong word. I thought it sounded like what I was trying to say fast. And I said something else. My grandmother was quite shocked at me. I think I told her we were going right to hell. So there's such a little difference in some of the words. But after a few days it would all come back again.

At Brantford we'd get up at six o'clock, make the bed; then we'd go down. We slept in what they called dormitories. The basement was where your lockers were, and bathrooms and washrooms and the play-room. Upstairs was the school room. The floor above that was the dormitory where we slept. There was another floor above that, but it wasn't very big. I'd been up there but I never had to sleep up there. But some of the children slept up there. I think there was on the average about 78 girls there and about 60 to 65 boys. Altogether there were maybe 135 kids.

The girls would get up and make the beds, and then we'd go down-stairs to wash and be ready for breakfast. About six thirty we had to be done. The dining room and kitchen were all down on the floor with the playroom. We'd be out of the dining room and in the playroom by seven. Then we'd get our assignments. After you got to be ten or eleven years old you were at school a half-day. The other half-day you worked in, say, the kitchen. Two weeks at a time we'd work in the kitchen. Then maybe another two weeks we'd be in the sewing room. We made all our own clothes—the boys' shirts, uniforms, and all. Of course, there's umteen hundred pairs of socks and stockings that had to be mended. And then there was the laundry room. Some of the girls would have to work in there. So you had to kind of move around. I guess we did the cleaning, too. So we went to school a half-day, and yet we finished when we were supposed to by age fourteen.

School started at nine, and you were there till noon. Then you ate your dinner. And then in the afternoon you went wherever you were supposed to be—what you had to do—until four o'clock. Five o'clock was our supper hour. Between four and five we had playtime. After supper you had to do your homework. At seven o'clock we had prayers every night for half an hour. On Sundays we had church. We had Sunday school, and we had evening prayers. So time went pretty fast.

It was during the Depression when I was fourteen. I came home in July. I couldn't go back to school because at that time you had to get to town on your own to go to high school. And you had to have clothes, but I didn't have clothes. So I didn't go to school.

I went to work when I was fifteen. I did housework in Chatham [Ontario]. My mother had worked there before she was married. And you were chaperoned. I knew how to do the basics because we had to take our turn in the kitchen at Brantford. We had to learn how to wash dishes, clean. So I was taught to cook, and I stayed there for six years. All I earned was $5.00 a week. But then you could buy lots with $5.00 a week.

I went on from there when I was twenty-one. I left, and I went to Detroit. I got twice as much money there—in Birmingham, about fifteen miles out from Detroit. It was like being in the country. I went to a place where other girls had worked.

My mother's sister was four years older than I. She had worked there before she got married, so I knew where I was going and knew the people. I stayed there for four years. I left there to get married. I didn't get married until I was twenty-five.

I don't think there is any difference between the Delaware traditions today and the way they were when I was young. We didn't think much about language back then because lots of children spoke it, and most grownups did. In my time, people who were grownups, that's all they spoke. They spoke English, too, but at home and with their neighbors everybody spoke the Delaware language. The only time I ever heard my mother's mother speak English was when she went shopping. She had a basket with some eggs in it that she used to trade for groceries. She took the basket of eggs into the store. The only thing I remember her buying was corn meal. I don't know what else she bought, but that stuck in my mind. That's the only time I ever heard her speak English, when she ordered the groceries. The rest of the time she always spoke Delaware. My brother Richard does not speak the Delaware language as well as I do because he grew up at a different time. His children don't speak it because his wife is a Miami; she speaks her own language.

I don't know whether any of the Delaware children are learning our language in school or not. They did for a while, but the teacher we had got another job. The linguist from Thunder Bay University, Dr. John O'Meara, has been coming here; it'll be ten years this year. He knows everything, I guess, because if there are words I forget I ask him. But when Diane Snake [wife of the current chief, not related to Beulah Timothy] and I are carrying on a conversation in Delaware he can't keep up. He can't grasp it fast enough. So I think the language is a lot easier if a person learns it while they are little. John is working on the dictionary; he's just about finished.

I don't get a chance to talk to the little ones at all. So our people will end up with an Anglo knowing the language, but they won't. We'll have to try to turn that around.

Diane Snake has a lot of tapes that she got over the years. She'd like to have them put someplace where they'd be available so people could borrow them but bring them back. But lots of stuff gets lost like that. I have one tape of a man who has been gone quite a while. He just goes on and on and not so fast. He was a Pentecost minister. He reads the Bible in English, and then he turns around and translates it into Delaware. Then I've got another tape of a woman who sings hymns in the Delaware language. And Emily Johnson does "Noah's Ark" in Delaware. She's gone now. I'd say that tape was made in the 1970s. And then Diane did two or three legends that were translated into Delaware. They're written in Delaware and English.

There was one instance I never forgot. When I was in Chatham I went to the theater. I don't remember what the show was now, but they had a section in the theater for what they called "colored" people. And that's where I was put. I told the man whose family I was working for. Well, I don't know what he said, but they never did it again.

From an oral history interview conducted May 15, 1995, on the Moravian Reserve, Ontario, Canada.

TOM TOPASH

Potawatomi (Pokagon Band)

Vice Chairman, Pokagon Potawatomi Nation of Michigan (1986-1990)

Born December 1946 in Niles, Michigan

This southwestern Michigan–northern Indiana territory where I live is the tribal homestead area. It has been the home area for the Potawatomi for many, many generations, a long time before contact with the Anglo world. When this large tribal group was distributed by the oppressors, several fled toward Canada. A group went to Wisconsin, a group to northern Michigan, a group to Oklahoma and Kansas, all of whom obtained federal recognition. It took up until 1994 for our home group to receive this federal recognition. It is one of the ironies of the way the government works.

I don't spend a lot of time berating the government, however. I see myself as someone who will do the long hard work of building between communities instead of the easier, damaging work of tearing down. That same philosophy spills over into my work with the majority community. I spend time with all people. Additionally, I speak to organizations as well as individuals and look at them as ways of building bridges.

Mom was second-generation German-Irish through New York, and a slightly prejudiced person, but that wasn't conveyed to us children. I find that I am willing to look at all sides. Dad was a Pokagon Band Potawatomi member. They met and married in 1921. Probably was a case of "pretty young girl from Niles meets handsome athlete from Buchanan." Dad was only fifty-three when he passed away.

There wasn't, at the time of my upbringing, an obvious Native American component to our lives. We weren't raised Indian, with the beads and feathers and all the expectations and trappings of what it was to be culturally Indian. I'm describing an experience that many, many Indian people of my generation had.

Tom Topash

Potawatomi (Pokagon Band)

*Vice Chairman, Pokagon Potawatomi
Nation of Michigan (1986-1990)*

What I have discovered, and am continuing to explore over and again, is that the important components, the important beliefs, behaviors that were Native were subtly taught to us by my dad. He had easy humor, was amiable, always polite, willing to give and to share, and that meant of his worldly goods and his personality. He was beautiful, yet he had faults. He was an alcoholic but not what one would consider a negative or serious problem in the home. He just quietly watched his baseball games. I felt like his years of decline were very premature, his having been an athlete and a well-regarded person. It was sad that he didn't get fired up about his Native heritage. I say that as a person from what we call "the comeback generation." Why didn't he do that? My answer to myself is, "All the time he was being himself he was building the groundwork for his children to be able to do what they do."

It was kind of unique for a mixed marriage like theirs to be in a little white neighborhood. Because of his nature, the guys at the shop all called him "chief" and other stereotypical names. But they all appreciated him. They all remembered his athletic prowess, and I think they all felt a little bit better sharing a smoke with an Indian guy. They treated him like a regular guy. That made him feel a tad bit better I'm sure, because in the '50s they were almost all openly prejudicial. In this social environment, Dad could go to the bars or to the shop; Dad could go anywhere and be that well-liked man, making no waves anywhere, paving the way for his children. I thank him for my lack of anger toward institutions and other races.

There were a number of events that all came together a few years ago when we started to become a strong Native community. Before I describe the Native school I founded, I must tell you of the development of the spiritual community here in southwestern Michigan. You'll see the connection.

The spiritual community was first just a group of young guys coming together. The first ceremony we experienced happened up at Torch Lake in northern Michigan. There were three cousins: myself, my cousin Dan, and my cousin Steve Winchester who, by coincidence, attended at the same time. We were taught to build a longhouse. We were shown ceremonies. We were enthralled. Next, we built one right here in Berrien Center. Frank Bush, a local spiritual leader, became known to us. He came here and guided the whole process. Ka-baam! That was the beginning of the return of our spiritual practices, hence the development of a spiritual community.

This was barely ten years ago. It was a time of great excitement.

Everyone was thirsting for knowledge. The excitement settled as it took on a more mature aspect. Factions developed within the community, with some Indian groups practicing their Native spirituality in a fundamentalist fashion, while others practiced their spirituality in a more inclusive way. Inevitably, that happened, but I think everyone is riding the reins a little easier nowadays.

What I learned at that time was so exciting because we were seeing unity, unity because of our way of looking at the world. I was starting to see how holistic we Native Americans are in our thinking. Naturally, the religion is totally holistic. When an Indian says, "We are at one with the tree and at one with nature," it is an all-encompassing concept—holistic. As we shared while passing the feather—the talking feather—there were concerns of the people that needed to be healed. Many had problems with alcohol; many people needed to be healed of their problems of not being able to get along with peers in the workplace. Most important, though, was the need to have someone else to talk to who felt the way that other Natives did. It became a support group. The passing of the talking feather—the foundation for today's support group—was a thousands-of-years-old tradition.

During this time, educational research was developing in this country. Those that are reforming their schools and learning to do things better are looking closely at integrated instruction, or holistic and thematic instruction.

I took a leave of absence from my public school principalship in May 1994. From the beginning of July 1994 to September 1994 we opened a school. Opening was hasty, but that kind of leap or jump seemed to fit what was needed. There is now a permanent school in Sault Ste. Marie. This Indian community had been experiencing a lot of breakdown. It is the third oldest city in the United States, thus generations of oppression.

In the education vernacular, the school is called an at-risk school. We begin each Monday with ceremony, the smudging. We talk about the values of the Anishnabe way. We promote positive self-esteem and don't just talk about it. The teachings of the seven grandfathers are in pictorial, visual form in every classroom. The honor code, which says we are to honor life in all of its forms, is posted in each classroom, recited in every classroom. The Nishaabe language is taught every day. It's inevitable that when you teach the language, you're going to be teaching the values of the culture as well.

These children now have many advantages. Take, for example, our opening ceremony last week. I was standing there with the all-important eagle feather. When I began asking them, "What kind of kid are you?" they shouted back, "I'm a great kid."

When I ask, "Who are you?" they shout back, "I'm Anishnabe."

"What does it mean to be Anishnabe?"

Their hands were popping up all around. They weren't reticent at all. They said, "An Anishnabe is a respectful person; an Anishnabe person doesn't fight and tells the truth and everyone is honest."

That was our twice weekly assembly of kindergarten through grade seven, all those ages, two hundred children in a circle. "The Anishnabe person tells the truth; Anishnabe person does good service." Those are the values we had been teaching for the last year and a half. For the first time the kids were beginning to name those values that we'd been teaching.

I make the umbrella shape when I describe the Anishnabe curriculum because there is a major theme in every classroom, the broad tribal relationship to the environment, or to the solar system. That means that it's a wheel. The thousands-of-years-old traditions are available to us today, too. This school will grow strong.

When I moved to the Upper Peninsula, I started experiencing prejudice. Clerks would talk to the other people in front of me, then come to me and throw my change at me. That was discouraging. It even made me feel bad. I'm an adult, and I'm trying to put my mind in the emotions of those little ones. They get that all the time. It's very real.

I would like to see our community grow strong. If I could come back in a hundred years, I would enjoy seeing that the Pokagon Band people understand they are an intelligent people and that they no longer are keeping each other from advancing academically. Today most Indian people believe it's a "sell-out" to educate yourself. Lip service is given to education, but in reality most people don't want it to happen. This is totally subconscious. Most believe, "You've left the community; you're not really one of us." There's a mild prejudice there. "Whose education is it?" That's an important point. The experience of the "Indian schools" may be the factor that changes this. We need Indian schools.

The Pokagon Band hasn't experienced its biggest change yet. The change of moving from a diverse set of individuals to building ourselves into a community is an important question. Is it going to happen?

One of the teachings of the Anishnabe way that has not been emphasized, and therefore is sometimes missed, is the teaching of optimism. I would like our people to join in the traditional way in order to gain the optimism along with all the other wonderful values.

We have continued to allow others to define what sovereignty is. Individuals can begin to see that Traditional Red Road as a sovereign path. We must relearn that we are a sovereign people and, as such, we'll not continue to accept the treatment we have received. It's time to build . . . Ourselves.

The following is my prayer:

> We thank the Great Spirit, our Grandfather, who made the Father Sky with dancing stars, the Mother Earth of rock, soil and waters, the sun that warms.
>
> The Great Spirit brought upon this beautiful place the growing things. He made the crawling creatures, the swimmers, and the soaring winged ones. The four-leggeds he made to both teach and to become food for the two-leggeds, The People, The People who walk in balance with the universe.
>
> We offer our saymaa and repeat Megwitch with each coming of the dawn.
>
> Megwitch to the East
> Megwitch to the South
> Megwitch to the West
> Megwitch to the North
> Megwitch to all that is above
> Megwitch to all that is below
> The seventh direction is the center of the universe . . . look within.
>
> The drum beats as our heart. The high keening and deep chest sounds of song celebrate our journey. This is a journey of balance by Nishnawbe People. We walk in the circle of the seasons and in this cycle of generations.
>
> Uh ho! We wish for all to walk in beauty, walk in balance on this Earth—the Mother.

From an oral history interview conducted October 28, 1995, at Berrien Center, Michigan.

WAP SHING (JOHN MOHRINGER)

MIAMI

SPIRITUAL LEADER, MIAMI NATION OF INDIANS OF THE STATE OF INDIANA

BORN HAARLEM, THE NETHERLANDS

There are all kinds of things that I remember from when I was very young. For one thing, we never had a meal unless we had a prayer. We thank the Grandfather, and we thank the animals and the plants. We thank the people who fixed the food. When I grew up a little more, even though I wasn't in a lot of homes, I realized that some of them would say a prayer before the meal, but they never mentioned the animals, the plants, the land. That was one of those things that very early on I became aware of.

As I grew up, my mother used to take me to the land and to the dikes, and we would be gathering plants and seaweed and edible plants and medicines. Because my mother was looked upon as a medicine person, a lot of people came. If somebody was sick, they always went to her.

She always said a prayer when she harvested something. She always gave a Sama. I never knew what that meant because it is not a Dutch word. It wasn't until many, many years later when I was here that a Chippewa person told me Sama is tobacco. That's indeed what we offered. It is indeed what we put on the land when we took something. We put a little offering on Mother Earth, and she used that word Sama. Later I found that the Miami have the same word. Indeed, a lot of the Woodland People use the same word for it.

That was just one of those things that came to me much later, and I began to recognize some things because what my mother told me was never one story. There's so many little experiences that I now recognize and say, "Oh yes, this is what my mother used to do." But she never really talked a great deal about those things. She just simply did them, and I was supposed to do the same thing, and I did. She learned those

264

Wap Shing (John Mohringer)

Miami

Spiritual Leader, Miami Nation of Indians of the State of Indiana

things from her father, because Grandpa did the same things. What she did is what she was told to do.

We had morning prayer, and we had evening prayer. If the weather was halfway good it was outside. At daybreak, at sunrise, we made an offering to Four Winds and to Mother Earth and to Father Sky, and then we thought about one another, in a widening circle, for those people who are in trouble and in need. That's the way we started the day. Teachings that come in such a very informal way stay with you. The day doesn't start for me until I have faced the East and brought my offering and given thanks.

My mother was always talking about minjipee. I didn't know what minjipee was. Then she showed me one day that it was a very important food. That was corn, of course. The only corn I had ever seen was in kernels when it was imported from the United States. The Dutch, at that time, certainly didn't eat corn.

I was brought up in the Indian way, but I was not kept away from other religions either. During the war, the idea of preparing for ministry had been steadily growing in me. I was unable to go to high school during the wartime, but when the war was over I came out of the military in 1946. I wanted to enter some sort of ministry. But where to go? Well, I met some people, and they said, "You can do that in the United States without any great problem." So I was invited to come here. In 1947 I came into the United States to study. I studied in Chicago, at McCormick Theological Seminary and at the University of Chicago. Then I wanted to know more things, and I was at Milliken University in Decatur, Illinois. And I did some work at Butler University Christian Theological Seminary in Indianapolis. During all that time, one of the first people that I got acquainted with was a fellow by the name of Bigay. He was my roommate in Chicago. He was Navaho. When I came to the United States, I thought, this is a strange country. Everything is materialistic. But he was somehow different. We sort of clicked. We were able to talk about other than mundane things. He invited me to meet his parents in Chicago. Those people accepted me as a son, and I accepted them as my second parents. I found out right there that the environment I had come out of—my family—was very much like the Navaho People.

When I entered the Episcopal ministry it was kind of natural that I was drawn to Indian people, and they were drawn to me. I got to know Chief Mon-gon-zah of the Miami of Indiana. Then, in the late '50s, I was transferred to Oklahoma for about four or five years. Of course, in

Oklahoma there are an awful lot of Indian people, and again the contact was strengthened more and more.

When we got back to Indiana, Chief Mon-gon-zah was a blood brother to me. He and the Eagle Clan adopted me as a Miami. I learned a great deal in ceremonial from Chief Mon-gon-zah. I learned Miami ceremonial because the Navaho ceremony is quite different. It's a way of life, it's who you are and your relationship with everything. As Chief Mon-gon-zah said at the adoption ceremony, "You're adopted and you're not adopted because in a way you've always been part of us." More and more people began to contact me, and ask me things, and I learned more and more from a lot of the Elders. A lot of the Miami words were taught to me by the Eagle Clan and by Chief Mon-gon-zah and by Cha-ke-pe-ah, the granddaughter of the Old Chief, who lives in Muncie [Indiana].

So when the old chief passed on, the clan by that time considered me as their medicine man, so the installation of the new chief, Wa-ka-ka-kee, George Dorin, fell to me. Of course, prior to that we had the burial ceremonies for the old chief. Then more and more people of the other clans began to ask for my services. People considered me a spiritual leader and medicine person, but I was not ordained. It's just a gift from the Great Spirit. He prepared me from when I was really small, and it is that power that sustains me and teaches me. Sometimes I throw my hands up and say, "I don't know what, how, to do that. And then I see the old chief sitting opposite me, shaking his finger at my face, saying, "People need it; you do it. It is ceremony you don't know; you do it."

That happened with the Gathering of the Waters Ceremony in Cairo, Illinois, for the closing of the Always a River project in 1991. I understand somebody recently had another ceremony, and I understand they did it very much the way we did it in Cairo.

The Miami People have certain characteristics which, in a way, are a little bit like what you'd find in many other tribes, too. We are very much like a family. And in a family it is sometimes extremely difficult to find a consensus. They will argue about all kinds of things, important and not so important, and totally trivial from time to time, and they will fight one another tooth and nail. And one doesn't recognize the other, and the other in turn doesn't recognize somebody else. But there is continuity in the leadership of the Miami People that goes back for thousands of years and can be traced. There was Chief Godfroy, who was an important chief, and Chief Lafontaine before him. Some of them may not have recognized that chief. But they were chiefs and, in the main, they spoke for all The People, even in the turbulent times in which they lived.

John Bosin, who is a Kiowa from Oklahoma, was a very important teacher to me. So was Howard La Hureau, who lived near Fort Wayne, Indiana. His Indian name is Shepshe, and many people know him by that name. Shepshe was a Potawatomi and a Meday priest. Many, many of the things that I still practice and do were taught to me by Shepshe. He passed on, I think, in 1991. He has been of tremendous help to me and still is in so many of the things he has left me, both orally and in writing. Shepshe, after the old chief died, was very active with our People. He conducted weddings and burials and did a lot of counseling and teaching to our People, even though he was Potawatomi. He also helped politically in going to Washington with our People and for our People in gaining certain provisions that should have been there earlier. I do not know whether all of our People realize that, how important he really was, because he so often worked in the background. But his spirit is with us still and is working through me.

The way I taught my own children is how I try to teach the other young people. We started out with the Miami Junior Council having meetings from time to time. In a way, that has now been shifted to the Minnetrista Cultural Center because the Woodland workshop is a wonderful place where I can get people together for two and a half days. Not enough of our own [Miami] People are participating in that yet, but that's coming. It's something that has to grow. And if people do not feel a need for things, and they're not ready for it, then you might as well save your breath. But there are so many things that just by informally talking do come across because the question is asked.

We have never had any kind of organized things like a class. That's not the way we do. It's a highly individual, highly spiritual thing, and the teaching is done in a much more subtle way, but also a way that much better sticks in the people's memories because it becomes a part of their life.

One of the glorious things now is to have the area of the Seven Pillars and a longhouse. At our last longhouse meeting young people were there. And they're interested, and they're asking questions, and they're beginning to search things out. And that, I foresee, is going to multiply and eventually will truly again be the spiritual center of The People.

The removal to Oklahoma did force the people there to venture out earlier than the people did here. For a long time the people here did stick together and had, in a sense, the warmth and the comfort of knowing that they were all together. In Oklahoma, they're scattered over a much larger area. For the people here, many things go back to the Mississinewa Reservation, which was the last operable reservation we had. That is, perhaps, why even though people weren't forcibly removed, they were, in another sense, forcibly removed. It was economic necessity which caused people to have to go to the South Bend [Indiana] area, for example, where a clan like the Eagle Clan is much more close-knit than perhaps some of the other clans. Yet certain things have been preserved in Oklahoma which had not been preserved here.

Chief Floyd Leonard, two years ago [1991], gave me a copy of the way in which the Indian burials were done there. Something that had been lost here. I had some idea because it came over verbally, but now I had some of it in writing. On the other hand, I find on the part of the Miami people in Oklahoma, when they come here, they truly feel at home. They're back in home territory. Over the years, we didn't have anything to offer them because we didn't have any center. Now that the center's being rebuilt this is a tremendous advantage. But still many people are living outside and away from us and it will be a while for all to come together. I find that enormous pull; our people want to come together.

There was, for a while, among the people, just a matter of "if we can get the payments." It was just an economic thing: "Let's try to get as much as we can from an economic point of view." Now that those things are truly on the wane, people are beginning to say, "Hey, there are more important things." I think that eventually will pull all the people together.

The last person who really spoke Miami fluently was Mr. Bundy, whose name I bear, Wap Shing. He lived in Marion [Indiana] the latter part of his life. The Smithsonian was planning to ask him to tape, but they never got around to it until it was too late. My knowledge of the language is rather skimpy. I have gathered vocabulary over the past twenty some years, but since you don't have anyone to speak it with, you lose it. I have tried in my own little way to revive it. When I see people, I say Aiy-aiy but I don't really know in many cases what the correct pronunciation is. For example, for "I'll be seeing you," some say Ta-na-ky-a; and some say Tan-a-ky-a. I don't know what the proper pronunciation is, so I am very grateful we have some learned people and linguists who are now helping us with that.

I am very anxious to get some good solid material, but we'll still have difficulty in recapturing the language. Because language is a living thing, it expresses things that are in the here and now; we do not speak the language we were speaking in the 1860s. Many items we used then are no longer used. There are many new things that have come up for which we don't have words. We have them in English, but we sure don't have it in Miami. Who is going to decide what to call what? But some understanding and grasp of the language is so important for our young people because the language is an expression of what lives in the people—of their hopes, of their dreams, of their fears, of how they see things. We don't say "good-bye." That is far too final. We say Ta-na-ky-a because it is "I'll be seeing you." There is always that looking forward.

Miami people have no word for sin because it does not occur to us. There is no such thing as sin or guilt, so we don't have those words. So the language tells where people are spiritually.

As to what makes the Woodland unique, for instance, we didn't have rain dances here because we didn't need any rain dances here. In Arizona it's a bit different. The connection of Mother Earth and the rain is there. You have these different and very unique expressions within the dances. But when you go to the heart and the soul of it, it is said, "Truth is One." But there is somewhat of a problem in what I said. For example, the Miamis don't have a word for sin because it simply doesn't lie in the outlook and philosophy of Miami people and most Woodland people. But you go to the Southwest, and you do find a word for sin. And you begin to wonder how far are some of these things the result of the close proximity and the influences of the Roman Catholic Church on the people? I've found that in Mexico, in Arizona, even among the Navaho people.

For the Western Nations, their culture was intact when the settlers got there. But, here, people were moved from one area to another. Woodland tribes were pushed, and they had to move. It has been an extremely traumatic experience. It's surprising that so much of the culture still lives in The People.

In a way, you can compare that with a story of the Hebrew people. How is it that in the Diaspora, over hundreds and thousands of years, people still retain their identity; they retain their faith; they retain their values? For me, personally, the most important thing is to somehow transmit the respect, the awe, the love that my mother exhibited for everything. You feel, "Here is another day, and I haven't deserved it at all. In fact, everything is sacrificing for it: the sun is coming up; the plants are there; the flowers are blooming; the birds chirping. That's all a gift." You feel like a king or queen because, "All that, for me?" And then, "What is my part in this because I, too, am part of that wheel, and I'm also part of not just receiving but the giving." That, I think, is by far and away the most important thing because the Grandfather can take away everything. But if a person has that sense, what can hurt us? That's the whole of life. Does it make sense to you? It's the good and the evil, or seeming evil, both, that are part of the circle. But that goes beyond my understanding and yours, but that is what we accept. That is what we see. I can hardly believe what I am seeing, but this is what I accept. I fall down on the job, and yet I get another chance and another and another. And I might think, "Why would anyone or any thing do that for me, who the heck am I?" Yet it's there.

Supposing we get back our federal recognition, supposing the government does anything we ask of them, would that be in the interest of The People? Would that be for the good of The People? It depends on how The People use it. The gifts are there, it depends on what we do with the gift. Rejection from the federal government may also be a gift. A gift to strengthen us. It may be a gift so we will stand on our own two feet. Maybe a gift to really begin to see our goal in life as a Nation, as a person within that. On the circle, things become different; your vision widens, as opposed to the linear thing, a narrow road. Like Browning said in his little poem: "For a reach should exceed a grasp/ or what's a heaven for."

I tried to tell [the late] Chief Ray White that some time ago. The Bureau of Indian Affairs has really been keeping us on a leash and playing around. We are asking for recognition, but maybe what we ought to learn is that we have recognition. As a People. We are the Grandfather's Red People. A thousand times we're asking for the wrong things to start out with, and sometimes we get precisely what we ask for, and we are sorry.

Powwows, I think, have changed tremendously. The early powwows at the turn of the century were to create some kind of an economic base for the people. Promoters were willing to pay something for it, so they tried to make it colorful. The whole thing was catering to the public in order to make some money. So people wore totally outlandish outfits that were reportedly traditional but weren't at all. That's the time when even the Miami used the Western head dress because that is what an Indian had to look like. And they painted themselves up. Much of what was true had either been lost or was buried. And part of that is also because of the hobbyist groups. These groups had their dances. There is a dance still going on in Michigan, which sells all kinds of knickknacks and fake Indian things. They have little tipis that are made of plywood, and that sort of thing. There's a wooden Indian standing in front. But it draws people.

In this area, the Tecumseh Lodge grew out of a Boy Scout adventure. They happened to get a scoutmaster who had lived for years with the Lakota people. Ted Wiese got Lakota people to come over. He himself learned many things about the Lakota people. He had danced with the Lakota people. They formed a drum and started teaching the Boy Scouts some of the Lakota ways, Lakota songs, and how to be more correct historically. It pretty much left out all the Woodland people. But you have to look at what slender thread and what narrow road they came back to.

They call that group the Kunieh Society, and the Kunieh Society taught those boys. And when those boys grew up, they wanted to continue that because they had learned to love the songs and the pow-wow. What you got, on the one hand, is people who did a powerful job to preserve our Native culture. On the other hand, they became very picky. So it came about that a number of years ago, Cha-ka-peah and I were at one of the powwows, and somebody came up and said, "You have to leave the arena. You cannot dance in the dress you are wearing because that's not the way to properly dress up." On the one hand, they wanted to be perfectly authentic; then, on the other hand, when you became too authentic, the clothing didn't do the job. She was wearing her mother's traditional dance dress, which was perfectly fine, but it wasn't recognized as such. So there came somewhat of a rift between Native people and the hobbyists.

Now, for the Indian people, the powwow is becoming what it is supposed to be. It's a dance for the Grandfather. You dance for The People; you tread lightly on Mother Earth; you are together because you want to communicate; you want to give of yourself; give something back.

Every once in a while you still find shows, and it bothers me. But that's the way it's been for a long time and it is simply a matter of making money, making ends meet, paying the bills.

Every year, on Labor Day, the Tecumseh Lodge powwow is in Tipton, Indiana, and the traditional Potawatomi powwow is at South Bend, Indiana. It used to be in Menden, Michigan. Indian people are always sort of torn between the two because it was through the Tecumseh Lodge that many of them got back to the culture.

From an oral history interview conducted August 24, 1993, in Lebanon, Indiana.

RAYMOND O. WHITE, JR.

Miami

Late Principal Chief, Miami Nation of Indians of the State of Indiana

Born December 30, 1937, in Muncie, Indiana

Died March 3, 1994

My feelings about the English and others coming into America during the contact period are that, if it hadn't been for the American Indian, when they hit the East Coast, to nurse them back to health and feed them and show them how to grow corn and squash and other food, they would not have survived. They celebrate Columbus, but Columbus didn't discover America. I don't think people know exactly who the first European people were to touch North America.

As to where the Miamis were in the 1640s and 1650s when the Jesuits first made contact with them around Green Bay, Wisconsin, we've got sites here in Miami County, Indiana, that were documented four to six hundred years ago. You go back to the Iroquois wars, and it's known that the Iroquois came in through this area in Indiana and Illinois. They were killing off the tribes slowly, one by one. I think it is known that the Miamis, the Weas, the Piankashaws, the Peorias, and a lot of the other tribes left this area for a period of time as a matter of survival. We've got documented sites here in Indiana, like the Windsor Mounds and the Mountain State Park, that are 800 to 1,000 years old. We've got another site in Posey County, right along the Ohio River, that's called the GE Site; that's documented as 1,500 to 2,000 years old.

Archaeologists and anthropologists say the Miami Indians and the Potawatomi and the tribes that inhabited Indiana in the early eras had no distinct connection with the Adenas and the Hopewells. I say, "I don't think you're right." I think there is a direct connection. The Miamis didn't drop out of the sky 350 years ago. There is a direct connection with the early inhabitants 1,500 to 2,000 years ago.

I want to know what happened here 10,000 or 15,000 years ago, or

Raymond O. White, Jr.

Miami

Late Principal Chief, Miami Nation of Indians of the State of Indiana

1,500 years ago: who the inhabitants were, whether there was a direct connection, because there's too much similarity in the way the people lived 1,500 to 2,000 years ago and the way the Miamis lived when they were here 300 years ago. The early inhabitants in the areas along the Ohio River, the Wabash River, the Maumee River coming out of Toledo had sophisticated trade networks.

I've gotten some criticism because I've, in a sense, okayed scientists to go in and do cross-sections of sites that have been found so they can tell you and me what type of dwellings those people had; what type of medical treatment they had in the way of broken bones, and whatever else; whether they had arthritis; what their daily eating habits were; what their mode of transportation was; how they survived. In order for me to be educated, scientists have to have permission to do their research. It changes from year to year because of their explorations.

The Miamis had one of the greatest confederations any place in the United States. That's why Little Turtle was one of the greatest war chiefs any place in the country, the one that inflicted two of the greatest defeats on the American armies in the defeat of Harmar and Sinclair. Little Turtle could put 5,000 to 6,000 warriors on the line, and they weren't all Miami. They were the Confederation of Weas, Piankashaws, the Peorias, the Illinis, the Potawatomis, the Shawnees. There were probably some Chippewas, maybe some Hurons, Ottawas.

It wasn't any different back then—150 to 200 years ago—than what it is today. If somebody comes onto your property and starts tearing it up or starts burning your crops or your house, what are you going to do? You are going to resist, and you're going to fight back. But it was a little different back then. After the Miamis were denied guns and gunpowder, they tried a lot of resistance when it came to signing treaties. Little Turtle's popularity went way down, but he thought in his own mind it was a matter of survival: to save what Miamis and what land they had, to sign the treaties, or they all would have been killed off. That's basically the choice the government gave them: "Either you sign these treaties and take what we're going to offer you, or we won't offer you anything. And we'll still remove you, or we'll kill you off."

So we owe the Miamis and the Shawnees and the Potawatomis; they didn't have any choice other than to sign the treaties and get out of it what they could, get an allotment of land their people could live on.

I was talking to a lady from Bulgaria. She said, "You look more French than you do Indian." I said, "Well, I get it 'honest' because my grandfather was Richardville Lafontaine, who was of French descent."

The French took part in the sophisticated Miami trade networks. And they intermarried. So we had more influence from the French Canadians and the Catholics into the Miami tribe, maybe more so than any other tribe east of the Mississippi.

A lot of people say that all the women did in the tribes was to raise the kids and bear the kids and grow the crops and do all the hard work. But you've got some matrilineal tribes, and you've got some patrilineal tribes. With the Miami Indians, you'll find in most cases there wasn't a major decision made among the tribal leaders without first consulting with the women. The women always played a dominant role in decision-making. In a lot of the cases some of the women chose the chief. Male chauvinism didn't start with the American Indian. Miami women are very strong-willed. In most cases, they won't take "no" for an answer. In a lot of cases, our Miami women are stronger and have more determination than a lot of our Miami men.

One of the main reasons the Miami people traveled was to engage in hunting. If you look at the forestation of Indiana 300 or 200 years ago, you'll see why the Miamis didn't use horses. The Miami historic homeland is around the Maumee, the Wabash, the Miami, the Eel. There were a lot of different reasons why they lived around rivers and streams. It was their mode of travel and a form of fortification. Rivers and streams and, in some cases, swampland were a natural defense because the enemy couldn't get to them quite as easily from all directions. If you are on a swamp, you don't have to worry about somebody coming in from the backside of you.

Most Indian tribes always inhabited the areas around the main tributaries and the streams because it was not only their drinking water and their cleansing supply, but game had to come to the water, so it was a way they could do their hunting. It wasn't uncommon, in different periods of time, for tribal people to travel three to four hundred miles just to hunt game. Back in the 1640s and 1650s when the Jesuits first made contact with the Miamis up around Green Bay, they were probably up there as a hunting party.

The Jesuit priests said the Miamis were one of the best educated—knowledgeable and astute—people. They were basically a friendly tribe, except when another tribe would declare war on them. If the Miamis had not been a friendly tribe, they would never have invited the Delawares in after the massacre in Ohio. That's why the Delawares got into Indiana. The Miamis let the Shawnees come in. They let the Potawatomis come in. They were part of the Miami Confederation.

We don't want to use the white man's history about Little Turtle. We don't even have a true picture of Little Turtle because the only portrait of Little Turtle was burned when the White House was burned. We know that Little Turtle probably went to Washington, D.C., and visited with the president of the United States more than any other tribal leader in history did. Little Turtle died of the gout. He was in Washington one time when another gentleman supposedly said, when he found out Little Turtle had the gout, "Well, the gout is a gentleman's disease." And Little Turtle replied, "But, sir, I am a gentleman."

The sad part of it, when you read your history books about how great Indian tribes were, you read about the Battle of the Little Big Horn and the defeat of Custer. That's part of the stereotype. In all your movies—cowboy and Indian movies—they always go out to the Plains tribes and Southwestern Indians. A lot of kids and a lot of people around here in residence east of the Mississippi think all Indians live in tipis. It's not teepee; it's tipi. But that's not right. The tribes here lived in wickiups of cattail mats. They made them; they were lightweight. If people were just made aware of all the history of Indians in the state of Indiana, and teaching materials were made available to the teachers to teach the proper history of the state of Indiana, that could help eliminate a lot of the stereotypes. There's a lot of information available, but we need help. You are talking about a minimum of twenty-five to thirty tribes that people should have the privilege of being able to study and learn more about who inhabited the eastern part of the United States, the people we call the Great Lakes Tribes.

From an interview, March 6, 1993, at the headquarters building of the Miami Nation of Indians of the State of Indiana, Peru, Indiana.

CURTIS ZUNIGHA

DELAWARE/ISLETO PUEBLO

CHIEF, DELAWARE TRIBE OF INDIANS, BARTLESVILLE, OKLAHOMA

BORN 1953, IN ST. LOUIS, MISSOURI

My childhood was different from a lot of Indian kids around here. I was raised as a dependent of a career Air Force man. My dad was in the Air Force, and we traveled all over the world, living on Air Force bases, so I had an international upbringing. However, my Indian roots are firmly grounded in Copan, Oklahoma, at my grandma Edna Zunigha's allotment in the area that is now Copan Lake.

Probably my vision and awareness of a spiritual presence at my grandmother's home at Copan [is the most vivid childhood memory that I have]. [It occurred] late at night. I knew it was a supernatural presence—spirits, whatever the case may be. I wasn't frightened, just my senses were extremely heightened. And I knew something special was going on, but I didn't understand what it was. It moved about the room as I lifted my head and watched. Years later, the house was sold and moved. The new owners found me and asked if the house was "haunted." I knew then my vision was real. I'd say that was pretty significant since I don't often come in contact with that level of spiritual presence.

My father had more stories to tell growing up a poor Indian boy around here experiencing prejudice. I have, but not to the degree the generation preceding me has. But I know a fair amount of it goes on. Here in Oklahoma racism is alive and well. I've experienced it subtly in public accommodations and with some members of different non-Indian families that I've been around.

The Delaware sold their reservation in Kansas as a compact unit of property and moved down in the beginning of 1867 to the Indian Territory and tried to purchase an identical district and at least came

Curtis Zunigha

Delaware/Isleto Pueblo

Chief, Delaware Tribe of Indians

close to identifying that. But the Allotment Act actually occurred at the turn of the century, and it was that that broke up the tribal land holdings into individual allotments. Those assignments are still passed on from generation to generation. In a lot of cases families lost their allotments for one reason or another, including my family, which sold out to the Corps of Engineers for Copan Lake.

I keep referring to my grandmother because she was the Delaware. My dad was Indian. But his mom was Delaware, and his dad was Pueblo. One of the Pueblos of New Mexico is Isleto. That is what my grandfather, Vidal Zunigha, was. It was his relationship with my Delaware grandmother, Edna Wilson—their meeting in Chilocco Indian School—that ultimately produced a marriage and the mixed-blood lineage that my father had. And obviously it's passed on to me. And being a matrilineal society of people—therefore not having a mother to tie back to, Indian way, Delaware way—I do that through my dad. So that's the way I make my association to my Delaware heritage. My great-grandfather, Jim Wilson, represented the Delaware one time when he went to Washington, D.C., to deal with tribal claims. He had a heck of a time and got really sick and had to send for relatives to come get him out of the hospital.

My dad grew up like a lot of Indian boys around here. He would have been sixty-six [in 1994], so some of the Delaware men you talk to in that approximate age range could all relate to growing up and going to Indian boarding school and the old dirt-poor Depression days in little old Copan, Oklahoma. My dad, after going through all that and being sent off to boarding school all year long, didn't want any more of that. He had a lot of exposure to traditional Indian ways, but he had a different calling in him to get away. He chose the military as that route. So when I grew up, my connection with anything traditional is going back to Grandma's house, hearing her tell stories.

Until her husband died she was somewhat suppressed from participating in a lot of the traditional activities. My grandfather had really kind of gone over to the way of total assimilation. At one point he was an evangelist. Boy, he was really out there thumping that Bible, telling people all that kind of stuff. Those old Delaware ways weren't what he encouraged. My dad did not discourage me, but he did not have the knowledge and the exposure to be a teacher to me. However, it was the inspiration that my grandmother gave me of my identity, of my heritage, that kept it alive to the point that I chose to search out my own identity, after traveling around the world and having been connected to both sides of my family.

This position that I'm in now—this path that I have taken—I can't say that I have chosen. But for some reason, as I look back on it, it appears that it has chosen me. Once I accepted that, I've tried to make the journey as trouble-free as possible. I realize this is not my destiny but that of the Delaware people, and I'm committed to that. And all of that I have found and acquired on my own with the inspiration of my grandmother and the—well, I won't say encouragement—lack of discouragement from my father.

After I got out of the service, my uncle Wayne, my dad's little brother, encouraged me to get a business degree, an economics degree, because he was doing consulting work for Indian tribes. It appeared to be a lucrative calling, so I said, "Hey!" And I went to college, and in 1980 I received a bachelor of business administration degree; I majored in economics.

I have worked in the private sector with Lewis Ketchum's company, Red Man Pipe and Supply. I've worked in the public sector. In 1986 I got another degree—associate of arts in broadcasting, radio and TV—from a two-year college here in Oklahoma, Rogers State, and went to work there shortly thereafter in the development of a television station. So I have television and radio broadcasting—a professional background. I came back to work here at the tribe, 1989-1991, as a tribal manager and the project director for development of a system to administer our tribal claims money, which now totals over $4 million. Then, from '91 through, oh, a few months back, I was executive director of the American Indian Heritage Center, a nonprofit cultural preservation urban Indian organization in Tulsa.

My degrees have given me the education—then I got more or less on-the-job training—for the areas of my strengths, which I guess would be operations management and now with broadcasting. So public relations and conveying information in a public fashion seem to be my strong suits. That's the kind of expertise and energy I bring into this current position.

The oral history project with the Native American Heritage Center in Tulsa was a project we felt we could get funding for and something also to include the Delaware tribe, so I could continue to serve the tribe in a different capacity. Of course, it involved other tribes, too, but I just thought that once I got out of tribal operations and management, I could concentrate more on cultural preservation. These are projects that many other tribes are doing. This is just that time in the history of our tribes and organizations where there is a big, big effort going on in the preservation of cultural heritage for Indian tribes. So it makes sense for us to be a part of that right now.

In my journey I talked about earlier, in discovering my own heritage, I knew that—after having been around Indians long enough—the center of our culture has to be around our language, our religion, our spiritual beliefs. That is what establishes our identity, our uniqueness as Lenape. Therefore, the only religious icons left for me to learn from were down at the Philbrook Museum in Tulsa, Oklahoma—down in the vaults that they have there. So I made special arrangements to go down there and look at them.

They were more than inanimate objects. I felt a deep spiritual presence inside them. I don't understand why I felt them, but I did. And then I realized that this is just a part of what is inside me. This is something that is much more powerful than any kinds of words. It's hard to convey in words. Words don't express it. But I can say because of that feeling I knew, after having been around so many of my other tribal members who were also looking for this, this hunger for spiritual and cultural awareness, that this was the place to go to. And, working in conjunction with other tribal members, the Philbrook Museum, and in my capacity as American Indian Heritage Center director, working with Jim Rementer and other cultural specialists of the Delawares, it made sense to do something on the Delawares to serve as an inspiration for continued cultural awareness and to strengthen the new directions of our tribe. It was symbolic in many different ways, just as it was symbolic a hundred years ago when those ceremonies were being performed. That was the intent of this effort and I would say it has been successful in its organization and presentation. I think the jury is still out on how much inspiration it has given the entire tribe, but I can say it is a proud accomplishment for all of us and we all—the Delaware people that do see it—feel that spirituality, and that connects them with their Delaware identity, which makes them better Delawares, in my opinion. And that part's worth it.

Some of this relates to the 1990 Native American Graves Protection and Repatriation Act that was passed by Congress, with the express purpose of returning religious artifacts and sacred objects to the tribes. We want to develop a partnership where it is acknowledged that these belong to us, but we've got no place to keep them. A fine institution, such as the Philbrook Museum of Art, can help present this for everyone to learn more about the Delaware people. That opens the door for people to learn who the Delawares are, and to realize they are more than just an historic tribe; they're an alive and vibrant tribe right now. It identifies us as a spiritual and cultural People with a great history as opposed to what some people think is, "Oh, here's just another Indian tribe out there to get bingo and money and all that kind of stuff." That's not us.

As part of our community service we were asked to present something of a Native American/American Indian presence to the 12th National Workshop on Christian/Jewish Relations, which occurred in Tulsa, November 1994. Oklahoma being the home for so many tribes of Indians it made sense for all of these out-of-town folks to learn about the local color. But in our presentation we expressed that just as Christians and Jews have a deep religious basis to their identity, so do Indian people in their own way. We presented a lot of our cultural aspects couched in religious terms. I think it impressed both groups of people so much that dialogue began, because so many Indian people are also Christians. But Jewish people can relate a lot to Indians as tribes and their struggle for survival over the centuries. There is a lot of common ground for us to work to help each other out. That was just a regular part of community service.

I speak very little Delaware. I learned enough to say some prayers and say some things around the supper table and greetings. I'm an advocate for the teaching of it. I have a keen desire and a great hunger for learning it more. I have to credit Jim Rementer, who has served as our historian, for really being a savior of the process of retaining the Delaware language as this century closes out. It was never taught to me as I was growing up. I had to go out and seek it. Just in the last several years has an opportunity been created for being taught.

We have been providing teachers and classes and written material. I think advocacy for the retention of language as the foundation for our tribal identity is meeting with some success. I think there is a meaning in language that can't be directly translated. Those meanings are taught in a philosophical way. Loss of language is a loss of some of the spiritual meaning perhaps. Language is the basis for the distinction between cultures. When that is lost, you lose the distinction. When the edges are blurred like that, you become lumped in with others of a similar look.

Traditions passed on by my grandmother are the Delawares' struggle to retain their unique identity: spiritually, legally, culturally, politically.

All of those, all of those words. I think just telling those stories was the inspiration to me to continue that service, representing my family here in this generation, in this time.

My hopes for the future include Delaware boys marrying Delaware girls, having Delaware children, speaking the Delaware language, and keeping our community with a strong tribal identity rather than a people who have assimilated into mainstream white America, and the only connection with their tribal or Indian heritage is because their name is on a piece of paper and the government gives them a card.

As to preference for "Delaware, Indian, or Native American," personally, I don't have a problem with any of them. I only know how I identify myself—as Lenape first. I use Lenape more than Delaware. I identify more with the Delaware side than with the Pueblo side, but that is because of my environment. I'm here, I'm among these people. This is part of my life. It's hard to connect with the Pueblos unless I go back to New Mexico. Because most of my life is tied up with Delawares, I identify with that side of my heritage more so. As far as Indian or Native American, I prefer the name Indian in general for Indian people. Native American has more of a political distinction to me. But any of those are fine, and there are no absolutes. In this realm of "political correctness" there are no absolutes, so I think a lot of that is intent. Myself, I don't think you need to tiptoe so much in this realm of political correctness.

The Big House would probably have been unique to the Lenape because it was their religious ceremony. We still maintain certain dances, social activities, and our language as about the only things that make us culturally distinctive today. Nobody else has our songs. They might have similar songs, similar types of musical instruments, similar types of dances. But Delaware words in those songs, that's what makes them unique and special. That's about all we have nowadays. It doesn't mean we can't have more. We will—we will have more.

Growing up, it was all the claims era. We were making claims and weren't getting a lot back. Throughout the '70s we were starting to get money back from those claims. I'd say in my lifetime the greatest significant turn of events for this tribe has to have occurred in the last eight to ten years with the growth, rebirth of our cultural awareness. It went from being, in my mind, purely historical documentation to active learning as a social group in order to preserve it in an active and dynamic fashion, as opposed to a static fashion.

What I would like my daughter to carry forward is that her awareness of her Indian identity is couched in two different terms. One is in pride. The other is in responsibility, responsibility to keep her culture alive and in the right way. You have to learn that. So pride and responsibility are what I want her to have.

If you are going to claim your Lenape heritage, you have a responsibility. It is a wonderful gift. It wasn't one that we asked for. We were born with it. One could say it was an accident of birth. It was given to me whether I wanted it or not. But if you understand what being Lenape is about, that gives you a great sense of pride. Then it is your responsibility to keep it alive in your generation and to pass it on. It is something that we owe to those ancestors who suffered—generations who suffered and were deprived, were prejudiced against, were discriminated against. It is in their memory and in their honor that we keep alive that which they oftentimes fell on their knees and cried out to the Creator asking for strength to continue. It's those things, all those things—the religious artifacts, the language, the songs. All those things that make us a Lenape people were a gift from God. You don't mess with gifts from God. You treat them with a great degree of respect, and you take on that responsibility of keeping that gift alive. If you do, God says it will benefit your People. That's why we're still alive.

If people would just hear the message I said and understand why Indian people seek to keep their identity alive. If they can look past all of the discussions of sovereignty and economic development and tribal rights and this and that and understand that Indian people are doing this, as they should be doing this, in order to retain that identity. All of these other things that I said, including sovereign tribal rights, all these things are inherent in the unique group of people. But you don't tell others you're a unique group of people until you have an understanding of who you are, and that is that cultural and religious base. If the non-Indian community would understand that about Indian people they would understand that's what makes them a so-called sovereign nation. That's why certain laws and privileges and benefits and agreements made by treaty are given to Indian people, not because of the color of their skin but because they were a unique group of people that had just as many rights on this Earth as the Europeans who came over. When they understand that—that is why I have tried to reach out to Christian and Jewish communities and all these other communities and approach them through their religious leaders—that our identity is based on religion just as theirs is, it creates a much more fertile ground for compassion, for understanding, and for good relations. That's what I want to express to non-Indian folks.

You will probably get more eloquent answers from our tribal Elders, but everything I've said, everything I've presented I learned from them, whether it was from my long-deceased grandmother or some of the people in this community. This isn't Curtis Zunigha's message. I learned from them, and I'm just one of those eager students out there.

From an oral history interview conducted December 14, 1994, at Bartlesville, Oklahoma; headquarters building of the Delaware Tribe of Indians.

Afterword

Teachings

Michelle Mannering

The United States has been conceived as a nation "born modern," in Jack Greene's words, without a past, in particular without the rigid castes of birth and station embedded in European societies (*The Intellectual Construction of America: Exceptionalism and Identity from 1492 to 1800*). It has been imagined as a place where men and women, regardless of who they are, where they come from, or what they bring with them, may create new lives and new identities. On this continent the individual and the nation could both be made anew. Thus, the United States incorporated at its inception an acute tension between social order and individual freedom. Thus, too, the quest for reconciliation of order and freedom has composed an essential component of the democratic experiment.

The system of checks and balances designed to protect myriad minorities while implementing the consensus of the majority has its own hallowed place in the annals of political philosophy. And the celebration of freedom—of religion, press, speech, and pursuit of the elusive ideal of happiness—rings through centuries of American rhetoric and outward to peoples around the globe. The United States is also an idea. It is a nation conceived in difference and dedicated to diversity.

That diversity, however, also challenges the social order. It challenges the cohesion of a nation where rule is determined by the consent of the governed. And to these issues the narratives in this collection speak in a timely fashion. Assimilation versus separatism, integration versus segregation, have again become acute in the national discourse. Americans are divided over affirmative action and, once again, over whether all of us must speak English.

Yet the men and women recorded here also remind us that in our current debates are themes that run through the combined histories of the many peoples who make up the United States. Indeed, in the encounter between Europeans and the original inhabitants of this continent began both our struggle with difference and our celebration of it, the forging of a particular American identity. The idea of an America without a past overlooks the Native histories that have unfolded here for centuries. More accurately, America is a continent on which multitudes have met and have defined their identities, as Charles Taylor has recently written, "in dialogue" with others (*Multiculturalism: Examining the Politics of Recognition*).

In the United States, law has been fundamental to those dialogues. It is the white man's ground, as David Lee Smith says. And immediately striking in this collection is the intimate knowledge of law shared by the Native peoples interviewed. These pages resound with the names of statutes critical in U.S. history: the Indian Removal Act, the Allotment Act, the Indian Citizenship Act, the Indian Freedom of Religion Act, the Native American Graves and Repatriation Act. A distinct experience with the American struggle to accommodate difference distinguishes these individuals and their narratives. To overlook their centrality to the evolution of American identity, both individual and collective, is yet another act of removal, which, this time, separates all of us from our past.

Few Americans now know the tortuous history of U.S.-Native relations echoed in the story that Patricia Hrabik tells. In the first one hundred years of its existence, the United States deemed Native communities to be sovereign nations and defined its legal relationship with them by treaty. The federal government concluded more than three hundred formal treaties with Native Nations but abrogated most of them. By the end of the Civil War, continual abrogation had become a political, ideological, and philosophical dilemma for a nation whose fundamental principles included protection of the sanctity of treaties established under international law. In 1871, therefore, Congress forbade treaty making between Native Nations and the United States. Treaties already concluded remained valid, but the government sought new ways to determine the legal relationship between Native peoples and the larger society. The issue of sovereignty, as Grace Thorpe makes clear, remains unresolved and no less critical now than it was two hundred years ago.

The issue of citizenship reveals the persistence of our dilemmas and of our quest for reconciliation. After 1871, most Native peoples, neither sovereign nor citizen, had no clear path to the enjoyment of inalienable rights. As George Captain, Keller George, and others recount, children were taken from their parents and shipped to boarding schools with or without parental consent; freedom of religion for Native peoples was not made law until 1978. And the confusion over their place within American society continues. In 1924, all Native peoples were declared citizens of the United States. Yet, on February 14, 1996, the *Indianapolis Star* reported that the North Township Trustee office in East Chicago denied unemployment assistance to Casey Lewis, a Sisseton-Wahpeton Sioux, on the grounds that he was not a citizen of the United States.

These narratives relate individual histories and experiences but, as David Edmunds points out, they relate shared experiences and shared history as well. "All of these other things that I said," Curtis Zunigha recounts, "all these things are inherent in [this] unique group of people."

These cultures, like all cultures, like the American culture, have evolved through time, their traditions, like all traditions, transformed through experience and event. Today, in the fervor of our current dialogues, Amy Gutman has asked whether cultural identity is as much a right, as necessary to the pursuit of happiness, as the more familiar rights of freedom of speech, press, and religion (*Multiculturalism: Examining the Politics of Recognition*). In the pages of this collection one can find a multiplicity of individual answers to that question. The process of identity appears in the realities of daily living: both in the damage inflicted on Helen Rameriz's vocal cords and in the transfiguration, in Leonard Thompson's lifetime, of vision into television.

Here, too, is the strength of continuity. When newcomers came to this continent, Ray White remembered, "if it hadn't been for the American Indian, when they hit the East Coast, to nurse them back to health and feed them and show them how to grow corn and squash and other food, they would not have survived." Four hundred years later, the Native peoples who speak in this collection continue that tradition. They teach.

Index

Rita Kohn is Adjunct Professor at the Indiana University School of Journalism in Indianapolis. Her books include four Woodland Nations titles, *Spring Planting, Celebrating Summer, Fall Gathering,* and *Winter Storytime;* and *My Country 'Tis of Me: Discovering Citizenship Through Cultural Heritage* (with Katherine H. Lutholtz and Dennis G. Kelly).

W. Lynwood Montell is Emeritus Professor of Modern Languages and Intercultural Studies at Western Kentucky University. His books include *The Saga of Coe Ridge: A Study in Oral History, Monroe County History, 1820-1970,* and *From Memory to History* (with Barbara Allen).

R. David Edmunds is Professor of History at Indiana University. His books include *The Potawatomis: Keepers of the Fire; The Shawnee Prophet; Indiana and a Changing Frontier: The Art of George Winter* (coauthored); and *The Fox Wars: The Mesquakie Challenge to New France* (coauthored).

Michelle Mannering is Assistant Professor of History at Butler University. She is a former editor of the *American Historical Review.* In 1996 she received a grant from the Arts Council of Indianapolis to direct a Festival of Woodland Arts and Cultures at Butler University.

Evelyn J. Ritter is a painter of landscape, still life, and portrait work. Her oil paintings can be found in numerous private collections, universities, museums, and public institutions, and include numerous commissions.

Michael and Linda Shinkle are lifelong advocates of Woodland Nations cultures. Their work includes cofounding the Minnetrista Council for Great Lakes Native American Studies, Return to Pimiteoui: An Intertribal Powwow, and Prophetstown State Park Foundation, Inc.